STEPHEN JOLLY

1 Threave Castle. 2 Auchenmalg shore. 3 Mountain biking at 7stanes Kirroughtree. 4 Red squirrels attract many visitors to Eskrigg Nature Reserve. 5 A passion for whisky, Scotland and the restoration of old buildings was behind the 2014 reopening of the Annandale Distillery. 6 Taking it Slow on the Jubilee Path between Kippford and Rockcliffe.

ALAN IRVING

FORESTRY AND LAND SCOTLAND

DG/DF (SLOW BRITAIN)

ANNANDALE DISTILLERY

1

TERRY KETTLEWELL/S

HISTORY & HERITAGE

From hero kings to literary legends, a rich historical and cultural seam runs across Dumfries and Galloway, with reminders of times past coming in all forms. Memorials, artefacts, museums and outdoor artworks are all part of a cultural tradition through which the stories of the region's past unfold.

THE SAVINGS BANK MUSEUM

ELLISLAND FARM

HEARTLAND ARTS/S

SLOW TRAVEL

Dumfries & Galloway

Local, characterful guides to Britain's special places

Donald Greig
& Darren Flint

EDITION 2
Bradt Travel Guides Ltd, UK
The Globe Pequot Press Inc, USA

TAKING IT SLOW IN

Dumfries & Galloway

A SNAPSHOT OF THE REGION

Slow down and feel the pressures of daily life ease away. Dumfries and Galloway regularly comes in the list of top regions for quality of life. Plenty of outdoor space, lots of activities to enjoy, and beautiful scenery make this one of the best places in the country to unwind.

PETER NORMAN/WWW.WILDSEASONS.CO.UK

1 The Famous Blacksmiths Shop at Gretna Green. 2 The Wigtown Martyrs monument at Wigtown. 3 Early home savings boxes, coins and banks notes are on display at the Savings Bank Museum in Ruthwell. 4 Get a glimpse of Robert Burns's daily life in the kitchen of his home at Ellisland Farm. 5 The rare Beam Engine at Wanlockhead. 6 The interior of the fascinating Stewartry Museum. 7 Part of the Quorum sculpture near Murray's Monument.

ALISON SMITH

DG/DF (SLOW BRITAIN)

ALISON SMITH

200 MILES OF COAST

Rocky beaches, craggy cliffs, sandy bays, tidal mudflats, fishing villages and harbourside towns – these are just some of the scenes to be found along Dumfries and Galloway's 200 miles of coastline, from the eastern end of the Solway Firth to the Mull of Galloway, Scotland's most southerly point.

1 Portpatrick's picturesque seafront. 2 Painted cottages in Kirkcudbright. 3 'The Seat', an unusual resting place on the southwest Machars, looking out to Luce Bay. 4 Stunning Solway views walking from Rockcliffe to Sandyhills. 5 Traditional stake net fishing on the Solway Firth. 6 Of the many bays on the Rhins, Ardwell is one of the loveliest.

ANDY FARRINGTON

KEVIN EAVES/S

CREATIVE NATURE MEDIA/S

DG/DF (SLOW BRITAIN)

RODNEY HUTCHINSON/S

JAMES JOHNSTONE

7 The iconic Mull of Galloway Lighthouse. 8 Monks and royalty have made Hestan Island their home over the centuries. 9 Boats moored in the Isle of Whithorn's pleasant harbour. 10 Grey seals are not uncommon along the Solway Firth.

GEORGESIXTH/D

KEITH K/S

KEITH K/S

AUTHORS

Donald Greig spent many years working as a travel and wildlife publisher for companies in the UK and Australia, including seven years as Managing Director of Bradt Travel Guides, before settling in Dumfries and Galloway in 2014. In addition to writing for national newspapers and magazines (most frequently for BBC *Countryfile* magazine), he has worked for the National Trust for Scotland and was for several years a Trustee for Moat Brae, Scotland's National Centre for Children's Literature and Storytelling in Dumfries. He also works with Edinburgh-based children's publisher Barrington Stoke, specialising in books for reluctant and dyslexic readers.

Darren Flint worked across the UK and Australia before putting down roots in Dumfries and Galloway and being hooked on the region from the outset. After a career in tourism development and then conservation with the RSPB, he completed a Masters in Environmental Conservation at UCL. An avid naturalist with a fascination for Lepidoptera, he likes nothing better than donning his boots and uncovering those hidden corners we all dream about. He is currently the project officer for a number of community-led ventures in Dumfriesshire, including the award-winning Castle Loch in Lochmaben.

Donald and Darren are the authors of three walking guides: *The Dumfriesshire Dales*, *Galloway* and *Suffolk*, all published by Pocket Mountains.

They also run a small B&B: Summerlea House (Eastgate, Moffat DG10 9AB; ✆ 01683 221471 ⊛ moffatbedandbreakfast.co.uk).

DEDICATION

To the people of Dumfries and Galloway and all who come to visit; treasure this special place.

WITH SPECIAL THANKS

We were able to proceed with this new edition – at a time when the Covid-19 pandemic had hit independent travel publishers very hard – in part due to the extraordinary generosity of David Hananel. Thank you again, David.

Second edition published August 2020
First published 2015
Bradt Travel Guides Ltd, 31a High Street, Chesham, Buckinghamshire, HP5 1BW, England
www.bradtguides.com
Print edition published in the USA by The Globe Pequot Press Inc,
PO Box 480, Guilford, Connecticut 06437-0480

Project Manager: Emma Gibbs & Anna Moores, with thanks to Sarah Dickinson
Cover research: Pepi Bluck, Perfect Picture

ISBN: 978 1 78477 610 7

British Library Cataloguing in Publication Data
A catalogue record for this book is available from the British Library

Photographs © individual photographers credited beside images & also those from image libraries credited as follows: Alamy.com (A), Donald Greig and Darren Flint (DG/DF; Slow Britain), Dreamstime.com (D); istockphoto.com (I); Shutterstock.com (S); SuperStock: (SS); Wikimedia Commons (W)

Front cover Moffat (Allan Devlin)
Back cover St Ninian's Chapel, Isle of Whithorn (PJ_Photography/S)
Title page Lady Bay, the Rhins (Rodney Hutchinson/S)

Maps David McCutcheon FBCart.S

Typeset by Ian Spick, Bradt Travel Guides
Production managed by the Zenith Print Group; printed in the UK
Digital conversion by www.dataworks.co.in

ACKNOWLEDGEMENTS

We would like to express our gratitude to everyone we have been in contact with while working on this new edition. Your generosity of time and spirit has made all the difference. We also owe an enormous debt to our many guest contributors, whose expertise and insights are enlightening, and we say a resounding thank you to the several thousand people who follow our Facebook posts (slowbritain) and our B&B updates (Moffat Bed and Breakfast). Your feedback helps us to keep it all relevant and interesting.

On the Machars, we would like to thank Julie Muir Watt for her considerable contribution to the section on Whithorn, where ongoing exploration continues to reveal more about Scotland's cradle of Christianity.

Alison Smith has once again been enormously helpful in bringing to light people and places on the Rhins that we might otherwise never have found. Also on the Rhins, a sincere (if slightly sheepish) thank you goes to Stewart Adams and his son Steven, who one February day not so long ago rescued my car (and me, Donald) from a particularly tricky dirt track during a research trip for this edition. Had it not been for you (and your tractor), I might still be there now.

Finally, we would like to thank our editor Emma Gibbs and all the staff at Bradt for their patience and support, particularly Claire Strange, Anna Moores, Sue Cooper and, now off on much-deserved new adventures herself, Rachel Fielding.

AUTHORS' STORY

For several years before writing the first edition of this guide, we had been thinking about moving somewhere more rural. Eventually, after visiting various corners of the country, we decided that Dumfries and Galloway ticked all the boxes. Its combination of hills and coast, wildlife and birdlife, empty spaces, and its irresistible range of small towns and villages had instant appeal. And as a bonus, Moffat, the town in which we have settled, lies only around an hour from Edinburgh, Glasgow and Carlisle. For me, Donald, it was a return to the places of my childhood, for we used to have family holidays here in the early 1970s. For Darren it was a step into a new country. Now, seven years on, we can happily re-affirm that we made the right decision. There is nowhere else that we would rather be.

SUGGESTED PLACES TO BASE YOURSELF

These bases make ideal starting points for exploring localities the Slow way.

NEWTON STEWART page 198
The 'Gateway to the Galloway Hills': access to Galloway Forest Park and the 7stanes centre at Kirroughtree. Ideal for walkers and cyclists.

NEW GALLOWAY page 143
Compact and cultured, part of the idyllic Glenkens, with Galloway Forest Park and Loch Ken nearby.

GATEHOUSE OF FLEET page 165
An overgrown village with literary connections, peacefully located on the banks of the Fleet.

WIGTOWN page 204
Scotland's National Book Town is replete with cafés and popular with bird lovers, with two reserves nearby.

WHITHORN page 211
The cradle of Christianity in Scotland, a village atmosphere and easy access to the beaches of the southern Machars.

PORTPATRICK page 241
A delightful fishing village set around a picturesque harbour, within easy reach of the Mull of Galloway.

KIRKCUDBRIGHT page 181
'The Artists' Town' has a nationally important gallery, pretty cottages and a historic working harbour.

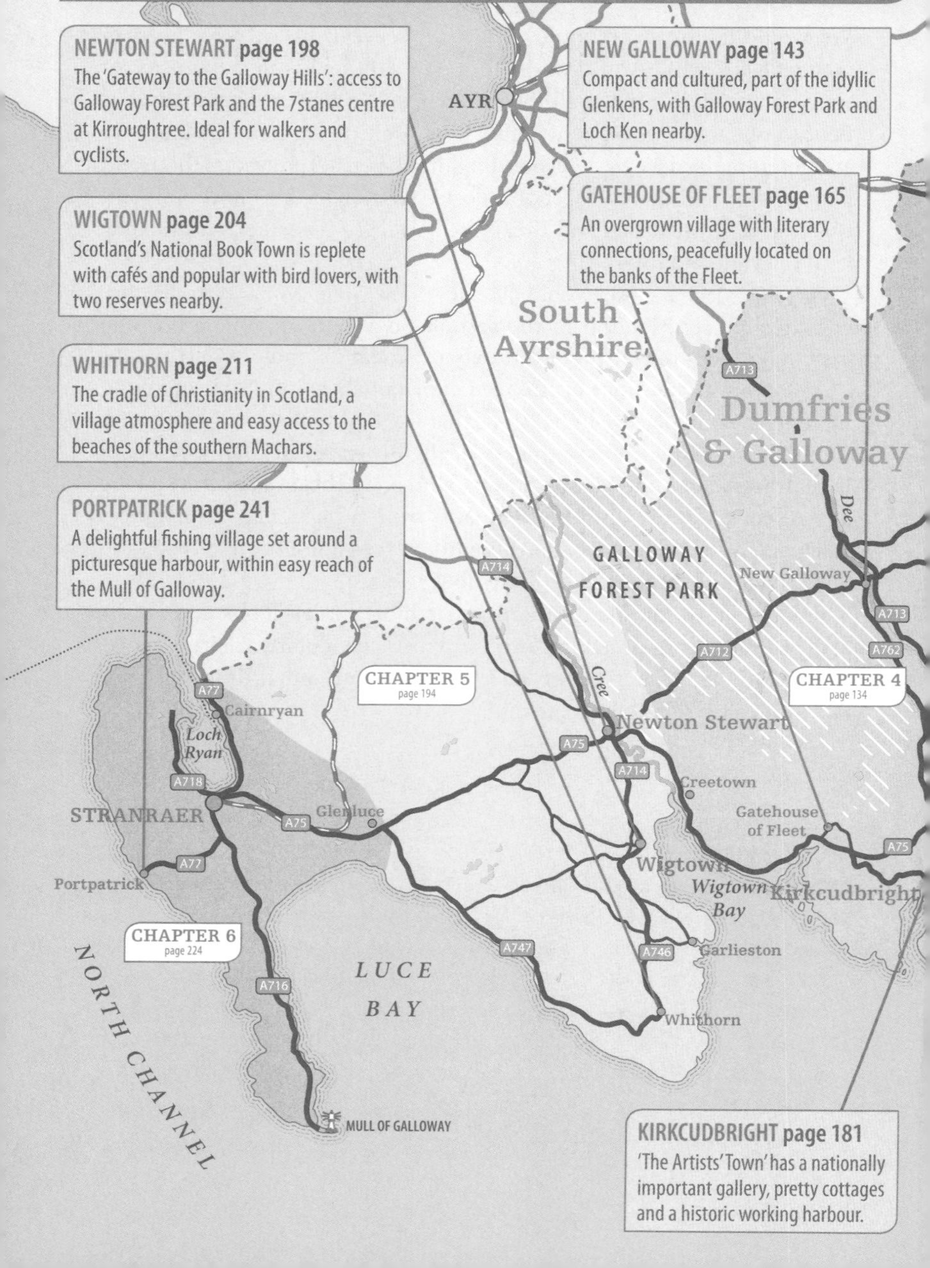

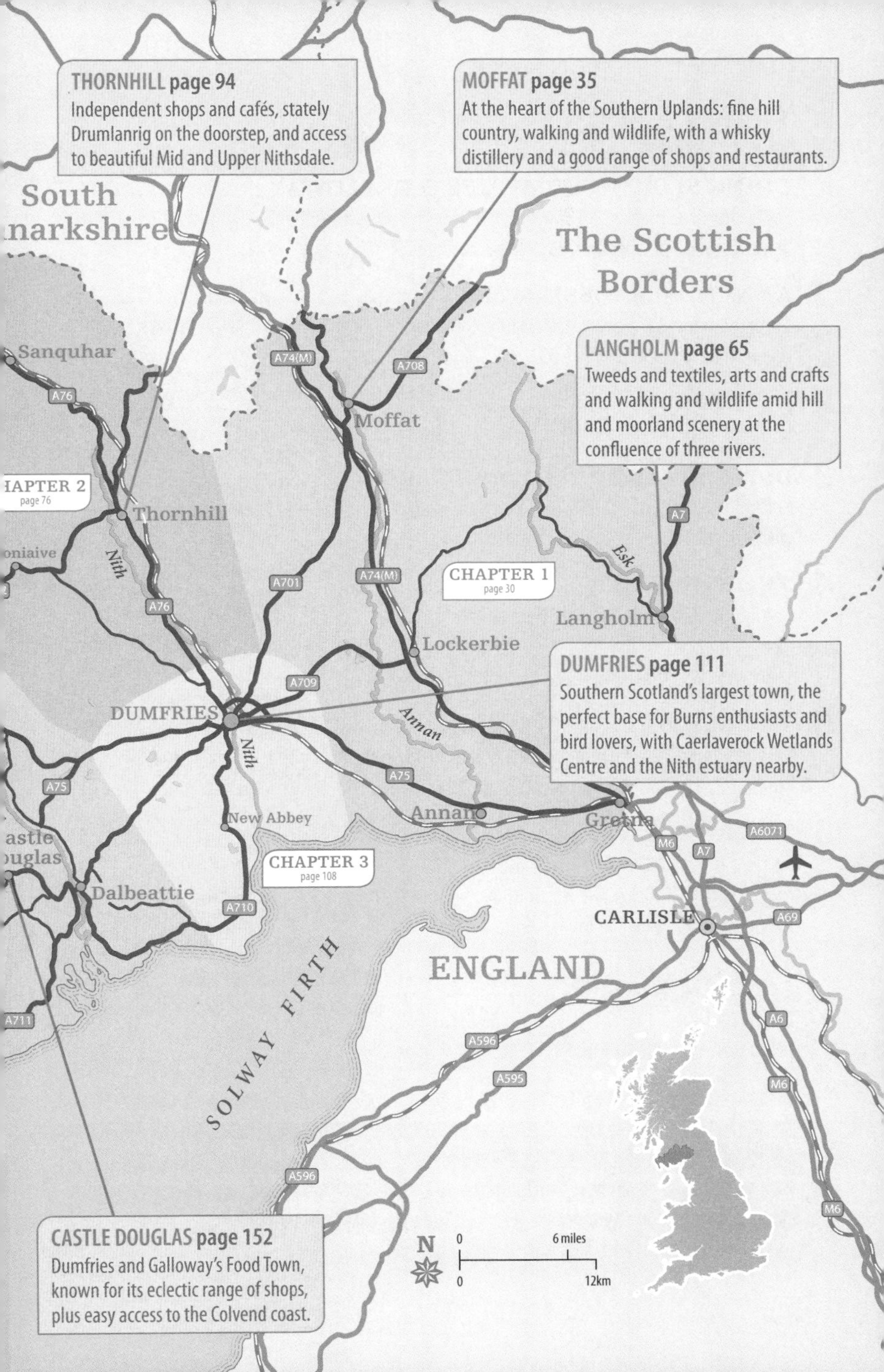
THORNHILL page 94
Independent shops and cafés, stately Drumlanrig on the doorstep, and access to beautiful Mid and Upper Nithsdale.
MOFFAT page 35
At the heart of the Southern Uplands: fine hill country, walking and wildlife, with a whisky distillery and a good range of shops and restaurants.
South
narkshire
The Scottish
Borders
LANGHOLM page 65
Tweeds and textiles, arts and crafts and walking and wildlife amid hill and moorland scenery at the confluence of three rivers.
Sanquhar
A74(M)
A708
A76
Moffat
APTER 2
page 76
Thornhill
A7
oniaive
Nith
Esk
A701
A74(M)
CHAPTER 1
page 30
A76
Langholm
Lockerbie
DUMFRIES page 111
Southern Scotland's largest town, the perfect base for Burns enthusiasts and bird lovers, with Caerlaverock Wetlands Centre and the Nith estuary nearby.
A709
DUMFRIES
Annan
Nith
A75
A75
New Abbey
Annan
Gretna
astle
uglas
A6071
M6
A7
CHAPTER 3
page 108
Dalbeattie
A710
CARLISLE
A69
SOLWAY FIRTH
ENGLAND
A711
A6
A596
A595
M6
A596
M6
CASTLE DOUGLAS page 152
Dumfries and Galloway's Food Town, known for its eclectic range of shops, plus easy access to the Colvend coast.
N
0
6 miles
0
12km

CONTENTS

A NOTE ON 'I' & 'WE'

With two of us involved in researching and writing this book, you will find references in the text to both 'I' and 'we'. Wherever 'I' is used, it is a comment from Donald.

GOING SLOW IN
DUMFRIES & GALLOWAY

Often described as 'Scotland's forgotten corner', Dumfries and Galloway is one of the country's most under-explored areas. Bordered to the south and west by coastline and to the north by wild moorland and hill country, the region has for centuries been seen as a remote rural outpost. The easiest access point is from the east, where the A74(M) follows, out of necessity, the north–south travel route of old, for the Annan Valley and Solway Plain offer the most viable place for a major roadway. This means many travellers enter and leave Dumfries and Galloway in less than an hour, heading for points north or south with ne'er a moment's thought for what lies east or west. And, it has to be said, the motorway route gives little away: the flatlands around Carlisle stretch up past the eastern end of the Solway Firth and the region presents a distinctly demure face. There are few geographical features of note along the route other than at the northern boundary where the Moffat Hills loom large to the east and the Lowther Hills to the west. What can be seen of those hills gives just a hint of the wilderness that awaits those who slow down and make time for a diversion, for Dumfries and Galloway is home to some of the most glorious scenery of the Scottish Lowlands, scenery which can still fill me to bursting every time I see it.

Accounting for one eighth of Scotland's total land mass, Dumfries and Galloway is a large region, by road almost 120 miles from Langholm in the east to Portpatrick in the west, and over 55 miles at its deepest point from Kirkconnel in the north to Kirkcudbright in the south. What's more, it is sparsely populated. Out of Scotland's 32 unitary authorities, it is the third largest by area but, with a population of just under 149,000 (National Records of Scotland, mid-year population estimate 2018), it has just 23 people per square kilometre. This compares with the Scottish average of 69, the UK average of 261 and English average of 407. Beyond

THE SLOW MINDSET

Hilary Bradt, Founder, Bradt Travel Guides

We shall not cease from exploration
And the end of all our exploring
Will be to arrive where we started
And know the place for the first time.

T S Eliot, 'Little Gidding', *Four Quartets*

This series evolved, slowly, from a Bradt editorial meeting when we started to explore ideas for guides to our favourite country – Great Britain. We wanted to get away from the usual 'top sights' formula and encourage our authors to bring out the nuances and local differences that make up a sense of place – such things as food, building styles, nature, geology or local people and what makes them tick. Our aim was to create a series that celebrates the present, focusing on sustainable tourism, rather than taking a nostalgic wallow in the past.

So without our realising it at the time, we had defined 'Slow Travel', or at least our concept of it. For the beauty of the Slow movement is that there is no fixed definition; we adapt the philosophy to fit our individual needs and aspirations. Thus Carl Honoré, author of *In Praise of Slow*, writes: 'The Slow Movement is a cultural revolution against the notion that faster is always better. It's not about doing everything at a snail's pace, it's about seeking to do everything at the right speed. Savouring the hours and minutes rather than just counting them. Doing everything as well as possible, instead of as fast as possible. It's about quality over quantity in everything from work to food to parenting.' And travel.

So take time to explore. Don't rush it, get to know an area – and the people who live there – and you'll be as delighted as the authors by what you find.

the main towns of Dumfries, Stranraer and Annan, all other settlements have a population of less than 4,500.

Our advice is not to attempt to cover all of the region in one go. Any one of the six areas into which this book is divided offers sufficient interest to fill a Slow week or more. And, despite its size, if you do want to cover more ground once you're here, the trans-regional A75 offers quick and convenient access to most points.

One of the comments we hear regularly from first-time visitors is 'I never knew that this was here!'. So what is it that takes them by surprise? Certainly the grandeur and variety of scenery combined with the sense of space and a distinctly slower pace of life rank highly. A day spent in the Dumfriesshire Dales or Galloway Uplands soon confirms – if confirmation were needed – that, while the north of Scotland undoubtedly has majestic mountains, you don't have to travel those extra four or five hours (if coming from the south) to find landscapes that impress. Here, you can be on a pristine sandy beach in the morning and at Scotland's highest village (and micro-brewery) by the afternoon. And speaking of travel times, it's worth pointing out that it takes less than an hour longer (according to the AA website) to get here from London than it would to reach Penzance. For those already in Scotland, it's even better. From Glasgow and Edinburgh it's only an hour or so to the northern reaches of the area, while from Aberdeen it's less than five hours. Distance, therefore, is not the obstacle that some may perceive it to be.

Wildlife, history and food and drink are also part of the attraction, and so too are regional specialities, festivals and events and beaches. There's also an increasing range of accommodation of increasingly high standard, while walking and cycling are as good as you'll find anywhere else in the country. This quiet corner of Scotland is starting to make its presence felt on the tourist map; now is a perfect time to come, while it's relatively undiscovered, its infrastructure keeps pace with an increasing number of visitors, traffic continues to flow smoothly and the local welcome is as friendly as you could wish for. For those who are familiar with Dumfries and Galloway (especially those readers who are resident), we hope that you find much in this book to enjoy and perhaps a story or two that will take you by surprise. For those who are just discovering the area, we welcome you to a part of the world which, in this day of mass-market living, remains true to itself and is resolutely and irresistibly real, a sure hallmark of the best of 'Slow'.

FEEDBACK REQUEST & UPDATES WEBSITE

We've scrutinised our sources and travelled the length of the region, but slip-ups can occur. If you spot an omission or error, or if you come across a new attraction or a story that you think should be shared, please get in touch, either directly with the authors (details on slowbritain.co.uk) or via Bradt: 01753 893444 or info@bradtguides.com.

Contact can also be made via the Facebook page that accompanies this guide: Slow Britain and you can also add a review to bradtguides.com or on Amazon.co.uk.

SOME PRACTICAL MATTERS

The unitary authority of Dumfries and Galloway is very much an artificial construct and there are a multitude of ways in which the region could be broken down: geographic features, historic names, regional divisions past and present… all are used depending on who you speak to, personal preference and what it is they're telling you. In the end we have opted for a mix of all of the above, which we believe is logical in terms of either travelling around the region or basing yourself in just one area, combined with the dictates of geography, how the region is viewed by local people and how you might come to view it yourself. Our aim has been to make sense of it in a way that is easy to get to grips with for first-time visitors but which has a familiarity for repeat visitors and those who live here.

Broadly speaking, we have broken Dumfriesshire down into its three valleys, Annandale, Eskdale and Nithsdale, with chapters progressing from north to south. Nithsdale itself is split into two chapters to allow greater space for coverage of Dumfries. For Galloway, we have taken the old, fondly remembered district of the Stewartry as one chapter, with the rest of the area broken down into its naturally occurring geographical divisions of the Machars (and Moors) and the Rhins. All have their own distinct identities and each area offers more than enough for a Slow holiday in its own right.

MAPS

Each chapter begins with a map complete with numbered stopping points that correspond to the numbers found within the text. These include all the main towns and sights, plus a few of the more unusual or remote features. To avoid overcrowding the maps we have also included a grid reference in the text for places that are off the beaten track. The symbol on these maps indicates that there is a walk in that area. There are also sketch maps for some of these featured walks and there is a map for Dumfries town centre.

It takes nine 1:50,000 OS Landranger maps to cover every corner of the region (numbers 71, 76, 77, 78, 79, 82, 83, 84 and 85). To make life easier we use the OS Custom Made service, which allows you to create a personalised map based on a precise area of your choice. See ordnancesurvey.co.uk.

ACCOMMODATION

On page 258 we list accommodation suggestions for each area. From smart hotels to glamping in shepherds' huts, each place has been chosen because it has a special quality, be that its location, character or service. Within the text, hotels and B&Bs are indicated by 🏠 under the heading for the area in which they are located. Self-catering options are indicated by 🏠, campsites and caravan parks by ⛺ and glamping sites by ⛺. For in-depth reviews and additional listings, go to bradtguides.com/D&Gsleeps.

FOOD & DRINK

Recommendations are very much our personal take on places we have enjoyed, that perhaps offer an interesting menu or local specialities, something quirky or a cracking view. Alternatively, they're simply included where there were no other options in that remote location. If you come across somewhere memorable we haven't included, please tell us about your find.

ONLINE CONTENT

Throughout the guide you will spot the symbol 👆 in the text. This indicates that additional information on a specific subject or attraction can be found online at slowbritain.co.uk, the website set up by the

A NOTE ON BEACHES, THE COAST & TIDES

The coastline of the Solway Firth offers a good choice of beaches: sandy, rocky or simply muddy and estuarine. Be aware though that the Solway tides run fast with a tidal rise of over 20ft, while in some places the tidal bore reaches 3–4ft and travels at six to seven knots. If you are in an area such as the estuary flats in the eastern end of the region or the merse further west, keep an eye open and don't take chances. If you're looking for somewhere to swim, generally speaking the more sheltered bays and coves of the Stewartry coast are the most popular. For walking and simply enjoying the sea air, there are also some stunning stretches of sand on the west coast of the Machars and the eastern Rhins. Specific beaches have been identified in the text and the website of the Solway Firth Partnership (solwayfirthpartnership.co.uk) has an excellent guide that details beaches with a 'Family Star Rating' and 'Adventurers Rating'. It also has links to tide times for specific locations.

An annual booklet on Solway Tides is available from many local newsagents and post offices for a small cost.

authors to accompany this guide. On the same website you will also find details of updates and/or reader feedback as it reaches us, plus photographs from across the region.

MOBILE COVERAGE & WI-FI

If accessing online content while out and about, you'll find that mobile/4G coverage is patchy, but you normally don't have to travel far for it to connect. Many cafés, B&Bs and other establishments also have Wi-Fi.

GETTING AROUND DUMFRIES & GALLOWAY

There is no denying that travelling around the area by public transport can be tricky, particularly when trying to get to some of the more out-of-the-way places.

Train

Three train lines run north–south. In the east the main **national West Coast line** runs through Annandale but has only one station, at Lockerbie. Some trains from the south do stop here en route to Glasgow or Edinburgh, while others only stop at Carlisle where you have to change.

The **Nithsdale line** is particularly scenic, passing along the eastern end of the Solway to Gretna and Annan, and then on into Nithsdale. From Dumfries it continues north up the Nith Valley to Glasgow via Kirkconnel and Sanquhar, the only station on the Southern Upland Way walking route (page 14).

Also scenic is the **western line from Stranraer** up the eastern edge of the Rhins into Ayrshire and on to Glasgow. The return journey offers particularly good views of the moors and, on a clear day, across to the Isle of Man.

Michael Pearson's *Iron Roads to Burns Country* offers lots of detail on and stories of these routes.

Significant chunks of the region, notably the Stewartry and the Machars, lost their lines in the Beeching cuts of the 1960s. Campaign groups are lobbying for stations at Beattock, Thornhill, Eastriggs and Dunragit, and for the Lockerbie–Dumfries and Dumfries–Stranraer lines, to be reopened. The wheels turn slowly, though, and it is likely to be many years before something (if anything) happens.

Bus

Bus services offer more options for getting around, with most places you could wish to visit having a service or two, although frequency can vary widely and even the more popular routes peter out in the evening and on Sunday. We advise not heading off on a day trip by bus without first making sure you can get back. Double check timetables and perhaps carry a local taxi number with you (although be warned, mobile phone signal can be patchy).

We have outlined key transport options at the start of each chapter. Local public transport information is provided by South West of Scotland Transport Partnership (swestrans.org.uk), or alternatively Traveline (0871 2002233 traveline.info). Local bus timetables can also be downloaded from dumgal.gov.uk/timetables.

Car

If driving, watch your speed. On the main trunk roads, which are often quiet in comparison with many other areas of the UK, it is tempting to put your foot down, but the exceptionally diligent local police are regularly out with mobile speed cameras. Note that unlike England, Scotland doesn't offer the choice of a speed awareness course instead of a fine.

Walking

The area is superb for walking. Most of the countryside, from mountain to forest and moorland to seashore, is accessible with observance of the Country Code. While contentious when it came on to the statute book, few landowners we speak to have any issue with Scotland's Right to Roam. That said, avoiding walking close to sheep (especially during lambing) and cattle is appreciated and advisable (and if you do find a

KNOW THE CODE BEFORE YOU GO

Everyone has the right to be on most land and inland water providing they act responsibly. Your access rights and responsibilities are explained fully in the Scottish Outdoor Access Code (outdooraccess-scotland.com) from Scottish Natural Heritage.

The key things to remember are:

- Take responsibility for your own actions
- Respect the interests of other people
- Care for the environment

lone lamb please leave it where it is as the mother won't be far away). Always leave gates as you find them and, no matter the time of year, if there is livestock around keep dogs on leads.

The absence on Scottish OS maps of dashed lines indicating footpaths and bridleways can make it harder to determine routes that have been used before or to know if you are likely to end up at an impasse a few miles in. Local bookshops hold a wealth of walking information, as does a Google search for any area you happen to be visiting. For ease of reference, we use a highlighter to add routes to our OS maps. There are numerous quality walking books to the area. Our own walking guides, *The Dumfriesshire Dales* and *Galloway* (Pocket Mountains' pocketmountains.com), each have a selection of 40 walks suitable for all abilities, in a handy pocket format. The classic Pathfinder Guide series also covers the area in a single volume. Dumfries and Galloway Council produces a fine selection of free walking and cycling downloads, available from dumgal.gov.uk (look under 'Leisure' and then 'Outdoor Access and Paths').

LOCAL & LONG-DISTANCE ROUTES

A number of local and long-distance routes cross the area including **The Southern Upland Way** (southernuplandway.gov.uk), which runs for 214 miles from Portpatrick on the west coast to Cockburnspath on the east, with a series of kists to find along the way. Shorter walks incorporating parts of the route can be followed and many are detailed in a leaflet available by making contact with the rangers through the website. From east to west, there is also:

Annandale Way annandaleway.org. From Moffat to the Solway at Annan (55 miles).
Sir Walter Scott Way sirwalterscottway.com. A 92-mile subsection of the Southern Upland Way, from Moffat to Cockburnspath.
The Glenkens Way gallowayglens.org/projects/glenkens-way. In development at the time of writing, this route will run from New Galloway to Carsphairn.
The Whithorn Way whithornway.org. Follow the footsteps of pilgrims of old on this 149-mile route from Glasgow to St Ninian's Cave.
Rhins of Galloway Coast Path f. Circular 84-mile path right around the Rhins.

Cycling

The many miles of quiet lanes and forest tracks offer cycling opportunities for all levels of ability, from a simple ride out along the estuary flats through to more hair-raising options such as an extreme black grade mountain bike run. In tandem with the development of the **South West Coastal 300** driving route (page 20), a comparable **cycling route** has been devised (sw300.net), taking in many of the region's sights.

Linking Sunderland and Inverness, **National Cycle Route 7** (NCR7) passes right through Dumfries and Galloway, taking in Gretna, Dumfries, Castle Douglas and Newton Stewart before crossing Glen Trool Forest on its way north. The Newton Stewart via Glasgow to Inverness section also forms part of the **EuroVelo 1 Route**, which starts in Portugal and follows the Atlantic seaboard through France and Ireland. In the east, the **NCR74** links Gretna to Lockerbie and Moffat on its 74-mile route northwards to Douglas (sustrans.org.uk).

A **Southern Upland Cycleway** is currently under development. A full guide is available from the Southern Upland Way website (southernuplandway.gov.uk), detailing which sections are good for cycling and alternatives for those that are not.

The area is also home to a number of the world-famous **7stanes trails** (7stanesmountainbiking.com), a series of seven mountain-biking trail centres that span the south of Scotland.

Dumfries and Galloway Council details a number of cycling routes in downloads available from info.dumgal.gov.uk/mapviewers/pathsmap.aspx. Click on the red dots for cycling routes. Information is also available at gosmartdumfries.co.uk and bikemap.net.

Trailbrakes Biking Holidays (trailbrakes.co.uk) has devised its own coast-to-coast route from Portpatrick across to Berwick-upon-Tweed, while **Galloway Cycling Holidays** (gallowaycycling.com) offers a range of suggested routes and can organise accommodation, transfers and luggage transfers.

A 125-mile **coast-to-coast** route from Annan to the Forth Road Bridge at Edinburgh has also been devised, details of which are given in *The Ultimate Scottish C2C Guide* by Richard Price, published in 2015.

TOURIST INFORMATION & ADDITIONAL RESOURCES

In addition to the sites listed in the following section, there are many Dumfries and Galloway pages on Facebook, including We Love Dumfries and Galloway and Dog Friendly Eating Places in Dumfries and Galloway. Local and site-specific Facebook pages are included throughout the guide. Details of information centres are given at the start of each chapter.

A NOTE ON OPENING HOURS *(see also page 28)*

Normal opening hours are as you would expect (⏲ 09.00–17.00 or 17.30 Mon–Fri), with many attractions detailing a last entry time either an hour or half an hour before the official closing time. Opening hours have been included in this guide in as much detail as is practicably possible. Months listed are inclusive, so Apr–Sep means from 1 April to 31 September.

Many places operate seasonal hours, meaning they close during the winter, generally from October to March or until Easter, taking Easter weekend as the start of the season. Some businesses close for lunch and some villages and towns still have half-day closing for banks, post offices and those shops that elect to take it. This is usually on a Wednesday.

The area has many lifestyle businesses, for whom opening hours are often not standard: hours can change from one week or month to the next.

We strongly recommend checking opening hours of individual attractions and businesses online before setting out. We have learned this the hard way!

Tourism organisations

VisitScotland visitscotland.com/destinations-maps/dumfries-galloway. Primary information provision is online, but there is an information centre in Dumfries (see box, page 110).

Visit South West Scotland visitsouthwestscotland.com. Lots of information on the website and it was also behind the new South West Coastal 300 route (page 20).

Local media

Local newspapers One distinctive delight of this region is the plethora of regional newspapers that are still available from local newsagents. Look out for the *Annandale Observer, Annandale Herald, Moffat News, The Galloway News, Dumfries and Galloway Standard,* and *Stranraer and Wigtownshire Free Press,* to name but a few.

Local magazines The award-winning, monthly glossy magazine *Dumfries and Galloway Life* (f) covers everything from arts and business to community and wildlife and is available from newsagents or by subscription. *Our Wigtownshire* magazine f is also available, covering life in the western end of the region.

Local websites

Slow Britain slowbritain.co.uk f Our own Facebook page is updated regularly with details of travels around the region and contains an archive of images, places to visit, accommodation and restaurants.

Dumfries and Galloway! What's Going On? dgwgo.com f A superb community-based online resource for news and information about what's going on in the region.

MAKING THE MOST OF SLOW DUMFRIES & GALLOWAY

Getting the most out of Dumfries and Galloway is a matter of taking time to discover and understand what makes the region tick, from the local economy to habitats and wildlife, history and culture.

ECONOMY

In terms of the economy, Dumfries and Galloway relies chiefly on **agriculture**, with centuries of sheep, dairy and beef farming having shaped the landscape and informed the development of a strong local food tradition. The south of Scotland (Dumfries and Galloway and the Scottish Borders regions combined) is the country's third-largest farming area, although farmers are increasingly diversifying, chiefly into renewable energy and holiday property. Nonetheless, this combined region is home to the largest numbers of dairy cattle, beef cattle, sheep and laying hens in Scotland.

Tourism is the second-largest sector, and this in turn is linked closely with the **creative industries**, the region's fastest-growing sector. The number of artists and producers living here is particularly high.

Forestry also contributes significantly. Dumfries and Galloway is one of the most wooded areas in Scotland, with large tracts – around 30% of the land area in total – given over to commercial forestry under Forestry and Land Scotland, which produces around 30% of Scotland's annual timber production. Galloway Forest Park on its own covers 299 square miles and is the largest forest in the UK.

Scotland's **renewable power** record is well documented and the country is progressing towards the Scottish government's goal of using renewable energy sources to provide 100% of the nation's gross annual electricity. Dumfries and Galloway plays a significant role, with wind farms scattered across its northern reaches.

GALLOWAY: A NATIONAL PARK?

In the west of the region, the unique mix of geography and landscape, wildlife, history and culture (and more besides) has prompted a campaign to be launched for Galloway to become Scotland's third national park. Check out gallowaynationalpark.org for more information.

THE BELTED GALLOWAY

The south of Scotland in general has a reputation for producing good-quality livestock with some notable native breeds. Galloway cattle are known for their hardiness, with the distinctive Belted Galloway being the most popularly celebrated subspecies. One of the most iconic – and much loved – sights of the region is that of Belted Galloway cattle, completely black except for a white stripe around the middle, set against a background of lush green hills.

Since the 1920s Belties, as they are commonly known, have been exported all over the world and herds are found today in mainland Europe, the USA, Canada, Australia, New Zealand and Africa. Even if you've never had much interest in cattle, it is difficult not to take a certain delight in this quirky looking breed. More information on Galloway cattle is available from the eponymous society at gallowaycattlesociety.co.uk and information specifically on Belties can be found at beltedgalloways.co.uk. For the story of one of the renowned early breeders of Belted Galloway, Miss Flora Stuart, see box, page 218.

The main private landowner is the **Duke of Buccleuch** (pronounced Buc-clue), said to be Scotland's second-largest land owner after Danish clothing billionaire Anders Holch Povlsen (strictly speaking the land is held in trust). He has two Dumfries and Galloway estates, one at Langholm, and the other, Drumlanrig, near Thornhill (page 91).

Two major developments that are expected to help drive development are the creation of the **South of Scotland Economic Partnership** (sosep.co.uk) and attendant South of Scotland Enterprise Agency, and the **Borderlands Growth Deal** (www.borderlandsgrowth.com), which brings together the five local councils of Dumfries and Galloway, Scottish Borders, Northumberland, Carlisle and Cumbria to promote the economic growth of the area that straddles the Scotland–England border.

HABITATS & WILDLIFE

Dumfries and Galloway is recognised for its biodiversity and scenic value and boasts many areas with Scottish Natural Heritage (SNH nature.scot) designations (some with multiple designations), from the three National Scenic Areas of Nith Estuary, East Stewartry Coast and Fleet Valley to Local Nature Reserves, Ramsar sites, Special Protection Areas, Special Areas of Conservation and Sites of Special Scientific Interest (of which there are 94 across the region). SNH has also designated almost 20% of Scotland as Wild Land Areas, all of which are in the north and west of the country, except for two in Dumfries and Galloway: Talla-Hart Fell (page 43) and Merrick, southern Scotland's highest summit (page 197).

Much of the Stewartry is also included in the **Galloway and Southern Ayrshire Biosphere** (gsabiosphere.org.uk), the country's first UNESCO Biosphere and, in their words, 'a world-class environment for people and nature'. At a local level Dumfries and Galloway Council has identified ten **Regional Scenic Areas**, from the Moffat and Langholm hills in the east across to the Rhins coast.

The region's habitats are classified by the South West Scotland Environmental Information Centre (SWSEIC swseic.org.uk), the local records centre, as fen and peatland, woodlands, wetlands, urban, upland, grassland, farmland and coastal and marine. SWSEIC's website also includes a breakdown of species types, from amphibians and reptiles to birds, butterflies and moths, fungi and lichens, and terrestrial mammals to name a few, along with helpful identification and distribution notes.

There are several **RSPB** sites (rspb.org.uk) in the region, all of which are detailed in the text, as well as the **WWT Caerlaverock Wetland Centre** (wwt.org.uk). The **South of Scotland Golden Eagle Project** (goldeneaglessouthofscotland.co.uk) is managing the reintroduction of Golden Eagles to the region, though at present numbers are low and they are found across a large area, so spotting them is far from guaranteed.

In addition to large areas of commercial forestry, there are also a number of ongoing small- and large-scale projects replanting 'natural' broad-leaved woodland by organisations such as the Borders Forest Trust and Moffat's Gallow Hill.

Alan Mcfadyen (scottishphotographyhides.co.uk) offers **wildlife photography courses** and exclusive use of his hides in the Kirkcudbright area (as featured in BBC's *Autumnwatch*). Adders, owls, kingfishers and pine martens are just a few of the species to be spotted.

KNOW YOUR BIRDS?

Local birdlife is abundant, but if you're not up to speed on the difference between a chiff-chaff and a dipper, there are lots of apps to choose from to help identify what's what. We use **Pocket Birds**, but there are many others available. One request if you do have an app is to resist the temptation to use the birdsong feature to flush out wild birds, as they need all the energy they have to get through the long winter and busy nesting seasons.

THE SOUTH WEST COASTAL 300

The enormous success of the North Coast 500 around the north of Scotland has prompted other Scottish regions to come up with their own versions. Dumfries and Galloway's is the South West Coastal 300 (visitsouthwestscotland.com/swc300), a 300-mile route covering many coastal and hill sites, from Moffat in the northeast of the region to the Mull of Galloway in the far southwest, and also up into neighbouring Ayrshire. Stunning hill scenery, fishing villages, dramatic passes, remote moorlands and country roads that hug the coastline all feature. All of the Dumfries and Galloway locations are included in this guide. We recommend choosing a selection of places and stopping for a couple of nights in each.

STARGAZING

Galloway Forest Park was designated as the UK's first Dark Sky Park in 2009 and astronomy and stargazing are an increasingly popular attraction there. Moffat became the UK's first Dark Sky Town in 2016 and has its own observatory (page 36).

SAVOURING THE TASTES OF DUMFRIES & GALLOWAY

One of the most noticeable things about Dumfries and Galloway's high streets is that many still have an independent butcher. This is in keeping with the region's reputation for locally produced meat, but it comes as a pleasant surprise in a day when for many people a pre-packed joint from a supermarket is the only option. Greengrocers, too, are not uncommon, and every town also has at least one baker. Town centre individuality and distinctiveness hasn't been completely lost here. Castle Douglas in particular is celebrated for its range of independent shops and is the region's official 'Food Town'; it even has its own high street brewery. In the far west, Stranraer now hosts an annual Oyster Festival (see box, page 234).

Local specialities suggest the region has a sweet tooth and include Moffat Toffee (available from the eponymous shop in Moffat), Cream o' Galloway ice cream, Galloway Lodge Preserves' range of marmalades, jams and jellies, and chocolate from the Cocoabean Company and Moniaive Chocolatiers (who are actually in Thornhill, not Moniaive). Locally produced meat and locally caught fish are both widely available,

RECIPES FOR SUCCESS

LOGAN BAKEHOUSE SHORTBREAD

Heading along to the west of the region, Jo and Lyn at the Logan Bakehouse (see box, page 248) make mouth-wateringly good shortbread, that great Scottish staple, from a recipe given to them by Jane Bentley of Drummore. It has an unexpected and delicious twist, as it also contains rosemary and seasalt.

Ingredients

Quantities given make 20–30 biscuits.

9 oz soft unsalted butter
3½ oz caster sugar
½ tsp fine sea salt
1 tbsp chopped fresh rosemary
9 oz plain flour
4½ oz corn flour
1½ oz granulated sugar, mixed with 1 tsp Maldon sea salt

Method

Preheat the oven to 180°C/fan 160°C/gas mark 4.

In a bowl, cream together the butter, fine salt, sugar and rosemary. Sift in both flours. Bring the mixture together by hand to form a smooth dough, roll it out on a floured surface (we like to make the biscuits quite thin – about 5mm thick) and cut out using a biscuit cutter. Gather the leftover dough together, roll out again and cut out more biscuits; repeat until all the dough has been used up.

Place the biscuits on a tray lined with baking paper, and bake for 15 to 20 minutes (we like them lightly baked). Take them out of the oven when they are still soft as they firm up when cooling. Sprinkle with the granulated sugar and Maldon sea salt mix and leave to cool.

CAFÉ ARIETE'S ECCLEFECHAN TART

Ecclefechan in the east of the region is known partly for its tart, a fruity concoction with a pastry base that is perfect for afternoon tea or dessert. At Café Ariete in Moffat (page 41), Vivienne produces a scrumptious tart using her own recipe, a version of which can be found on the Slow Britain website (page 11), where you'll also find a recipe for a Beltie beef and stout casserole.

the latter notably from smokehouses in the west of the region. A few producers to note are Galloway Smokehouse, Marrbury Smokehouse, Clash Farm and The Ethical Dairy. The Little Bakery in Dumfries has teamed up with the Galloway Cattle Society to produce the Galloway pie: Galloway beef in a rich gravy encased in a Scotch pie shell with a puff pastry top.

WILD FOOD: THE ULTIMATE IN SLOW FOOD?

Dumfries and Galloway's resident forager, Mark Williams of Galloway Wild Foods (gallowaywildfoods.com), works closely with a number of local restaurants and also runs courses, walks and scheduled and tailored events throughout the region and across Scotland. His website is a vast free wild food guide, providing in-depth information and recipes, as well as an examination of the broader issues around how foraging can fit into our modern world. We are grateful to him for supplying the following text.

Practised mindfully, foraging delivers good, clean, fair food for everybody. To find, identify, sustainably harvest, process, cook and eat wild ingredients is to connect with the land and seasons, affording a deep intimacy with one's food, restoring the vital connection between us and the land.

Local, organic, sustainable, healthy gastronomy is entwined in the very roots of wild foods and Galloway is the best place in the UK to learn about and gather it.

The warming influence of the Gulf Stream and the shelter from Atlantic storms afforded by Ireland means southwest Scotland enjoys a warmer, gentler climate than comparable areas on similar latitudes. This allows a vast range of species to thrive year-round. I can gather over 300 varieties of plant, fungi, seaweed and shellfish within 20 minutes' walk from my home in the Fleet Valley near Gatehouse of Fleet.

As a 'peninsula of peninsulas', Galloway boasts a huge variety of coastal habitats – from tidal estuaries of saltmarsh to rocky shores and opulent beaches – all fine hunting grounds for coastal foragers.

Inland, habitats become even more diverse – a patchwork of farmland framed by bountiful hedgerows, vast deciduous and coniferous forests rich in diverse fungi and upland moors full of aromatic herbs.

With our right to roam and responsibly gather leaves, seeds and fungi for personal use enshrined in Scottish law, the largely unspoiled wild delights of southwest Scotland are there for all to enjoy for free.

An increasing number of **distilleries and breweries** is spread across the region and whisky, gin, rum and beer makers are all covered in the text. Surprisingly, there is even a **wine** producer here, Glebe House Winery (glebehousewinery.co.uk) just outside Ecclefechan.

Farmers' markets are held regularly; details are posted on dgmarkets.org.

FESTIVALS & EVENTS

A wide range of festivals and events takes place across the region throughout the year – far too many to include them all here, but a few of the main ones are detailed below. In addition, classical music is well represented by **Absolute Classics** (absoluteclassics.co.uk), which brings world-class talent to the region, while **Driftwood Cinema** (driftwoodcinema.org) screens movies across the region in villages and small towns.

The Big Burns Supper bigburnssupper.com. A stonkingly good musical & arts bash held each year in Dumfries over the course of 7–10 days at the end of January.
Spring Fling spring-fling.co.uk. 'Scotland's Premier Art and Craft Open Studio Event', which takes place primarily in May across the region.
Dumfries & Galloway Arts Festival dgartsfestival.org.uk. Scotland's longest-running rural performing arts festival, usually held in May.
The Eden Festival edenfestival.co.uk. A family-friendly music event, held just south of Moffat and over a weekend, usually in June.

SOME HISTORICAL PERSPECTIVES

While travelling around the region you are likely to come across – repeatedly – a few historical aspects of local and national life which may require further explanation.

'The Galloway Hoard', a collection of over 100 objects, was discovered in Dumfries and Galloway in 2014. It is described by the National Museum of Scotland in Edinburgh, where it is now housed, as 'the richest collection of rare and unique Viking-age objects ever found in Britain or Ireland'. Check out nms.ac.uk for full details and for touring exhibitions.

The **Solway Military Trail** (solwaymilitarytrail.co.uk) pulls together, in four separate driving trails, military sites from more recent times on both Cumbrian and Dumfries and Galloway sides of the Solway.

The southwest end of the **Merlin Trail** (merlintrail.com) also crosses the region, incorporating sites associated with the legendary wizard and – according to some accounts – the real Merlin, a 6th-century Druid living in southern Scotland.

And on a more prosaic, vernacular note… the region's **built heritage** is worthy of further exploration – visit dumgal.gov.uk/article/16042/Listed-buildings as a starting point; over 3,400 buildings, objects and structures that are considered to have special historical or architectural interest are listed.

REIVERS & THE 'DEBATABLE LANDS'

The eastern end of Dumfries and Galloway, beyond the Solway, is demarcated by a land boundary with neighbouring England, where over the centuries two warring nations came face to face. This has been a vital geographical pinch point in the development of not just Dumfries and Galloway, but of Scotland as a whole, and the skirmishes that played out here in times past were particularly persistent and violent. From the 13th to early 17th centuries the area from the Solway near Carlisle northeast through Canonbie and up to Langholm belonged to neither England nor Scotland and was known as the 'Debatable Lands'.

The people who lived on either side of the border were in a permanent state of turmoil, with their lands often pillaged by armies travelling north or south. Deprived of their livelihood, the practice of 'reiving' took hold and was passed down through the generations. 'Reiver' comes from the early English for 'rob' and has given rise to the modern 'ruffian'. Both Scottish and English would undertake daring raids into each other's lands, most commonly in winter when long hours of darkness provided cover, to steal cattle and generally wreak havoc. Reiving was an accepted way of life based on tribal affiliations rather than nationality, for raids between clans were just as common as cross-border incursions. It was only with the Union of the Crowns in 1603, on the accession of James VI of Scotland to the throne of England, that order began to be restored.

Visitors to the northern end of Annandale might wish to head for the Devil's Beef Tub (page 45), a scenic spot with reiving associations. If you visit the Langholm area in southern Eskdale, we have included a walk 'in the footsteps of the Border Reivers' (see box, page 68).

COVENANTERS & THE 'KILLING TIMES'

When James VI (James I of England and Ireland) died in 1625, he left to his son, Charles I, a Scottish church divided. During his reign he had attempted to re-establish episcopacy in Scotland, a policy that was resisted by the Presbyterians. On acceding to the throne, Charles I took up where his father had left off and in 1637 at St Giles Cathedral in Edinburgh a new liturgy was read publicly for the first time, effectively bringing the Church of England to Scotland. The resulting riot led eventually to the widespread signing in 1638 of the National Covenant, which demanded a Scottish Parliament and General Assembly free from the interference of the monarch. Those who signed the Covenant

BRUCE, BURNS & BARRIE

Bruce, Burns and Barrie are three of the most notable names associated with Dumfries and Galloway.

Robert the Bruce (1274–1329), who led the Scots in the Wars of Independence and famously defeated a much larger English army at Bannockburn in 1314, was descended from the Lords of Annandale. Four Bruce trails cross the region (one walking trail, in Dumfries, and three driving trails), detailed on the website of the Medieval Heritage Bruce Trust (🖱 brucetrust.co.uk).

Robert Burns (1759–96), famous the world over as Scotland's national bard, lived the last nine years of his life in Dumfriesshire and is buried in Dumfries itself. VisitScotland (🖱 visitscotland.com) has devised a Burns Heritage Trail incorporating sights associated with him.

And for the child in us all, JM Barrie (1860–1937), author of *Peter Pan*, had strong associations with Dumfries; the garden in which he invented Neverland is part of Scotland's National Centre for Children's Literature and Storytelling at Moat Brae (see box, page 116).

became known as Covenanters. Thus started a tumultuous period of extreme repression that lasted until the accession of William and Mary in 1689.

During this period, southern Scotland, and the southwest in particular, was strongly Covenanter and over 300 ministers in the Lowlands left their churches, many choosing to hold open-air services in the hills, gatherings that became known as Conventicles. Such services were particularly risky as it was an offence punishable by death to preach from anything other than the Book of Common Prayer, drawn up by Charles's Commission in 1637.

The appointment of John Graham of Claverhouse (known as either 'Bonnie Dundee' or 'Bluidy Clavers' depending on which side you stood) in 1681 to bring the southwest to heel marked the start of a particularly brutal campaign in which dissidents were tracked down and executed. In total 82 people were killed in Dumfries and Galloway by Claverhouse and his supporter, Sir Robert Grierson of Lag, Steward Depute of Kirkcudbright, in a period that has become known as the 'Killing Times'.

In many of the churchyards across the region today you will come across Covenanter graves, some of which have been identified in the text of this guide. Many churches also still hold Conventicles once a year, to which all are welcome.

COMMON RIDINGS

The tradition of Common Ridings stems from the 13th and 14th centuries, when local townspeople would ride out to patrol the boundaries of their town to protect it against marauding invaders, be they from across the border or simply from neighbouring clans, and to ensure that their rights – to fishing and common land, for instance – were not threatened.

The oldest Common Riding in Dumfries and Galloway is Langholm's, which has taken place continuously every year since 1759. (Annan's first took place in 1680 but has not been held continuously.) Others are held at Lockerbie and Sanquhar, while the Dumfries ride-outs (as they

DUMFRIES & GALLOWAY ON SCREEN: THE *OUTLANDER* EFFECT

The filming of Diana Gabaldon's *Outlander* in many parts of Scotland has had a disproportionate effect on tourism, with locations used in the series seeing, on average, a 45% rise in visitor numbers between 2014 and 2018.

Dumfries and Galloway has a particular connection to *Outlander* as leading man Sam Heughan comes from New Galloway. However, the only location used in the region was Drumlanrig Castle (page 91), which doubled as the Duke of Sandringham's estate in episode 11 of season two. A French couple who stayed at our B&B were delighted to discover this, since they had, prior to coming to Scotland, made their way to Sandringham in Norfolk, believing the Duke to be a real historical character and the Queen's country retreat to be his estate.

Perhaps the most famous scenes filmed in the region are those from the 1978 version of *The 39 Steps*, which feature Robert Powell as Richard Hannay filmed in locations from Cairnsmore of Fleet to the Moffat Hills.

Cult British horror film *The Wicker Man* (1973) with Christopher Lee, Britt Eckland and Edward Woodward was filmed in the Stewartry and on the Machars (page 217) and Rhins. The trials of the production are well documented: filming in the region in October and November, with artificial blossom on the trees to make it look like May was (perhaps unsurprisingly) not a happy experience!

More recently, parts of the first *Mission: Impossible* (1996) were filmed (from helicopters) along parts of the region's rail network, while much of *The Vanishing* (2018) with Gerard Butler was filmed at the Mull of Galloway.

In real life, the region is home, for some of the time at least, to various well-known personalities, including Joanna Lumley, Martin Shaw (*The Professionals, Judge John Deed*) and Gary Lewis, who played the father in *Billy Elliott* (2000) and Colum MacKenzie in... *Outlander*, of course.

are called) are part of the annual Guid Nychburris (Good Neighbours) festival, marking the anniversary of the town's elevation to royal burgh in 1186.

At every Common Riding there are annually selected key players: the cornet, cornet's lass and standard bearer, all of whom travel to Common Ridings in other towns as well as taking part in their own. Common Ridings tend to be held around the same date in the summer for each town annually, a day in which 100 or more riders plus many more followers and spectators congregate early in the morning to start the proceedings off, when riders are wished 'safe oot, safe in'. Once the riders return there are festivities throughout the rest of the day, with everything from horse races to musical parades.

FURTHER READING

In the course of researching this guide we have dipped into many books. Listed below is a small selection which we gratefully acknowledge (dates refer to editions we have used).

The Antiquities of Scotland (vol 1) Francis Grose. Published 1797 and available as a print-on-demand title from Gale ECCO Print Editions via Amazon.

The Buildings of Scotland: Dumfries and Galloway John Gifford, Penguin Books 1996

The Galloway Highlands Dane Love, Carn Publishing 2014

The House of Elrig Gavin Maxwell, Longmans Green & Co Ltd 1965

The Kirkcudbrightshire Companion Haig Gordon, Galloway Publishing 2008

The Queen's Scotland: The Border Counties ed. Theo Lang, Hodder and Stoughton 1957

The Queen's Scotland: Glasgow, Kyle and Galloway ed. Theo Lang, Hodder and Stoughton 1953

The Raiders S R Crockett, T Fisher Unwin 1902

The Solway Firth Brian Blake, Robert Hale Ltd 1966

The Wigtownshire Companion Haig Gordon, Galloway Publishing 2008

STOP PRESS: CORONAVIRUS

As we put the finishing touches to this new edition, countries around the world are starting to ease restrictions brought in due to the coronavirus pandemic. Owing to the impact of the crisis on tourism, some businesses or services listed in the text may no longer operate, and opening hours may differ from those detailed. We will post any information we have on the authors' website (slowbritain.co.uk) and we would, of course, be grateful for any updates you can send us during your own travels, which we will add to the site for the benefit of future visitors.

MAKING THE MOST OF THIS GUIDE: A NOTE ON USING THE INDEX (PAGE 264)

In compiling the index for this guide, we have aimed to create a truly useful tool to help you get the most out of your time in Dumfries and Galloway and we would encourage you to make full use of it. The index is more than just a means of finding your way to a single reference. It condenses into a small number of pages the contents of the guide, providing an at-a-glance overview of what you can find within these pages.

We have also used the index to draw together themes that run throughout the book – references to subjects that are spread across chapters in single entries which, when seen together, add up to more than the sum of their parts. For example, although we include a section in the introduction on habitats and wildlife, there are references to both throughout the guide, and if you look up 'wildlife' in the index you will find entries on a great range of related subjects, from 'adder' to 'WWT Caerlaverock Wetland Centre'. Similar 'themes' which you might find useful to peruse range from 'beaches' and 'birds and birdwatching' to 'walks and walking', where you will discover that, in addition to the mapped routes that are included in the guide, there are suggestions for a huge range of other walks.

Happy exploring!

Donald and Darren

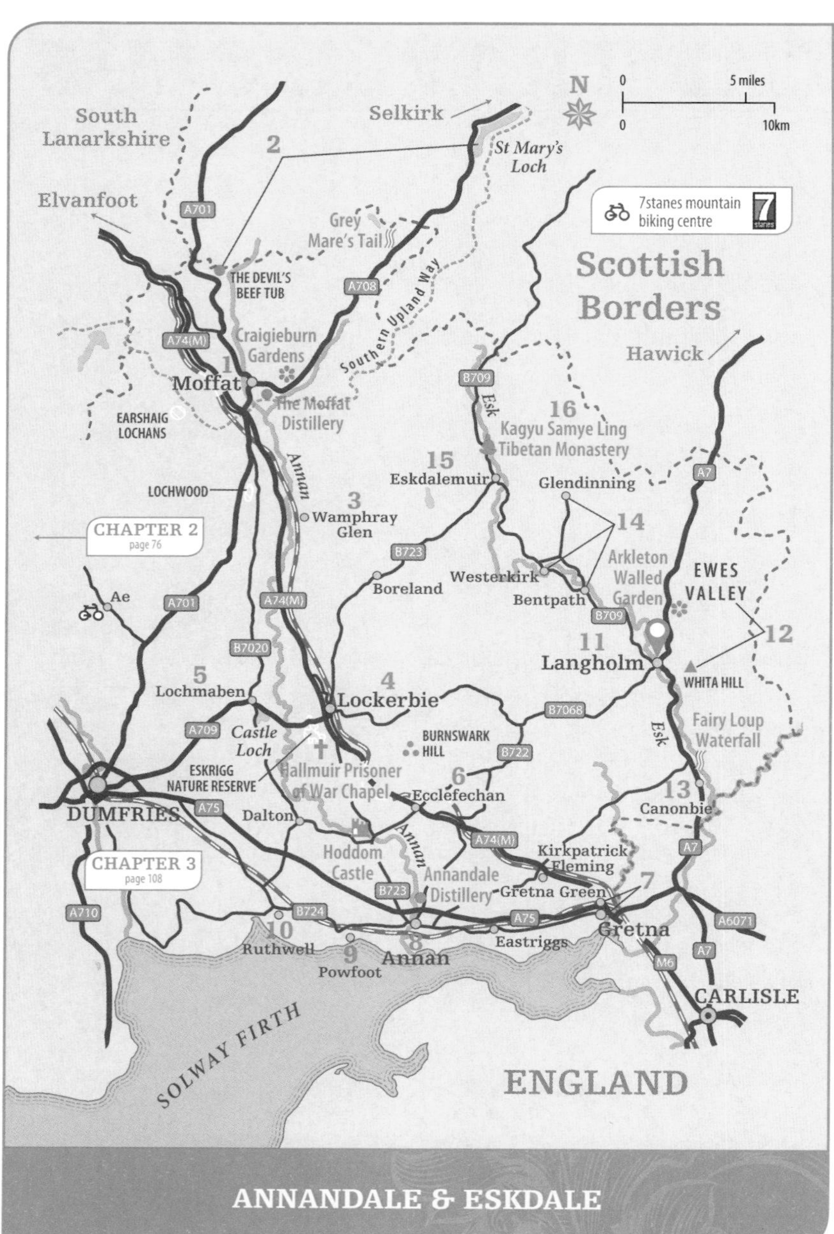

ANNANDALE & ESKDALE

1
ANNANDALE & ESKDALE

Annandale and Eskdale account for the entire eastern end of Dumfries and Galloway, abutting South Lanarkshire to the north, the Scottish Borders to the east, the border with England to the southeast, and sloping down to the shores of the Solway Firth directly to the south. Residents of the area are proud of it but feel a frustration that, of the millions who pass through on the A74(M) motorway each year, more don't stop to visit. It's a shame as there is much here to discover and enjoy, far more than may at first meet the eye. In fact, it's an ideal area for exploring slowly.

This is a sizeable area: 31 miles from **Moffat** in the north down to **Gretna** at the border with England, and just under 18 miles from **Lockerbie** eastwards to **Langholm**. The rivers **Esk** and **Annan** rise in the north and flow southwards to empty at the eastern end of the **Solway**. They cut a clear line along the valley bottoms, running through forests and between steep hills, past communities on their banks that have developed over centuries. Spending time in this area is a delight for anyone who loves the outdoors. For **walkers** in particular there is a pack of routes to choose from, whether undertaking all or part of a long-distance trail, or simply devising a shorter loop for a bit of fresh air. **Fishing** is also popular, with a good choice of beats on a selection of rivers. More information about fishing on the River Annan can be found at riverannan.org and fishpal.com. **Birdwatching**, **canoeing**, **horseriding** and even **carriage driving** can all be enjoyed by expert and novice alike.

You can encounter a wealth of history on the ground, from early **prehistoric stone circles** through **Roman forts**, to memorials to more recent events such as the Lockerbie disaster. There are also connections with **Robert the Bruce**, William Wallace, the Covenanters and the Jacobite Rebellions. The last few hundred years have given rise to numerous famous sons and daughters, including the engineer **Thomas Telford** and philosopher **Thomas Carlyle**. Although **Robert Burns** neither came from nor lived in this particular part of Dumfries and Galloway, he did visit and there are one or two places hereabouts that will be of interest to Burns enthusiasts. For romantics incurable or otherwise, **Gretna Green** tells the story of elopements past and marriages present; this small village immediately north of the border is (in)famous worldwide thanks to the historic differences in marriage law between Scotland and England.

The people, communities and economic activities of Annandale and Eskdale are diverse – to say the least – and range from farmers caretaking the land in serene valleys and on isolated hilltops to retired plant hunters running exotic gardens, incomers from the south who have escaped to set up B&Bs, and community trusts who have acquired lochs and raised funds to develop wildlife centres. There's even a monastery in the hills, the first Tibetan Buddhist centre to be established in the West. The work of Forestry and Land Scotland is also much in evidence, with conifer plantations making up 27% of land use in the Annan catchment alone.

GETTING AROUND

Annandale is bisected by the A74(M) motorway from Moffat in the north to Gretna in the south, with the A7 heading off northeast through Eskdale, passing through the town of Langholm and on to the Scottish Borders. The two valleys can feel a world apart, separated by river valleys and rolling hills in the south, and craggier hills, isolated moorland and forestry plantations with more circuitous secondary roads in the north. If you're travelling any points between Gretna and Moffat, we recommend following the route of the old main road, now the B7076, which runs parallel to the A74(M). With barely any traffic, it is a gentler option than the A road and is very spacious for a B road.

PUBLIC TRANSPORT

The region's public transport is adequate but isn't viable for reaching the more remote parts. If you're happy to move from centre to centre, then the bus network is fine but there's nothing in the way of an integrated public transport system, and getting around is generally easier by car. The main west coast **train service** runs through the area, but there is only one station, at Lockerbie, served by infrequent Avanti West Coast services and the more frequent TransPennine Express. While this is useful for arriving and departing from points further afield, with no other stops within Annandale or Eskdale, wider travel needs to be linked in with local buses. Scotrail services between Glasgow and Newcastle pass along the Solway Coast after departing Dumfries, with stations at Annan and Gretna Green.

The Annandale local **bus services**, plus the longer distance inter-regional routes, use the county town of Dumfries as the main hub, with services fanning out through the area. Moffat is well served by the frequent daytime X74 and 101 Stagecoach services. Lochmaben and Lockerbie are also well served, with Stagecoach/Houstons 81/381, while along the Solway, the Stagecoach service 79 between Dumfries and Carlisle stops off at Ruthwell, Cummertrees, Annan and Gretna. Stagecoach also operate the 380 service between Lockerbie and Moffat, which is useful for linking with the train services.

The Eskdale bus services for Langholm and on to Eskdalemuir and Kagyu Samye Ling Buddhist Monastery are a bit more hit and miss. The FirstGroup service 95 from Galashiels to Carlisle is the most frequent way for getting into Langholm, but this isn't linked to the rest of Dumfries and Galloway. Other routes operate via Lockerbie, with a weekly Thursday 103 service by Houstons, and a daily, if infrequent, McCalls 112 service to Eskdalemuir with the option to then change at the village church for Houstons 124 service on to Langholm. There is also one bus daily, service 123, between Langholm, Canonbie and Annan.

Local public transport information is provided by South West of Scotland Transport Partnership (swestrans.org.uk), or alternatively Traveline (0871 200 2233 traveline.info). For general observations on public transport, see page 12.

CYCLING

Away from the main A roads, cycling is an enjoyable affair, if a little strenuous over the more hilly sections, particularly for those of us not as fit as we used to be. The lanes are generally very quiet, save for the odd farm vehicle, and are a joy to explore throughout the changing seasons. As part of the Sustrans cycle network (sustrans.org.uk), **Route 7** runs from Gretna, along the Solway to Dumfries, before linking in to **Regional Route 10** up to Moffat over a mix of quiet roads and traffic-free sections. The easiest way to cover a lot of distance north–

TOURIST INFORMATION

There is no VisitScotland information centre in Annandale and Eskdale.

Langholm Tourist Information Market Pl, High St, DG13 0JQ
www.welcometolangholm.co.uk Apr–Sep & Oct–Jan (reduced hours); check online for latest opening times
Moffat Information Point Moffat Woollen Mill, Ladyknowe, Moffat DG10 9EG
year-round
Visit Moffat visitmoffat.co.uk. No premises but its website and Facebook page are packed with local information; requests posted for information usually solicit lots of responses.

south is to take **Route 74** between Gretna, Lockerbie and Moffat, although this is not the quietest route as it runs parallel to the A74(M) for numerous sections.

CYCLE HIRE

Annandale Cycles Caledonian Place, Moffat DG10 9EG 01683 220033
annandalecycles.com

WALKING

With the flat of the river valleys, wide open beaches on the Solway Firth, and the dramatic hills of the Southern Uplands, the two valleys of Annandale and Eskdale offer routes and distances for all tastes and fitness levels. Local visitor information centres (see box, above), along with most libraries, town halls and many shops and post offices in the area, stock a wealth of walking information, including OS maps, leaflets and books. One of our other books, *The Dumfriesshire Dales: 40 Favourite Walks* (Pocket Mountains) includes routes of varying length across the area, and Dumfries and Galloway Council produces a range of free walking and cycling downloads that can be found at dumgal.gov.uk (look under 'Leisure' and then 'Outdoor Access and Paths'). On top of this, a quick search on the internet for the area you are visiting will soon turn up numerous routes of interest.

Two long-distance paths also cut through the region. The **Southern Upland Way** passes Beattock and Moffat on its 214-mile route from west coast to east, and both the full route and suggestions for shorter day walks are detailed on southernuplandway.gov.uk. The Annandale Way (annandaleway.org) runs for 55 miles from the source of the River Annan above Moffat southwards to the Solway at Annan. It, too, offers plenty of choice for shorter circular day walks. Three we recommend are the spectacular hills around the Devil's Beef Tub at the route start, the three-mile loop of Castle Loch, Lochmaben at the halfway point, and Annan to the Solway estuary at the walk's end.

UPPER ANNANDALE: MOFFAT & THE NORTH

A glance at an OS map reveals a mass of thumbprint contours spiralling from the upper reaches of the Annan, where it rises just north of Moffat, down towards Lockerbie 16 miles to the south. To the west, stretching over to neighbouring Nithsdale, are the Lowther Hills, empty and bleak in parts, rising only to 2,500ft, but no less striking for that. To the east, the Moffat Hills reach only a little higher, to almost 2,700ft, but are full of drama. This area was historically of great strategic importance, for whoever controlled Upper Annandale controlled access to the north and south; today it is dotted with sites of Roman forts and the remains of medieval castles.

Moffat is the only town of any size and makes a good base from which to explore the area, with plenty of accommodation options, access to the surrounding countryside and a new whisky distillery. The River Annan rises just north of Moffat and runs almost due south along the centre of a corridor lined by hills. The joy of this area, though, lies not just in this central river valley but in the hidden places on either side.

1 MOFFAT

Annandale Arms (page 259), **Hartfell House** (page 259), **Summerlea House B&B** (page 259), **Cauldholm Bothy** (page 259), **Wee Hartfell Cottage** (page 259), **Moffat Camping and Caravan Site** (page 259). Moffat offers an exceptional range of accommodation; see page 259 for more recommendations.

A former royal burgh and Victorian spa town, Moffat quickly charms most visitors with its mix of quirky shops and cafés, village atmosphere, range of architecture and new distillery. Located amid some of the Southern Uplands' grandest scenery, it's only around an hour's drive from both Edinburgh and Glasgow, thus it works well for both short

THE WALKERS' TOWN

Moffat sits in the midst of glorious walking country, a perfect base from which to reach some of the highest ground in the south of Scotland: Hart Fell (2,652ft); Ettrick Pen (2,269ft); Loch Fell (2,256ft); and Queensberry (2,285ft). It's also the starting point of the 55-mile **Annandale Way**, which runs southwards to Annan, and the midpoint of the **Southern Upland Way**, which runs for 212 miles from Portpatrick on the west coast of Dumfries and Galloway to Cockburnspath on the east coast of the Scottish Borders. The section from Moffat to Cockburnspath has also been dubbed the **Sir Walter Scott Way** due to connections with Scott's life and work. A selection of walks ranging from five to 14 miles is detailed on visitmoffat.co.uk.

Hopefully they won't be needed, but in an emergency contact the volunteer-run **Moffat Mountain Rescue** (01683 222800 moffatmrt.scottishmountainrescue.org).

breaks and as a base for a longer holiday (most of our B&B guests stay for anything from two to ten nights). Walkers and cyclists are in their element as nature abounds, and there are good birdlife and wildlife spotting opportunities in the area.

Moffat is also the UK's first **Dark Sky Town**, having adapted its street lighting to reduce light pollution, and the Moffat Astronomy Club (moffatdarksky4.wixsite.com/moffatastronomy), with their new observatory and 16-inch Meade telescope at Hammerlands, would be pleased to hear from visitors. There are also three fixed telescope piers around the town.

Visitors are also welcomed by the **Friends of Gallow Hill** () to assist in their mammoth tree-planting task on the northern edge of town. Since being acquired from the Earl of Annandale in a community buy-out in late 2016, the hill has been planted with over 17,000 trees, with another 20,000 to go. This is also one of the nearest and easiest hills to town for walking.

Moffat has long been a staging post on the national north–south route and, as a result, its broad high street is lined with more hotels – traditional coaching inns – than you would expect in a town of 3,000 or so people. Visitors are not a new phenomenon here. Although wool was the original economic mainstay, it was overtaken by tourism following the discovery of the health-inducing sulphurous waters of the well in the nearby hills. Rachel Whitford, a bishop's daughter, was walking in the hills east of Moffat in 1633 when she quenched her thirst with a drink from a spring. She recognised the tang as sulphur – a taste of 'stale eggs whipped up with Lucifer-matches' – and thus an industry was born. By the start of the 18th century Moffat was attracting the celebrities of the day, including Robert Burns, and in 1881 a railway branch line was opened from Beattock to cope with the increasing number of people coming to take the waters. You can still walk up to **Moffat Well** today, where the smell is as eggy as ever. Waters were pumped down from the well to the old Bath House (now the Town Hall), such was the demand.

Visitors also come to Moffat for the range of events that take place throughout the year. The Scottish Rootes Enthusiasts' (sre-scot.co.uk) annual **Classic Car Rally** in late June is now one of the biggest two-day classic car events in Scotland. At **Hogmanay** every pub and hotel in town is buzzing, the Town Hall is packed to the gunnels for its superb ceilidh (tickets can be hard to come by), and the evening culminates in a high street fireworks display that punches above its weight for a wee town in the hills. Accommodation for both events gets booked up, so advance planning is advised. **Gala Week** (Aug) and **Christmas Fair** (Nov/Dec) also draw visitors. The **Moffat Walking Festival** (walkmoffat.co.uk) in October has been held intermittently over the years and is back on the calendar, while the new (hopefully annual, but check for details) **Moffat Eagle Festival** (visitmoffat; late summer/early autumn), marking Moffat's status as Scotland's first 'Eagle Town', includes a programme of events organised in conjunction with the South of Scotland Golden Eagle Project (see box, page 42).

"At Hogmanay every pub and hotel in town is buzzing and the Town Hall is packed to the gunnels for its superb ceilidh."

Moffat has several claims to fame. The **Star Hotel** on the high street features in the *Guinness Book of Records* for being, at only 20ft wide by 162ft long, the narrowest hotel in the world. **Chapel Street** is said to be the shortest street in Scotland (though it's given a run for its money by the miserly named Ebenezer Place in Wick, in the far north of the country), while the pharmacy on the high street, Thomas Hetherington, is Scotland's oldest, dating from 1844.

The town's most famous son is **Air Chief Marshall Hugh Dowding** (1882–1970) of Battle of Britain fame, who was born in Moffat and whose ashes were laid to rest beneath the Battle of Britain window at Westminster Abbey. There is a memorial in his honour in Station Park and a service (with fly-past, weather permitting) is held here each year in September. If you're interested in World War II history, especially aviation, take a walk down The Glebe, a quiet residential cul-de-sac off the main southern road into town, for the unexpected sight of a full-size replica **Spitfire** (an MK IX Supermarine Spitfire PT 462, to be precise) in the unlikely setting of the front garden of a private house. The owner, a Spitfire enthusiast, had this built having flown the original in Florida during a flying course. A noticeboard in the garden at the bottom of the drive gives more information.

Another local man to make a very distinctive mark was engineer **John Loudon McAdam** (1756–1836), whose family home was in the Stewartry (page 135) and who died here on his way back to London, having been in Scotland for his annual summer visit. The name may well ring a bell, though it's not so much the man you may know of, but rather

THE MOFFAT DISTILLERY

Old Carlisle Rd moffatdistillery.com Friends of the Moffat Distillery. Moffat's newest attraction is a whisky distillery, planning permission for which was only granted in the final days of preparing this new edition.

Nottinghamshire-born Nick Bullard moved to Moffat from Ohio, USA in 2015, looking for somewhere to raise his family after many years working internationally as a consultant. 'After travelling so much I wanted to create a life that meant I could work locally and fit into the community,' he says. After contemplating a diverse range of possibilities, his interest in whisky won the day and thus a plan to build a distillery in the town took shape. The starting point was to create blends, and with the support of major players such as Diageo and Distell, his first whisky, The Moffat, was brought to market in December 2018.

Fast forward and his Dark Sky Spirits Company has two more blends: The Doonhamer, in honour of Dumfries (page 109), and The Muckle Toon, in honour of Langholm (page 65). (Nick also wanted to create a blend in honour of Gretna, but alas, trademark regulations disallowed the name 'Laird of the Rings'.)

Not content with blends, though, Nick is – as any whisky connoisseur would be – eager to produce his own single malt, and so he is now building his own distillery on the eastern edge of Moffat, where around 100,000 bottles a year will be produced in due course. The distillery will also have a visitor centre and tours will be run: milling, mashing, fermenting, distilling, casking, bottling and labelling will all feature.

Keep up to date with Nick's progress and the latest developments on his Facebook page: Friends of the Moffat Distillery.

the process for improving roads that he invented. The 'macadamisation' of roads resulted in a harder, more durable surface and did much for travel and communication. When tar was added to the process, the description became 'tarmacadamise', leaving us with the abbreviated 'tarmac'. McAdam's grave can be found in the Holm Street cemetery.

A tour of the town

Moffat is busy most of the year (other than in January, when the town is distinctly sleepy), with the population swelling in summer with an influx of visitors. Coach tours pull into the large **Edinburgh Woollen Mill** complex at the bottom of town, next to which is **Station Park** with a putting green and a boating/pedalo lake. Also down this end of town is the community-run **Moffat Museum** (Harthope Hse, Churchgate, DG10 9EG ✆ 01683 220868 🖱 moffatmuseum.co.uk ⏲ seasonal), with informative displays that include a Roman brooch found in the nearby hills in 1787 and the oldest longbow discovered in Britain. Merlin, with whom Moffat and the surrounding area have strong associations, is also covered. Moffat itself lies on the **Merlin Trail** (🖱 merlintrail.com), the website of which also includes details of the **Moffat History Trail**.

"A statue of a Blackface ram stands atop its cairn of stones, erected partly to honour Moffat's historic sheep market."

Opposite the museum stands the late 19th-century **St Andrew's Church** (down the side of which Santa abseils each Christmas for the annual lights switch-on), while just around the corner, at the bottom of the high street, is the old **Holm Street churchyard**, with the last remaining wall of the pre-Reformation church (c1600). What is obvious when walking around the site is the varying heights of the ground. In 1747, the churchyard was covered in an extra 4ft of soil to create more space for burials.

The pleasantly browsable **High Street** lends itself to a gentle amble up one side and down the other, but do watch out when crossing over as it's easy to forget that traffic runs in both directions on both sides of the road. At the top of the High Street a statue of a Blackface ram stands atop its cairn of piled-up stones, erected partly to honour Moffat's historic sheep market but also, say some, in memory of Sir Walter Scott's contemporary, poet James Hogg, 'the Ettrick Shepherd', who was known to drink in the town. Fondly referred to as the **Moffat Ram**, it's known more formally as the Colvin Fountain, having been presented by

CRAIGIEBURN GARDENS: A TASTE OF THE HIMALAYAS

Janet McGowan is the owner of Craigieburn Gardens (A708 Selkirk Rd, DG10 9LF ✆ 07557 928648 f ⏲ Easter–Oct 10.30–18.00 Tue–Sat & bank hol Mon) and the inspiration behind its inception. She has kindly supplied the following text.

Craigieburn is a gem of a garden hidden in a fold of the Moffat Hills, where a series of waterfalls tumble into a deep gorge that runs through ancient woodland. Begun 25 years ago, it is now reaching its peak of maturity, though it continues to evolve and develop. Himalayan plants always did well here, but the garden took on a distinct Himalayan flavour when Datenji Sherpa joined the team, expanding the planting into woodland and making a Sherpa garden in part of the steep-sided gorge. Here the fabled blue poppies, giant lilies, primula and bizarre cobra lilies of the Himalayas thrive in the cool moist air and lush vegetation that is so reminiscent of the foothills of that region. Festoons of Buddhist prayer flags add to the otherworldly illusion.

But it would be a mistake to think of Craigieburn only as a Himalayan garden. My prime passion is for herbaceous perennials and a vast range from all over the world pack into Craigieburn's six acres. They flourish in deep twin borders, weave through cottage borders and light up shady woodland. A border of hellebores in the spring garden kicks the season off, and an autumn garden planted with late treasures brings the display to a glorious end until the first frosts of winter put the garden to sleep again. An exuberant bog garden, ferns, hardy orchids, bulbs and many rare treasures add further diversity, while magnolias, hoherias, rhododendron species and bamboos provide the framework for year-round spectacle.

A nursery at Craigieburn sells many of the plants that can be seen in the garden and a cosy bothy is also available for self-catering stays (page 259).

businessman William Colvin in 1875. Noted for its peculiar lack of ears, it was sculpted by one William Brodie, who is perhaps better known for the diminutive Greyfriars Bobby in Edinburgh.

For a local delicacy, pop into the **Moffat Toffee Shop** (f) on the High Street. **Well Street** has a range of more specialised shops including Wallace Brothers butcher on the corner (excellent steak pies and haggis), the independent Moffat Books, Harvest Time traditional delicatessen, the Ram Shack record shop (as in vinyl), and three vintage/antique furniture and bric-a-brac shops: Lothlorien Antiques, Reloved and 27 Well St.

Fishing enthusiasts should head for the **The Green Frog** (Hammerlands, DG10 9QL ✆ 01683 221220 ⌖ thegreenfrogmoffat.co.uk), a short distance out of the town centre, with its long standing clear water and spring-fed lochan and also to **Selcoth Fishery** (selcothfisheries.com) a few miles east of town. Gardeners should make a bee-line for **Craigieburn Gardens**, also east of town (see box, opposite).

FOOD & DRINK

Annandale Arms High St, DG10 9HF 01683 220013 annandalearmshotel.co.uk. Excellent dishes using locally sourced food, served in the pleasant restaurant or dog-friendly bar.
Brodies 1–2 Altrive Pl, Holm St, DG10 9EB 01683 222870 brodiesofmoffat.co.uk. See ad, 4th colour section. Good food in a smart, friendly and relaxed setting. Start off with a drink in their gin bar (see below).
Buccleuch Arms High St, DG10 9ET 01683 220003 buccleucharmshotel.com. Wholesome food with a touch of seasonality; mostly British but with the odd wild card thrown in for variety. The South African *bobotie* is particularly good.
Café Ariete 10 High St, DG10 9HF 01683 220313. Welcoming café with an eye-catching sculpture of a ram (*ariete* means ram in Italian) made from old books. This is a family affair: owner/manager Russell Murray is usually on hand, dad Mitch is sometimes around, and mum Vivienne is responsible for the wickedly tempting range of cakes. The best soup in town. Call ahead to order take-away food.
Claudios Burnside Rd, DG10 9DX 01683 220958 claudiosmoffat.co.uk. Tasty, authentic Italian food in an *trattoria*-style setting. Originally opened by Claudio Capriglione and his wife in 1996 and now run by their children, chef Claudia and Davide front of house.
The Gin Bar at Brodies 1–2 Altrive Pl, Holm St, DG10 9EB 01683 222870 brodiesofmoffat.co.uk. See ad, 4th colour section. Comfy chairs, vintage décor and a choice of 75–80 gins (or thereabouts)! Perfect for a relaxing drink with friends or a pre-dinner aperitif.
The Green Frog Hammerlands, DG10 9QL 01683 221220 thegreenfrogmoffat.co.uk daytime only. Popular and friendly café a short way out of the town centre (with masses of parking), complete with gift shop, soft play, duck pond, bunnies and guinea pigs out the back, and a small garden centre.
Harvest Time 24 Well St, DG10 9DP 01683 221177. Delicatessen and wholefoods shop packed with local goodies and more. Julie's quiche and cakes are legendary hereabouts.
Hugos 4 Bath Pl, DG10 9HJ 01683 221606. Bar and restaurant downstairs, sports bar upstairs. Specialises in Scottish tapas, but also offers traditional breakfasts, sandwiches and afternoon teas.
Limetree Restaurant Hartfell Hse, Hartfell Cr, DG10 9AL 01683 220153 hartfellhouse.co.uk dinner only Tue–Sat; winter variations. Exceptional food in an intimate setting, where chef Matt Seddon keeps it all seasonal and local. A little pricier than elsewhere, but worth every penny. Booking advised.

SOUTH OF SCOTLAND GOLDEN EAGLE PROJECT

Dr Catherine Barlow, Project Manager at South of Scotland Golden Eagle Project (goldeneaglessouthofscotland.co.uk), has kindly supplied this snapshot.

The South of Scotland Golden Eagle Project is a partnership project of conservation and land-management organisations, aiming to reinforce and boost the small, isolated and fragmented population of golden eagles in the south of Scotland to healthier levels.

Golden eagles have a long history in southern Scotland. Populations were once healthy, with the species playing an important part as an apex predator in the ecosystem. Over the last couple of centuries human activity and changes in land use have caused populations here to fall to as low as three breeding pairs.

Through a series of translocations over a period of five years and greater co-operation between stakeholders, the South of Scotland Golden Eagle Project aims to increase numbers of golden eagles in the region and to prevent the loss of this wonderful species from southern skies.

From their release area in the Moffat Hills the young, translocated eagles have begun to explore and interact with resident breeding pairs and locally fledged young. It is hoped that in time the eagles will rediscover long-forgotten eyries and become a more familiar sight in the valleys of southern Scotland.

THE MOFFAT HILLS

Craigieburn Gardens Bothy (page 259), **Moffat Wigwam Holidays** (page 260)

The scenery around Moffat is among the most thrilling in the region. Here, too, is a good selection of **birdlife**: peregrine, merlin and golden plover may be spotted, to name a few, and possibly even golden eagle.

Our suggested tours focus on the north and east of the region to immerse you in the surrounding countryside, areas that sit just inside the boundaries of Dumfries and Galloway and which also stray into the neighbouring Scottish Borders region. Unfortunately, public transport isn't an option for these routes, so driving is your best bet, or cycling if you're a very fit, regular cyclist.

Immediately to the west of Moffat are the Lowther Hills, most of which are covered in the Nithsdale chapter (page 76). However, **Earshaig Lochans** and **Lochwood** are both within close reach of Moffat.

2 St Mary's Loch to the Devil's Beef Tub

Head out of Moffat on the A708 and within a few minutes of leaving the town you are into the **Moffat Water valley**, in our opinion one of the most beautiful in the Southern Uplands. What starts off as a broad river valley gradually narrows, passing the entrance to **Craigieburn Gardens** (see box, page 40; look out for the brightly coloured prayer flags) just under three miles from Moffat and creating an ever-changing vista as you wind your way eastwards. To the north and east lies the Talla-Hart Fell Wild Land Area, including the peaks of Hart Fell (2,652ft) and White Coomb (2,697ft), Dumfriesshire's highest. Around 7½ miles from Moffat, stop at **Carrifran Wildwood** (🖱 carrifran.org.uk; the gate on the left-hand side of the road is almost hidden, keep an eye open for it), an ecological restoration project spearheaded by Borders Forest Trust (🖱 bordersforesttrust.org) that 'seeks to recreate a valley of wooded wilderness in the Southern Uplands with the rich diversity of native species that existed there thousands of years ago'. Wander up the valley and enjoy the silence and the views. Over 600,000 trees have been planted here since Millennium Day.

Continue on from Carrifran another 2½ miles to the National Trust for Scotland's **Grey Mare's Tail Nature Reserve** (📍 NT185148; see box, page 44), where the 200ft waterfall is the fifth-highest in the UK. A short walk takes you to the viewpoint at the bottom of the falls; alternatively, if you're feeling energetic, climb up the right-hand side of them on a steep path that offers excellent views of the waterfall, the Moffat Water valley and an unfolding mountainous landscape en route to isolated Loch Skeen (around one hour each way). For a much longer walk, continue on over the hilltops of Lochcraig Head and the Corbett of White Coomb. It will take about five to six hours, but the effort is rewarded with far-reaching views to the Lake District's northern fells and the Cheviots in Northumberland.

From the Grey Mare's Tail, carry on for another five miles, passing into the Scottish Borders region, to the small **Loch of the Lowes** and, immediately after it, **St Mary's Loch**, a tranquil spot popular with sailors, tourers and walkers and, at three miles long and over half a mile wide, the area's largest natural loch. (Sailors might wish to make contact with the **St Mary's Loch Sailing Club** 🖱 stmlsc.org.uk). The **Glen Café** (🕒 Easter–Oct daily), located between the two lochs, is a popular stopping point, while at the head of St Mary's Loch stands an old house (now private) that used to be Tibbie Shiels Inn, a fabled watering hole in these parts that was frequented by Sir Walter Scott and James Hogg. A **statue** of the latter stands on the hillside overlooking the lochs and the former inn. A lovely **walk** of just over nine miles runs around St Mary's Loch.

THE GREY MARE'S TAIL NATURE RESERVE

Richard Clarkson is the National Trust for Scotland ranger who manages the Grey Mare's Tail Nature Reserve. If you visit the reserve, there's a good chance you might bump into him. He has kindly supplied the following text.

Grey Mare's Tail's wild and rugged landscape contains many habitats and species of international, national and regional significance. It is also well known as an internationally important geological site and is famous for its graptolite fossils. The considerable geological and wildlife interest is recognised by its designation as a Site of Special Scientific Interest (SSSI), and it is also included within the designated Moffat Hills Special Area of Conservation (SAC) for supporting eight habitats of European importance.

Deservedly, the reserve has the reputation of being botanically outstanding. While keen botanists will need to venture into remoter parts of the reserve to seek out scarcer upland species like dwarf cornel, alpine saw-wort, pale forget-me-not and the exceptionally rare fern oblong woodsia, there are many botanical delights to be seen close to managed paths. Globeflower, starry

Beyond the café, another couple of miles brings you to the waterside hamlet of **Cappercleuch**, where an old AA box stands on the left. Turn left here and stay on this road for 12 miles as it winds its way up through the hills, passing first **Megget Reservoir** and then **Talla Reservoir**. Views of hills and moorland abound, especially at Talla, and there's an ever-increasing sense of isolation as you wend your way along the narrow road. Over 500 acres of land to the west and south of Talla were previously part of the **Talla Gameshope Estate**, which was purchased by the Borders Forest Trust in late 2013. The aim is to restore large areas of hills and upland valley to their natural state after centuries of use as an upland hill farm. Keep an eye open up here for golden eagles. You never know, you might be lucky!

"Views of hills and moorland abound, and there's an ever-increasing sense of isolation as you wend your way along."

On passing through **Tweedsmuir**, turn left at the junction with the A701 for the return leg to Moffat. Around eight miles from Tweedsmuir, look out for a lay-by on the right with a cairn marking the **source of the River Tweed**. From here it flows eastwards for 97 miles through the Scottish Borders region to Berwick-upon-Tweed on the east coast. 'Annan, Tweed and Clyde rise a' oot o' ae hillside' goes an old Borders saxifrage and lesser twayblade are just a few that can be seen from the Loch Skeen path. Although not accessible, from late March it is possible with the aid of binoculars to spot purple saxifrage flowering on precarious rocky sections alongside the waterfall.

There is a rich animal life to be found here, too. Peregrine falcons nest on the craigs around the waterfall every year and can be observed via a TV link to a nest camera. Other frequently seen birdlife includes raven, buzzard, wheatear, stonechat, dipper, grey wagtail and kestrel, but also watch out for ring ouzel, red grouse, merlin, sparrowhawk and, if you are lucky, ospreys fishing in Loch Skeen. A recent project to reinforce the population of golden eagles in southern Scotland has also increased the chance of seeing this magnificent bird. Although the mammal community is quite secretive, the path to Loch Skeen usually holds a few feral goats and on the higher slopes there are occasional glimpses of mountain hare. The reserve is also home to Britain's rarest native freshwater fish, the vendace. This species has thrived here since it was introduced to Loch Skeen as part of a species recovery programme in the late 1990s.

saying, since the rivers Annan and Clyde also rise in this area, the former flowing south and the latter draining northwest.

Continue on the A701 and after another two miles or so, on the left-hand side, stands another cairn, known locally as the **Postie Stone**, commemorating James McGeorge and John Goodfellow, the guard and the driver of a Royal Mail Coach who lost their lives here in a snowstorm in 1831. Both are buried in the Holm Street graveyard in Moffat. Despite the warnings and the bad weather, they tried in vain to get the mail through Moffat to Tweedshaws and perished for their troubles.

Just beyond here the hills drop away sharply as the road runs along the top edge of the cavernous and carnivorously named **Devil's Beef Tub**, a huge hollow in the hills, the headwater of the River Annan and the watershed between the Annan and Tweed rivers. Celebrated as one of the most impressive landmarks of the Southern Uplands and possibly the most famous of Dumfries and Galloway's geological features, it is surrounded by four hills and is the site of some rare mountain plants and the occasional cluster of ash and hazel trees, a reminder of the forests that once thrived here.

The name was gained from its reputation as a place the Border Reivers (page 24) would hide their stolen cattle. From the road it's a long drop down, 1,351ft to be precise, and in winter the weather up here is usually several degrees colder and harsher than it is five miles further down the valley in Moffat. Just a few hundred yards beyond the viewpoint stands another memorial, this one commemorating **Covenanter John Hunter**, who was shot by Douglas Dragoons on the hillside opposite in 1685.

From here, continue downhill, twisting and turning your way back into Moffat.

3 Wamphray Glen

Wamphray Glen, once a popular spot with spa visitors seeking the picturesque in remote corners, lies eight miles south of Moffat. Wamphray Water flows down from the hills into the River Annan, running over several waterfalls and through a wooded glen. A **walking route** is shown on a sign at the junction of the Old Carlisle Road from Moffat with the Boreland road (NT121962), and you can park here or up the hill at Wamphray Parish Church (NT131965). The main attraction is the walk through the woods along the river and the **three cascades** known as The Pot, The Washing Pan and Dubbs Cauldron.

Passing the old mill beyond the falls, the route climbs up to **Wamphray Parish Church**, where among the fine 19th-century funerary monuments is one to Dr John Rogerson of Wamphray, who after studying medicine in Edinburgh joined many other Scots in travelling to Russia to pursue his career. Rogerson became physician to the sexually voracious Catherine the Great, at which time he also acquired the dubious responsibility of checking all of her lovers for venereal disease. His gravestone commemorates his service to 'His Majesty the Emperor of Russia' and not to Catherine herself, for he remained in Russia after Catherine's death and served succeeding emperors up to and including Alexander I.

Just over the hill from Wamphray, the **Chariots of Fire Equestrian Centre** (Nether Boreland, Boreland DG11 2LL 01576 610248 chariotscic.org.uk) offers riding and carriage-driving instruction and experiences.

MID ANNANDALE

Mid Annandale is the location of a number of historic towns and the village of **Ae** (pronounced as in the vowel 'A'), a place as diminutive as its name (the shortest place name in English in the UK), sitting on the edge of the much larger **Ae Forest**. Built in 1947 by the Forestry Commission (now Forestry and Land Scotland), the village was home to the workers involved in planting some 25,000 acres of conifers after World War II, making this one of the largest forests in the UK.

Also in this area is a little-known curiosity... an outdoor collection of **forestry ploughs** (NX985923) that represent the development of tree-planting technology. They can be reached on foot by following the Riverside Walk Trail from the Forest of Ae car park at Ae. More information is available from forestryandland.gov.scot

The **7stanes mountain biking centre** (NX985896) at Ae has trails for all abilities, plus walks varying from short circuits to longer hikes.

4 LOCKERBIE & AROUND

Nether Boreland (page 259), **Somerton House Hotel** (page 259)

Lying on the main road and rail routes between London and both Glasgow and Edinburgh, Lockerbie is the first sizeable town north of the Scotland–England border. From the motorway there is little to see other than the large grey mass of the Steven's Croft Power Station: not an auspicious start, you may think, but notable for the fact that it is the UK's largest wood-fired biomass station.

"Lockerbie's history is worn proudly and also with a cheeky wink: quirky sheep sculptures add a light-hearted touch."

Lockerbie lies within the parish of Dryfesdale, a name taken from the Dryfe Water, which rises east of Moffat to the north and flows southwest to join the River Annan. It's also a name adopted for one of the beers by micro-brewery **Lowland Brewing** (lowlandbrewery.co.uk), which is based here. They produce several beers you might come across locally, notably Dryfe Blonde Twa Dugs Session IPA, and Rabbie's Drouth Best Bitter.

It was in Lockerbie that the American game of **Pickleball** was first played in the UK (something like a cross between tennis, badminton and table tennis), and the town is also known for **curling**: three times Olympian David Murdoch hails from here. The curling season runs from October to March; contact the ice rink if you fancy a go (14 Glasgow Rd, DG11 2AR 01576 202197 lockerbieicerink.co.uk) or check when sessions are being run on trycurling.com.

In the 1950s Lockerbie was the eighth richest town in Scotland. Today it's a more modest place but its history is worn proudly and also with a cheeky wink: quirky **sheep sculptures** add a light-hearted touch to the high street (and had our dog very excited – and confused – the first time he spotted them) and are a tribute to the great Lamb Fairs of days past. People would flock (no pun intended) to Lockerbie from miles around for the livestock sale, the money from which bought Lamb Hill to the east and built the Scottish Baronial **Town Hall**, with its slightly fanciful clock tower, at a cost of £10,000. It is said that at the market's height up to 70,000 lambs would be waiting to be sold on Lamb Hill. Now that would have been quite something.

Lockerbie's more recent history has been dominated by the tragic bombing on 21 December 1988 of Pan Am flight 103 as it passed overhead, which killed all 259 people on board and 11 residents on the ground. The victims of that horrendous event are remembered in a number of memorials, all of which are detailed on the website of the **Dryfesdale Lodge Visitors Centre** (dryfesdalelodge.co.uk). At the lodge itself, west of Lockerbie on the A709, is a remembrance garden and exhibition. There is also a striking **stained glass window** showing the flags of the nations of all those killed in the main hall of the Town Hall. It can be viewed when the Town Hall is open (mornings) and at other times by request (01576 202632).

East of Lockerbie, at **Tundergarth Church** (NT175808), the Watch Room has also been refurbished as a memorial. The nose of the Pan

CHEWING OVER A BIT OF HISTORY

The Jardines' (see opposite) early stronghold was Spedlins Tower, built in 1500 and which still stands on a loop of the Annan, opposite where Jardine Hall once stood. Although in private hands today it has a tale attached that is worth telling. The story goes that the Jardines moved from here in the late 17th century to escape the bogle (ghost) of an unfortunate miller, James Porteous, who fell victim to the poor memory of the first baronet, Sir Alexander Jardine (whose portrait, incidentally, hangs today in Annan Museum, page 61). Porteous suffered the baronet's displeasure for apparently setting fire to a mill and was locked away in the tower dungeon. Off rode Sir Alexander to Edinburgh with the key in his pocket, completely forgetting about the poor man. When he remembered he sent a messenger back post-haste but it was too late and the miller had died of starvation. Time likes to embellish a tale, and it is reported that in the throes of his terrible hunger the miller had gnawed off his own hands and feet. To this day it is said that if you poke a stick into the dungeon at Spedlins it will come back chewed.

Am plane came down in the field immediately opposite the church. A visitor's book is full of heartfelt messages written to lost loved ones and it is difficult not to be moved at this quiet, solemn spot.

Dryfesdale Parish Church is now on Townhead Street, but it used to be up the Dryfe Valley until the river changed course one night and washed it away. A second church was built, but it too fell victim to the elements. And so the third, current, church was located in the town itself. Built high with a raised entrance, it has stood since 1898.

In the graveyard are stones of well-known local families, notably the **Jardines**, whose seat, Jardine Hall (now demolished), used to stand northwest of Lockerbie. It was William Jardine (1784–1843) who, with James Matheson, founded the incredibly successful conglomerate **Jardine Matheson** in Canton in 1832. One of the original Hong Kong-based *hongs* (trading houses) from the days of Imperial China, the company is still in operation today and is still controlled by Jardines' descendants. William Jardine himself is commemorated in the old cemetery in the nearby town of Lochmaben (page 51).

Collectors and secondhand enthusiasts should head for the **Lockerbie Antiques Centre** (142 High St, DG11 2BX) and also to **Cobwebs Antiques** (30 Townhead St, DG11 2AE), a veritable treasure trove packed to the gunnels. If you're lucky, owner Irene Henderson will be there as she, too, is a veritable treasure trove, of local history. From her we learned of the Grahams, who set up the poor house in nearby Ecclefechan (page 53) before the village grew to house the workers for Hoddom Castle (page 54), to where they would walk each day.

Note that there's **no tourist information centre** in Lockerbie; details of what's going on can be found in the Town Hall on the high street.

FOOD & DRINK

On the B7076, five miles north of town, is the café of the **Lockerbie Lorry Park** (lorry not obligatory), an excellent place not just for a fry-up, but also for a range of good home-cooked food and unashamedly indulgent desserts such as bread and butter pudding and jam roly-poly. Truckers and farmers are regulars, and we've even spotted the local undertaker here (not on official business) – all looked after by the cheery ladies behind the counter.

Just Be Bistro 53 High St, DG11 2JH ✆ 01576 205715 f. The main retreat for teas, coffees, scones and lunches.

Somerton House Hotel 35 Carlisle Rd, DG11 2DR ☎ 01576 202583 🖱 somertonhotel.co.uk. Open to non-residents, Somerton's bright conservatory makes a pleasant setting for lunch or dinner. Traditional food, tasty and good value – a reliable choice.

Eskrigg Nature Reserve

📍 NY126805; just southwest of Lockerbie, abutting the A709 Dumfries Rd; car park accessed from the A709: just before leaving Lockerbie, turn left into Vallance Dr & then immediately right on to Eskrigg Farm Rd. Follow this for 300yds & the car park is on the right.

Lockerbie Wildlife Trust's Eskrigg Nature Reserve is a fine example of a community-based habitat-restoration and wildlife project, and its history makes for interesting reading (🖱 lockerbie-wildlife-trust.co.uk). There's a whole ecosystem to explore here, but the star attraction is the healthy population of **red squirrels** supported by the Scots pines. We saw 14 of them on one visit.

Hallmuir Prisoner of War Chapel

📍 NY128793 f Ukranian POW Chapel Lockerbie

On the Dalton Road, 1½ miles southwest of Lockerbie is a utilitarian, white-painted corrugated-iron building with blue windows. It's more than it seems, though, for this is a chapel, and the last remaining building of a World War II prisoner of war camp. The history of Ukrainian expatriation to the UK during World War II is well documented. The men who came to Hallmuir were just a few of the 8,500 former soldiers of the Ukrainian Galicia Division, previously part of the German army and subsequently interned by the British in Austria when Germany surrendered to the Allies, then moved to Italy, whence to Scotland in 1947 rather than leaving them to be handed over to the Russians.

Many of the Ukrainians who came to Scotland during World War II chose to stay when the war ended and the chapel is a unique memorial to them and their descendants. The interior is both vivid and moving, a small outpost of the Ukrainian Orthodox Church in lowland Scotland.

In recent years the chapel has suffered from the elements, but moves are afoot to both ensure the future integrity of the building and, funding permitting, create a visitor centre. The chapel is not open as a matter of course, though it is still used for worship. Access needs to be arranged in advance through the Facebook page.

5 LOCHMABEN & THE ROYAL FOUR TOWNS

Hightae Inn (page 259)

Lochmaben has long held a place at the heart of Scottish history, renowned as the home of the Lords of Annandale, ancestors of **Robert the Bruce** (1274–1329). Bruce was brought up in this area; his family is said to have lived in a castle that stood on Castle Hill, though there is little left to see (the site is now the second green of the local golf course). Ruins of a second castle, believed to have been built by Edward I of England in the late 13th to early 14th centuries and once the strongest fortress in the Scottish borderlands, can be seen on a peninsula in nearby Castle Loch.

At the head of the wide main street stands the small but elegant **Town Hall** with a regal statue of Bruce on a plinth outside, plus a statue of one

CASTLE LOCH, LOCHMABEN: THE POWER OF COMMUNITY

Darren Flint, co-author of this guide, is also Project Officer for the Castle Loch Lochmaben Community Trust (castleloch.org.uk)

After standing empty for a number of years a little white cottage on the side of Castle Loch came on to the market, not overly unusual you may think in this area of plentiful little white cottages. However, what made this spot special was it came with 280 acres of loch, surrounding woodlands and fishing rights. This isn't something that happens every day and the residents of the town of Lochmaben, which nestles up to the northern edge of the loch, and the surrounding Royal Four Towns, were mobilised into action and seized the opportunity to purchase this for future generations. After much form-filling, hoop-jumping and consultation, the fundraising and acquisition of the loch were completed in early 2014.

Castle Loch is now managed by Castle Loch Lochmaben Community Trust (CLLCT) with the support of a stalwart team of volunteers. Thanks to their efforts, there is now a good path offering a three-mile flat and varied circular walk around the loch taking in the best of the history and habitats, with plenty of opportunities to enjoy the wildlife. And, also thanks to them, Castle Loch took the top award in the RSPB's Nature of Scotland Awards for best Community Project in 2015, and in 2018 the Queen's Award for Voluntary Services – the OBE for volunteering.

Take the waymarked walk around the loch and enjoy what each season has to offer, be it the winter migration of geese and wildfowl, returning sand martins and warblers in spring, darting dragonflies in summer, or the enticing year-round opportunity to see otter and rare willow tit.

Reverend William Graham in a recess above the door. Graham oversaw the enlargement of the Town Hall in 1869 and, from the satisfied look on his face, he was obviously happy with the results.

Lochmaben today is very much a local town with a strong community presence, a shining example of which was the acquisition of **Castle Loch** (see box, page 51). This is one of three lochs that surround the town, the other two being Kirk and Mill lochs, slightly to the north. Dinghy sailors can take to the waters on Castle Loch through the **Annandale Sailing Club** (annansail.co.uk) and **fishing** is also allowed by permit, which can be bought at Pettigrews on the high street and at castlelochfishery.co.uk (from where further information about fishing is also available).

"Bruce granted lands and privileges to the 'King's kindly tenants', conferring upon them a preferential position."

In the area around Lochmaben are the Royal Four Towns of **Greenhill**, **Heck**, **Hightae** and **Smallholm**, notable for their protected status that dates back to the time of Robert the Bruce. It is said that Bruce granted lands and privileges to the 'King's kindly tenants', conferring upon them a preferential position, to provide garrisons and food supplies for Lochmaben Castle, and since then the good citizens have enjoyed the protection of successive kings and parliaments against local officials and landowners.

A few miles south of Lochmaben on the road to Dalton, animal lovers will enjoy **Mossburn Community Farm** (DG11 1LE 01387 811288 mossburn.org) with its menagerie of rescued animals (pretty much everything apart from cats, dogs and donkeys).

A wealth of information about Lochmaben can be found at lochmaben.org.uk. Local information leaflets are available in the Town Hall.

FOOD & DRINK

Barony Country Foods Unit 4, Laverockhall Farm Rd, Lochmaben DG11 1RE 01387 811928 baronycountryfoods.co.uk. Smokehouse and shop offering an enticing range: smoked salmon, venison, shellfish, grouse and more.

Graham's Bakery 29 High St, Lochmaben DG11 1NG 01387 811421. Small café within the bakery; eat in or take-away; sausage rolls, sandwiches and sweet temptations.

Hightae Inn High Rd, Hightae DG11 1JS 01387 811711 hightaeinn.co.uk eve only. Quality food from local ingredients, always popular. Booking essential.

Pink Flamingo Vintage Tea Room 6a Bruce St, Lochmaben DG11 1PD ✆ 01387 810883. Retro tea room offering 'yummy food for all occasions' served from a cracking (not literally) range of china. Breakfast, lunches, home-baked cakes and loose-leaf teas.

6 ECCLEFECHAN & AROUND

The shortened version of Ecclefechan's name is bandied around freely and more than once we've heard the joke told of someone who 'missed the 'Fechan bus', so don't be surprised if you come across variations on this theme during a visit to the area. This strange name is derived from the Celtic for 'small church' and dates from pre-Roman times.

Ecclefechan has survived good times and bad and made a not insignificant contribution to history as the birth and burial place of philosopher and essayist **Thomas Carlyle** (1795–1881), whose description of economics as 'the dismal science' may ring true with many in today's economically vexing times. **Carlyle's Birthplace** (DG11 3DG ✆ 01576 300666 nts.org.uk late Mar–Nov & 4 Dec 10.00–17.00 daily; free 4 Dec for Carlyle's birthday; National Trust for Scotland), with its modest three rooms and knowledgeable staff and volunteers, is on the high street.

"The shortened version is bandied around – more than once we've heard the joke told of someone who 'missed the 'Fechan bus.'"

A series of six information noticeboards is dotted down the main street, telling the history and development of the village and, through that, something of the wider story of the area.

Ecclefechan Church is now closed but the **graveyard** next to it is not. As well as being the final resting place of Carlyle, it is also where one **Archibald Arnott** is buried. Born at nearby Kirkconnel Hall, Arnott was the physician who attended Napoleon Bonaparte during his confinement to St Helena and was the only doctor that Napoleon would countenance in his dying days.

Burnswark Hill

NY185788

Directly north from Ecclefechan is a detour worth taking up Burnswark Hill. It's about three miles from the village centre and can be walked or driven (a pleasant circular walk can be started in Ecclefechan or from Tundergarth Church near Lockerbie). At the summit are the ramparts of an Iron Age fort, with Roman siege camps to the north and south.

The view from up here is terrific, a panorama taking in the eastern end of the Solway Firth with the mountains of Cumbria to one side and Criffel to the other.

Archaeologists have been trying for 300 years to determine exactly what Burnswark's role was. A training ground for Roman soldiers and occupation by local tribes people have both been suggested, but excavations in 2016 threw up another possibility: could this be the start of the push northwards from Hadrian's Wall that culminated in the building of the Antonine Wall across central Scotland at the northernmost frontier of the Roman Empire? That's what a growing body of archaeological opinion suggests, supported by excavations made by the Trimontium Trust (trimontium.co.uk).

Hoddom Castle & around

Kirkwood Real Farm Holidays (page 259) **Hoddom Castle Caravan Park** (page 259)

Built 1437–84, Hoddom Castle (NY156730) was initially called the Castle of Hoddom Staines ('staines' means stones) as it was constructed from an older castle of the same name that stood on the opposite side of the river and which was said to have been the home of a branch of the family of Robert the Bruce at the start of the 14th century. It was a Herries property from around 1449, Herries being one of the old Galloway families that are still in the area. The castle today is partly ruined and partly used as a centre for the surrounding caravan park, where a bar and restaurant is open to non-residents.

A couple of interesting diversions on foot can be taken from here (leave your car in the parking area just above the gates into Hoddom Castle). The first is a visit to the cemetery on the banks of the Annan, reached downstream along the riverbank. The **graveyard** is on the site of a monastery built for St Kentigern (or Mungo) in the 7th century. There is little left to be seen of the monastery complex, but look out for the ghoulish skull and crossbones motif that adorns many of the gravestones, part of a tradition of 18th-century folk art in which heraldic emblems were often combined with symbols of mortality and immortality such as coffins and hourglasses.

This is an exceptionally peaceful spot in which to while away an hour or two, with a bench on the riverbank perfectly sited for a picnic. Come early in the morning or at dusk, sit quietly and watch for ripples at the water's edge and you might be lucky enough to see an otter. This is also one of the most beautiful stretches on the Annan for **salmon fishing** (permits can be bought at Hoddom Castle; see the Fish Annan page of fishpal.com) and a salmon trail with information boards along the riverbank, accessed from the castle, charts the life cycle of a salmon from egg to Atlantic migration. Keep an eye open for kingfishers and also look out for passing female goosander ducks with their red heads and long serrated beaks. We have seen them flying back and forth along this straight stretch of the Annan and under the handsome stone bridge.

"Keep an eye open for kingfishers and look out as well for passing female goosander ducks with their red heads."

The other option is to set out from Hoddom in the opposite direction, along the Dalton Road from the car park and then turn left up stone steps and carry on up the hill for the 360° views at **Repentance Tower** at the top. The tower dates from around 1560 and various stories explain its name, but all conclude that it was built to atone for some act of treachery.

Nearby Dalton has not one, but two **distilleries**. One is the home of **Oro Gin** (DG11 1DU 01387 840381 orogin.co.uk) and the other is the rum-producing **Ninefold Distillery** (Dormont Home Farm, DG11 1DJ 01387 840116 ninefolddistillery.com). Both run tours and Oro Gin also offers food.

A taste of farming life is offered at nearby **Kirkwood Real Farm Holidays** (DG11 1DH 01576 510200 kirkwood-lockerbie.co.uk; page 259) when you book one of their driving activities. Quad biking, 4X4 and tractor driving are all offered, in addition to courses in wildlife photography and salmon fishing on two stretches of the Annan.

LOWER ANNANDALE

From Gretna Green westwards to Ruthwell, the landscape shelves gently down to the shores of the Firth. The River Sark runs immediately south of Gretna, its winding course demarcating the border between England and Scotland for several miles before it empties into the eastern end of the Solway. The flatlands of the **Solway Plain** spread out in stark contrast to the hills and rugged coastline that characterise so much of the rest of Dumfries and Galloway. The appeal here is in the sudden and unexpected views across the Solway, the stories of centuries past, the enormous contribution of the area to World War I and II, and a few social quirks and anomalies thrown in for good measure.

7 GRETNA & GRETNA GREEN

There are few who haven't heard of Gretna and many who, regardless of whether they have been here or not, will offer an opinion. It is certainly a place that inspires love (literally) or loathing. The divide stems primarily from the whole razzmatazz that surrounds the Gretna marriage industry. There is a tale worth telling here though, one of legal precedent, thwarted love, scandal and intrigue.

First let's clear up the confusion between Gretna and Gretna Green, for they are two separate places, albeit right next door to each other. **Gretna Green** is the small hamlet known for its history of marriages, whereas neighbouring **Gretna** is, like the town of Eastriggs (page 58) a little further along the Solway, a planned town that was built during World War I.

"Let's clear up the confusion between Gretna and Gretna Green: they're two separate places, right next door to each other."

For centuries the main coaching route ran right past the Famous Blacksmiths Shop in Gretna Green. The Scotland–England border lies immediately south and the blacksmith's was the first place you came to. This was the fortuitous circumstance that led to its fame, for when the 1754 marriage act was introduced in England, making it illegal for those under 21 to wed without parental consent, the blacksmith of the day spotted an opportunity and, taking advantage of the liberal laws in Scotland, offered to conduct weddings over his anvil for any couples who were struggling to wed across the border. (Unlike in England, where marriages were only legal if conducted by a minister, in Scotland the ceremony could be officiated by just about anyone so long as it was in front of two witnesses.) Needless to say, the idea took off and spawned a tradition that, despite fluctuations over the centuries, is as strong as ever.

These days the **Famous Blacksmiths Shop** (⚲ NY321685) is open for business as usual and you don't have to be getting married to have a look around. Whatever day you visit there's a good chance you may witness (not officially, you understand) a wedding taking place, for these days the blacksmiths host weddings in the sort of numbers –

around 1,000 each year – that would make traditional churches weep with envy. The cottage also houses a museum and exhibition with a range of fascinating items, including letters from forlorn maidens beseeching the blacksmith priests to find them a husband, for these self-made businessmen-ministers were also regarded as matchmakers by girls from far and wide. It really is a piece of living history. There's also a tea room, gift shop and speciality food hall with an enticing range of goodies, all usually bustling with a coachload or two (or more) of visitors from all around the world.

It didn't take long for other local businesses to cotton on to their potential as wedding venues. **Gretna Hall**, just across the motorway and built originally in 1710 as a manor house for the Johnstone family, offered a more refined and genteel retreat in which couples could wed. Today it is still offering the same service and operates as a hotel. And just around the corner from it can be found the **Old Toll Bar**, which in 1830 found itself the first house in Scotland when the main route north was diverted. It was too good an opportunity to be missed and the toll keeper was soon pulling in passing couples for a quick service that he would perform himself, for a small fee of course.

FOOD & DRINK

In addition to the tea room at Gretna Green, fine food (sourced locally) and afternoon teas are available to non-residents at both **Smith's Hotel** (Gretna Green DG16 5EA ☎ 01461 337007 smithsgretnagreen.com) and **Gretna Hall Hotel** (Gretna Green DG16 5DY ☎ 01461 338257 gretnahallhotel.com).

Bruce's Cave

NY265705

On the subject of traditions and myths, while you're in this area you might want to pop up to **Kirkpatrick Fleming** a few miles northwest of Gretna to take a peek at Bruce's Cave, the spot to where the eponymous leader is said to have retreated in the winter of 1306 after defeat by the English. The cave is on the Cove Estate, where the main house (now holiday apartments) is surrounded by its own caravan site. Sir Walter Scott first told the tale of Bruce in his cave in *Tales of a Grandfather* in 1828. While he was here, it is said Bruce watched a spider spinning a web. Time and again it failed, falling and then starting again, and thus Bruce was inspired to rally once more before going on to succeed against all the odds at the Battle of Bannockburn. From this episode comes the saying 'If at first you don't succeed, try, try and try again'.

The cave makes for a fun trip, with a short walk down through the woods to a walkway and platform attached to the hillside high above the Kirtle Water.

WEST OF GRETNA

Heading west from Gretna, glimpses of the Solway to the south reveal ever-changing views of ever-changing waters and sands stretching across the estuary to Cumbria. Through the village of **Rigg** with its curious village hall (Mansfield Hall) and on to **Eastriggs**, thereby giving rise to an anomaly that we haven't yet been able to get to the bottom of. Specifically, why is Eastriggs west of Rigg? If you know, we'd be delighted to hear. Eastriggs is known as the Commonwealth Village for it was built to house workers who were brought in from all over the Commonwealth to the nearby munitions factory (see opposite).

THE WORST RAILWAY DISASTER IN BRITAIN

Dumfries and Galloway holds the unenviable distinction of being the location of three of the worst transport disasters that have ever occurred in Britain: the Lockerbie bombing in 1988, the sinking of the passenger ferry *MV Princess Victoria* off the west coast in January 1953 (page 236) and the tragic Quintinshill rail disaster just north of Gretna Green on 22 May 1915.

The circumstances that led to Quintinshill were a mix of signaller error and a 'failure to operate rule 55', which required safeguards to be put in place should a train be stationary on a running line. As a result, a southbound troop train travelling at high speed and carrying a Royal Scots battalion headed for Gallipoli ran into a stationary passenger train at Quintinshill. The resulting carnage was compounded shortly after when a northbound express ploughed into the wreckage, spilling hot coals across the carriages and starting a fire.

In all, 227 people were killed and 246 injured. The disaster accounted for 42% of the casualties suffered by the Royal Scots during World War I. George Meakin and James Tinsley, both signalmen on duty at Quintinshill at the time, were tried for involuntary manslaughter and found guilty in what proved to be a controversial verdict. Both had an unblemished record and both would have to live with their conscience. Tinsley was sentenced to three years penal servitude and Meakin to 18 months, but both were released after just 12 months.

A display about the Quintinshill disaster is included in the Devil's Porridge exhibition at Eastriggs (see opposite).

In recognition, the streets are named after different countries, regions and cities of the Commonwealth, thus you might see Delhi Road, Brisbane Way or Vancouver Road, for instance. Australia, New Zealand, Canada, India and South Africa are all represented.

The Devil's Porridge

Stanfield, Annan Rd, Eastriggs DG12 6TF NY246664 01461 700021 devilsporridge.org.uk daily, but usually closed for most of Dec & early Jan

During World War I reports were brought back from the front that Britain was losing the war due to lack of ammunition. Following the shell and ammunition crisis of June 1915, Lloyd George, then Minister for Munitions in Asquith's coalition government, resolved to do something and set about a project that was to see the construction of the biggest factory on earth.

A site was needed and the stretch of land along the Solway at Eastriggs fitted the bill. There was nothing here, it was close to mainline transport connections and ships could come up the Solway and dock at Annan. So in September 1915 work began, progressing at an urgent pace. Production started nine months later and, by September 1916, the factory was shipping out 800 tons of cordyte each week, a highly explosive mix of nitro-glycerin and nitro-cotton to be used as propellant in munitions.

The construction of the factory was an immense achievement in every sense. Not only was the site enormous, stretching for nine miles from Dornock to Longtown and two miles wide, but the running of it was a complex operation, not least in eradicating as far as possible any fire risk. Workers, the majority of them women, were inspected every time they entered the factory by the 'women police', who paid particular attention to bodices to make sure there were no buttons that could drop off and cause an explosion in the highly volatile propellant mix. There were 125 miles of rail track on the site and fireless steam engines were used, specially constructed with composite wheels to ensure there were no sparks from the rails.

Around 30,000 people worked here and so a whole social infrastructure had to be created. Churches and schools were built, and so too were cinemas and dance halls. And, of course, housing. There was no way the surrounding towns could absorb such a huge influx of people and so two purpose-built settlements were created, one at

Eastriggs which until that time had been only a single farmhouse, and the other at Gretna (page 56).

The architects of these towns were Courtney Crickner and Raymond Unwin, both keen supporters of the Garden City movement that had been pioneered by the Cadbury Bournville settlement in Birmingham and Port Sunlight near Liverpool. The towns they created were the most modern in Scotland and after the war attracted the attention of the US government, who had become aware of the limitations of their own public housing and the detrimental effect it had on their war effort. Congress voted to allocate US$50 million to create better living conditions and US architects subsequently looked to the UK for inspiration, including to the developments on the Solway.

"The architects were Courtney Crickner and Raymond Unwin, both keen supporters of the Garden City movement."

The Devil's Porridge engagingly presents this fascinating story in a super purpose-built centre with a small café. As for where the name comes from, it's thanks to Arthur Conan Doyle of *Sherlock Holmes* fame. During the war he visited the factory and observed the women workers kneading by hand the mix of nitric acid and cotton waste in large vats. It was this mixture that he subsequently termed 'The Devil's Porridge'.

The exhibition also includes a section on the Quintinshill railway disaster of 22 May 1915 (see box, page 58).

8 ANNAN

Waterside Rooms (page 259)

Annan's fortunes have fluctuated since the town was made a Burgh of Barony by the Bruces in the 13th century. Industries have come and gone, from shipbuilding and the bustling work of a busy port to whisky distilling and, in more recent times, nuclear power at the local (now decommissioned) Chapelcross Power Station on a site that is currently being evaluated for future economic development. Despite such ups and downs, an air of determined survival adheres to Annan's **High Street**, with its attractive red sandstone buildings that tell of more prosperous times and of another local industry, quarrying. What's more, there are several reasons for the town to be optimistic: the redevelopment of the historic Annandale Distillery (page 63) nearby; the ongoing work of the Annan Harbour Action Group (page 62); and its development as **'Annan the History Town'** (f), with plans and hopes for a summer History Festival and, if funds can be raised, the redevelopment of the Victoria Hall Complex in the centre of town.

In case of inclement weather, Annan has one of the region's few cinemas (**Lonsdale Cinema**, Moat Rd, DG12 5DE ✆ 01461 206901 🖱 annancinema.co.uk), an appealingly small affair with super-comfortable seats, which is one of Scotland's last remaining family-operated, privately owned local cinemas.

The broad curve of the high street is dominated by the 19th-century Scottish baronial tower of the **Town Hall** (✆ 01461 204914), inside which, fixed to the east wall of the council chamber, is the **Brus Stane** (Bruce Stone) 👆, which is believed to have been part of the original motte and bailey castle of the Bruce Lords in the 12th to 14th centuries. Access to view the stone is by appointment only.

Annan Museum (Bank St, DG12 6AA 🖱 annan.org.uk ⏲ Apr–Oct Mon–Sat) is a good place to get to grips with the history not just of the town, but also of East Dumfriesshire in general. Temporary exhibitions are staged downstairs and there's a permanent exhibition upstairs with everything from an engaging video of local fishermen explaining the different types of nets and talking about characters past and present, to portraits of the local gentry, old photos of the area and an exceptional

THE BELL RINGERS RAID

We are grateful to Alan Thomson of the Annan Harbour Action Group for recounting this story.

In 1626, raiders from Annan stole the original bell from the 12th-century St Michael's Church in Bowness-on-Solway in Cumbria. According to legend, due to bad weather, drink being taken and a hot pursuit, the raiders had to ditch their trophy overboard. In retaliation the Cumbrians raided Dornock and Middlebie in Dumfriesshire and made off with a new pair of bells.

Traditionally, on induction, the minister of Annan linked with Dornock would petition the vicar of Bowness for the return of his bell. These days, it's evolved into an annual event in August, when Scottish Coastal Rowing teams row out from Annan harbour via Waterfoot and across the Solway to Bowness where they are initially repelled by English forces, as represented by the pupils of the local school with water pistols, but eventually they prevail and retrieve their prize. The first team over brings back the bell and the second the stand. On return to the harbour the bell is assembled and rung.

Bronze Age sword in remarkable condition. Among many other exhibits are displays relating to the RAF presence during World War II, the development and decommissioning of Chapelcross, and a glass case full of items from the Common Riding tradition.

Annan Harbour was a major point of emigration in the 18th and 19th centuries. Today a few boats still make use of it but it's an ongoing job to stop it silting up completely. The quay has been partially restored and in late August is the location of the **Annan Festival**, organised by the Annan Harbour Action Group (annanharbouractiongroup.co.uk). Boats, vintage cars, crafts and artisan food and drink producers all feature. The Action Group can also run rowing sessions in its St Ayles skiffs if you fancy having a go, and organises the annual 'Bell Ringers Raid' in August (see box, page 61).

If you go down to the water at Whinnyrigg (NY209648; take Seafield Road south of the town) you'll not only get a good view across to Cumbria, but you'll also see nets in the water. Fishing along the Solway is mostly with **haaf nets** and other forms of 'fixed engines' – nets secured to the shore or seabed. Haaf nets consist of a single net mounted on a wooden frame that is carried into the water and held there by the fisherman.

"Haaf nets consist of a single net mounted on a wooden frame carried into the water and held there by the fisherman."

This historic spot has been much used over the centuries for crossing the Solway, notably just to the east at Bowness Wath ('wath' means ford), which was used by cattle drovers crossing between Bowness in Cumbria and Annan up until 1863. In the 19th century the **Solway Viaduct** was built, forming a safer crossing point until falling into disuse and then being demolished in 1934. The viaduct was a lifeline for local workers who had a habit of running across it for last orders at the pub, since closing time was half an hour later in England than in Scotland.

The **Annan Shore Walk** is a lovely loop of around five miles signposted from Annan Town Hall, passing boards with information about local fishing methods such as haaf nets, and taking in the Solway Viaduct and the grassland and sand flats of the Annan Merse, a Site of Special Scientific Interest (SSSI) with populations of wading birds. Full details can be found online at the local community website, **Annan Online** (annan.org.uk; click on 'Local', then 'Activities', and then 'Walking' for a downloadable booklet).

Annandale Distillery

Northfield, Annan DG12 5LL NY195683 annandaledistillery.com daily; 60-minute tours starting on the hour between 10.00 & 16.00; see ad, 4th colour section

Just north of Annan, the Annandale Distillery reopened in 2014 for the first time in almost 100 years, thanks to the determination of Dumfries-born Professor David Thomson and Teresa Church, who describe their project as a 'labour of love'. Thomson and Church are owners of MMR Research Worldwide, a global sensory and consumer research company, so this is something of a departure from their normal area of work, but one that is fuelled by their passion for David's home region and a fascination with whisky production in the area.

The distillery dates from the 1830s and in its time has been owned by an exciseman, the son of a former mayor of Liverpool, and international brand Johnnie Walker. From 1924 to 2007 it was owned by the Robinson family, who were producing the then famous 'Provost' brand of porridge oats from their mills in Annan with the distillery maltings, kiln and mash house converted into a grain-drying plant and the bonded warehouses used for housing cattle.

Now the impressive listed building has been painstakingly refurbished and produces two styles of whisky honouring two of Scotland's most iconic figures, both with strong ties to the Annandale area. The single malt, smoky, peaty Man O' Sword is inspired by Robert the Bruce, and the non-smoky Man O' Words pays tribute to Robert Burns, who is said to have visited the site during his career as the local exciseman.

FOOD & DRINK

Café Royal 95 High St, DG12 6DG 01461 202865. Reputedly the favourite restaurant of local lass Ashley Jensen, who came to fame in the TV programme *Extras*. Much loved for its fish and chips – 'best chippy in the toon' as one reviewer comments on Facebook. Eat in (or at the garden tables) or take-away.

The Maltings Coffee Shop Annandale Distillery, Northfield, Annan DG12 5LL NY195683 annandaledistillery.com. Soups, sandwiches, afternoon teas and 'hearty plates' in the atmospheric setting of the converted maltings.

WEST OF ANNAN

West of Annan the A75 sweeps northwest towards Dumfries, veering away from the Solway and crossing gentle hills that shelve down to the water. The more interesting option is to stay south of the A75 on the

B724 and take a couple of diversions, one right down to the shoreline at Powfoot and the other to Ruthwell, an unassuming wee place with a couple of unexpected attractions.

9 Powfoot

Terraces of red-brick cottages around the most English of village greens come as something of a surprise at pretty Powfoot, built as a holiday village on the Solway shore at the turn of the 20th century. Right at the end of the road you'll find the designated parking area, which also offers easy access to the beach.

Enjoy the gigantic sky and views of the Cumbrian mountains, and take a walk out over the sands but be aware of the tide times and do not venture out too far at the cusp of low tide; the Solway is notorious for its racing, treacherous tides. Look out for a strange circular structure about 600yds from shore; all that now remains of a tidal swimming pool.

This is a good spot for birdlife. We stood here at dusk one evening mesmerised by a huge flock of wheeling birds above the sands, behaviour typical of knot, wintering here from their Arctic breeding grounds.

FOOD & DRINK

Del Amitri The Powfoot Hotel, Links Av, DG12 5PN ☎ 01461 700300 thepowfoothotel.com. Something of a local institution, with views out across the sands. Lunches and dinners served daily.

10 Ruthwell

Four miles west of Powfoot brings you to Ruthwell, famous for two things, both connected with Reverend Dr Henry Duncan.

The first is the **Ruthwell Cross** (Historic Environment Scotland; free), an 18ft-high stone Anglo-Saxon preaching cross that is thought to date from the 8th century and is in remarkable condition. It is one of Scotland's rarest treasures. Carved with scenes from the New Testament, the cross was deliberately broken in 1642 so it could be more easily hidden – and protected – during the Reformation. Duncan restored it in 1818 and it was later installed in a specially built apse at Ruthwell Church, where it can still be viewed today. The church is kept locked but a sign is posted with directions of where to collect the key from a nearby house.

Duncan is remembered as a man of vision and compassion (not to mention as a geologist: he discovered the first dinosaur quadruped fossil footprints in Britain, at Cornockle Quarry north of Lochmaben), and it is these qualities that led him to establish the world's first savings bank, the Ruthwell Parish Bank, in 1810 in the building that now houses the endearing **Savings Bank Museum** (DG1 4NN ✆ 01387 870640 🖱 savingsbanksmuseum.co.uk ⏲ all year but check times). He also founded a couple of local newspapers, through which he encouraged the local population to start saving. Talk about a canny Scot!

ESKDALE

Eskdale is more sparsely populated and remote than neighbouring Annandale and tends to look as much to the Scottish Borders region and south to Carlisle as it does to the rest of Dumfries and Galloway due to its geography and associated road and transport connections. Public transport is a trickier option here and driving is the best way to get around, especially once you venture up into the hills. The scenery is inspiring and the attractions are varied, from the old mill town of **Langholm** in the south, now reinventing itself as a cultural centre for arts, crafts and theatre, to the village of **Eskdalemuir** (one of the wettest in Britain, but don't let that put you off) set in glorious countryside, and the nearby **Kagyu Samye Ling Buddhist Monastery**.

11 LANGHOLM

Eskdale Hotel (page 259)

Langholm sits snugly in the valley of the Esk at the confluence of the River Esk, Ewes Water and Wauchope Water, its white stone buildings bearing testament to the quarries of days past on neighbouring Whita Hill and its watery geography demanding such a proliferation of bridges that one enthusiastic guidebook writer in the 1950s declared 'So many bridges, so many waterways! Why, at first glance this Muckle Town of Langholm seems like a little Venice'. Comparisons with La Serenissima aside, Langholm nonetheless holds its own as a place of culture, cuisine and curiosity, all of the best possible local sort. The latter in particular has recently garnered attention as a result of one man's passion for chillies, an interest that – unexpectedly – took the town by storm and has earned Langholm an unlikely reputation as the 'Chilli Capital of Scotland'.

Known as the 'Muckle Toon' (the 'big town') in the 19th century, Langholm had a reputation internationally for the tweed woven in its mills, an industry that, at its peak around 1890, employed some 1,200 people. Although the last mill closed in 2013, there has since been something of a resurgence with a host of small textile companies choosing to base themselves here, including the memorably named Yarns to Yearn For. The work of the **Langholm Initiative** (langholminitiative.org.uk), a public-private partnership development trust, has been instrumental, helping to revitalise the Eskdale area in general through projects focusing on industry, landscape, music and the arts.

Three projects in particular are relevant for visitors. **Welcome to Langholm** (welcometolangholm.co.uk) manages the visitor information centre on the high street; **Wild Eskdale** (wildeskdale.co.uk) offers a range of wildlife experiences in the surrounding area; and the hugely ambitious **Langholm Moor Project** is exploring the possibility of purchasing 11,000 acres of moorland, all part of a larger SSSI, being sold by Buccleuch Estates, to create the Langholm Moor Nature Reserve. Check out the Langholm Initiative website for the latest details or make contact with Kevin Cumming from Wild Eskdale.

Langholm Moor is important locally and nationally for watching rare species of birds of prey, including hen harriers and other raptors. Between 2008 and 2018 it was also the location of a controversial project designed to determine if the moor could support a mix of conservation and driven grouse shooting and to deliver other wider biodiversity. Check out langholmproject.com for the full story.

With such a wealth of stunning countryside on its doorstep, Langholm makes a great base from which to walk in the surrounding hills, to spot the local fauna and flora, or to **fish** the beats of the Esk. It is also an area of inspiration for a wide variety of artists and crafts people. Artist **Julie Dumbarton** (juliedumbarton.com) is based here and attracts an international following to her courses in oil painting, while designer **Daniel Lacey** (daniellacey.com) creates stunning furniture – 'heirloom pieces', as he justifiably describes them – from his workshop in an old whisky distillery, and jeweller **Lisa Rothwell-Young** (lisarothwell-young.co.uk) specialises in ethical fine jewellery from her town-centre studio. Ask at the tourist information centre for details of other local artisans who welcome visitors.

Historically, Langholm was the site of the highly significant **Battle of Arkinholm** in 1455, when supporters of James II defeated the Black

Douglases who had controlled the area for so long, and thus ended a civil war. It was after this time that many local families came to prominence, names that are still heard today across the area: Scott, Beattie, Irvine, Glendinning, Maxwell and Armstrong.

The town is closely associated with the great engineer **Thomas Telford** (1757–1834), born in the tiny settlement of Glendinning (see box, page 73) to the northwest and who at a young age was apprenticed to a local stonemason. Telford left a bequest to the Langholm Subscription Library (as it was then), the interest on which was used to buy a fine collection of books. Some of these can still be seen in the **Langholm Library** (accessed from the Market Place at the back of the town hall and not to be confused with the public library on Charles Street), leather-bound volumes with 'Langholm Library Telford Legacy' tooled on the spines. Today they are stored upstairs in a temperature-controlled space, but they used to be kept in a splendid barrel-vaulted room on the first floor that has since been put to alternative use as a practice room for the town's **pipe band** (the addition of a false ceiling has improved the acoustics no end). Listen out for the band; if you're here on a sunny day you may find them in the car park.

Outside the library door stands a statue of **Admiral Sir Pulteney Malcolm**, one of Langholm's many famous sons and daughters, all of whom are detailed on a noticeboard towards the northern end of the High Street. Several Malcolms made the grade for their contribution to military and economic life; another, Sir John, is commemorated by the Malcolm Monument on Whita Hill (page 70) above the town. Pulteney and John were just two of the 17 children of parents George and Margaret, who farmed at nearby Burnfoot.

The library was built on land gifted by the Duke of Buccleuch, whose local estate has owned much of the surrounding countryside since the mid 17th century. Today, **The Buccleuch Centre** (DG13 0AW ✆ 01387 381196 🖱 buccleuchcentre.com) on the western side of the Esk is one of the main arts and entertainment venues in southern Scotland.

The library was also at one time frequented by Chris Grieve, better known as **Hugh MacDiarmid**, whose family lived here from 1899 to 1913. MacDiarmid is commemorated by an engaging modern installation on Whita Hill (page 70). If you plan to visit the Hugh MacDiarmid memorial, pick up a copy of the leaflet from the tourist information centre which explains what all of the panels mean.

Langholm circular walk: in the footsteps of the Border Reivers

❋ Landranger map 79, Explorer maps 323/324; start: Kilngreen car park NY364848; 6 miles/2½ hours (including breaks); moderate

The 'Muckle Toon' has many fine walks, with numerous circular routes all beginning from this walk's start point. This moderate route on hard-surfaced tracks and grass-hill paths with some steep sections provides a fine mix of habitats, history and upland views. Kilngreen car park is just north of the town centre (A7), on the edge of the River Esk and is accessible by buses 95/103/124. There are lots of refreshment options in Langholm.

From **1 the car park** head away from the town, upstream along Ewes Water, and cross at Ewes Bridge. By the pillars at the estate entrance and sawmill go left through the wooden gates and follow the path left around the field edge, **Langholm Castle** ruins stand in the centre of this field. Follow the path along the bank of the River Esk, pass the elegant **Duchess Bridge**, cast in 1813 and the first cast-iron bridge in Scotland, and on past the pheasant-rearing sheds.

The path bends right, then away from the river, and up to **2 Holmhead Farm** (NY354858). Follow the track around to the left in front of the steading, and on past North Lodge staying on the main woodland track. After about half a mile the woodland opens up and offers views of Potholm Farm and the Eskdale hills.

At the track junction, by the wooden bench, take the left fork down the hill, and pass above Potholm Farm to the **3 T-junction** (NY355878). Turn sharp right and follow the track as it meanders up the hill. Cross the stile and turn immediately right, following the line of the fence as it climbs up between Wrae Hass and Potholm Hill.

Just before the brow of the ridge, cross the stile on your right, through the field and over the next stile. Follow the old stone dyke (wall) as it climbs **Potholm Hill**, and, on a clear day, enjoy the 360° views along the Ewes and Esk valleys, and down to the Solway Firth and mountains of the Lake District behind.

The high street and river make for a nice circular loop, starting from the riverside car park, heading along the street and, next to Truly Scrumptious café, cutting down the 'Lairds Entry' to reach the river (at one time this was the only way down to the river, and was thus the entry to Rosevale House, home of the banker and lawyer 'laird', John Little). Cross the river, take a moment to wander around the church

Continue following the dyke down off the hill, over the ladder stile and alongside a more robust wall. Keep straight ahead when this wall bears sharply left, and continue to the summit of **4 Castle Hill** (NY361862). As you begin to descend, head for Langholm through the scrubby hawthorn trees that scatter this hillside, pass the footpath marker and join the rough track. Cross the ladder stile and carry on downhill to the road, passing Pathhead and returning to Ewes Bridge and the car park.

Shorter route: if time is tight, there is a pleasant alternative. Follow the first two stages of the above route, as far as the North Lodge, at which point turn a sharp right on to a track that follows along the far side of the wall (instead of continuing straight ahead on the main woodland track of the longer route). Stay on this track, ignoring any side paths, as it passes through attractive woodland, to emerge and continue along a field edge. The path then turns a sharp left between two fields and after about 200m reaches the path, from the longer route, coming off Castle Hill. Having joined the longer route, continue back to the car park in Langholm.

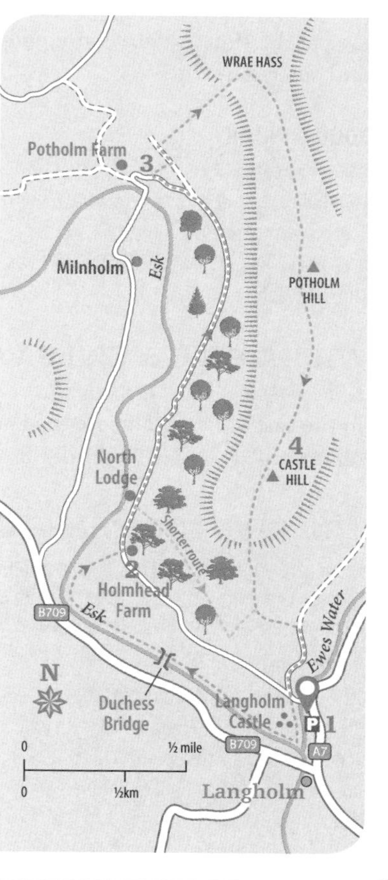

and riverside gardens before strolling back along the bank. The scant remains of **Langholm Castle**, built in the 16th century by Christopher Armstrong, brother of notorious reiver Johnnie Armstrong, stand in grounds across the double-arched stone bridge on the western side of the river at the north end of town. (Incidentally, the Eskdale Hotel holds a small collection of artefacts and a DVD relating to the Clan Armstrong.)

Every summer Langholm comes alive to the sound of pipe bands, cheering crowds and horses cantering through the streets for the annual **Common Riding** or Riding of the Marches. Langholm's is a particularly fine celebration, usually held towards the end of July. If you're in the area at the time, we'd recommend it highly as a day of grand tradition and entertainment.

FOOD & DRINK

Eskdale Hotel Market Pl, DG13 0JH ✆ 013873 80357. Conveniently located in the centre of Langholm, serving teas, coffees, soups, sandwiches and fuller meals in the small bar.
Truly Scrumptious 70 High St, DG13 0JH ✆ 013873 80402. Offers a good selection of teas and coffees in fine bone china, along with sandwiches and fuller dishes in a charming vintage tea room and garden.

12 WHITA HILL & EWES VALLEY

▲ **The Wagon at Arkleton** (page 260)

To the east of Langholm are the Langholm and Newcastleton hills, with **Whita Hill** (⚲ NY379847) the first summit, easily accessed by a road

THE KIRKTON BELL RINGS OUT

There is another tale attached to this curious churchyard feature that was told by one John Elliot of Langholm in a lecture he gave to a local archaeological society in the 1950s and which is reproduced in a book called *The Ewes Valley* by Brenda L Morrison and R Bruce McCartney, who have kindly given permission for it to be reproduced again here.

Mr Elliot tells us: 'No doubt you have heard the story of the wedding at Kirkstyle which was so tragically interrupted by the ringing of this self-same bell at dark midnight. Perhaps it might be worth telling again.

The fun was getting fast and furious when suddenly there was a toll of the bell. One or two people noticed it, but no-one mentioned it and they went on with the dance. Another sharp toll, at which womenfolk looked at one another a little scared. The men affected to make light of the incident and the merriment was resumed but in a more chastened spirit. Again came the ominous sound – doubled in number and intensity. This could be ignored no longer. The dancing ceased and the more daring of the men volunteered to venture into the kirkyard – dead of night though it was – and investigate this mysterious ringing of the bell. Just as they entered, however, there was heard a more clamant toll than ever and the men ran helter-skelter back to the house. Do not blame them, for these were the days of Burke and Hare and everything relating to the kirkyard was eerie and regarded with fear and superstition. But their being safe in the from the northern end of town. They are not the highest hills but the views from up on the moors, one of the few remaining large areas of moorland in southern Scotland, take in the Solway plain, the eastern end of the Firth to the south and west, and the lovely Ewes Valley to the north. Towards the top of the hill you can park by Jake Harvey's eye-catching steel and bronze **Hugh MacDiarmid memorial**, based on the idea of an open book – obviously so when you see it. To get the most out of it, pick up a leaflet from the tourist information centre in Langholm (page 34), which explains what all the different panels mean. At the summit of Whita Hill, the obelisk of the **Malcolm Monument**, almost 100ft high, was erected in 1835 in honour of Major General Sir John Malcolm, 19th-century governor of Bombay and envoy to Persia. If you're up here in the summer, keep an eye open for adders, which can sometimes be spotted. We've also seen red grouse among the carpet of ling heather.

North of Langholm the A7 follows the course of Ewes Water along **Ewes Valley**, a strikingly beautiful stretch surrounded by hills on either side. At **Kirkton**, look for a local curiosity. Here in the churchyard

house did not stop that fearsome ringing of the bell.

Consternation reigned and at last the company deemed it an occasion on which the aid of the minister should be invoked. So a deputation set out to the manse, and, rousing the minister, they told him – what he himself could now hear – how the kirk bell was being rung by unseen hands whose could be no other than Auld Nick himself. The minister reproved them for their foolish fears and, greatly to their comfort, volunteered to accompany them to ascertain the cause of this unseemly occurrence. They had got to the brig over the Kirktoun Burn when there was another series of loud and insistent peals. They looked to the minister – but he was down on his knees saying "Let us pray"– after which they betook themselves to the wedding.

All the long dread night that bell kept ringing and once, when day dawned, there was eager anxiety to ascertain the cause. It was then discovered that someone had maliciously tethered the minister's goat to the bell rope hanging loose from the tree, and every movement of the goat straining at the tether caused the bell to toll. Great was the indignation at the Kirkstyle, but the culprit was not discovered until many years later, when a well-set-up man visiting his native valley from America, made the astounding confession that he was the scamp who had done this scandalous thing.'

of **Ewes Kirk** (NY369908) a bell hangs in the fork of a tree. It has been here for well over 150 years, some reports say 300 years, and hung originally in the first church that stood here, but was later moved to a tree in the churchyard when the church was demolished. That tree had to be felled owing to its condition and the bell was eventually re-hung in an adjacent tree. And there it is to this day.

Beyond Kirkton, look out for the turning on the right, opposite the Ewes Community Hall, to **Arkleton Walled Garden** (DG13 0HL 013873 80830 the-walled-garden.co.uk seasonally, check online for details), where Kate Knott has taken in hand the walled garden of the Arkleton Estate, which was acquired by her grandparents in the 1960s. (It was previously the home of Walter and Dorothy Scott-Elliot, who are – macabrely – remembered primarily for having been murdered by their butler – though not while staying at the estate.)

Kate, an artist by trade, is reclaiming and replanting the garden with cutting flowers, which she uses in her flower-arranging workshops. Events are also held here (it's a romantic spot for a wedding), the garden is open in season for visits, and a glamping wagon is available for booking (page 260).

13 CANONBIE & THE DEBATABLE LANDS

For 300 years Canonbie was at the heart of the so-called Debatable Lands (page 24) until eventually James V lost patience and in 1530 made his move, imprisoning various local lairds for their lack of action, notably Johnnie Armstrong of Gilnockie Tower (see below). Then, in 1552, a physical barrier, **Scots Dike**, was built between the two countries, running between the rivers Esk and Sark. Most of it has disappeared from view, but a section is traceable in the Scotsdike plantation, west of the A7 between Canonbie and Longtown.

This quiet area today makes a pleasant base for exploring, fishing and walking.

The **Gilnockie Tower Reiver Centre** (Hollows, Canonbie DG14 0XD gilnockietower.com), a couple of miles north of Canonbie, is the only habitable Armstrong Tower still in existence from the original 90 or so pele towers in the area. Once a roofless ruin, it has been completely refurbished and is now open to visitors. Renowned historically as fierce reivers (page 24), the clan's (slightly) more recent claim to fame was

THOMAS TELFORD

From early beginnings at remote Glendinning, Thomas Telford (1757–1834) rose to become one of the greatest engineers the world has known. Telford either worked or advised on an astonishing number and range of projects in a host of countries, including Scotland, England, Ireland, Sweden, Poland, Germany and Austria. It seemed there was no civil engineering challenge to which he couldn't rise, including roads, bridges, aqueducts, churches, manses, canals, harbours and docks. His boundless energy and vision were vital in the dawn of the Industrial Revolution, opening up transport routes, improving trade and industry and advancing his home country at an unprecedented rate. He was also the founder and first president of the Institution of Civil Engineers. In all his time, though, he never forgot where he had come from, often referring back to his early days in Eskdale and ultimately bequeathing part of his estate to the libraries of Langholm and Westerkirk, which are still in use today. Telford's final days were spent in London and he is buried at Westminster Abbey.

welcoming astronaut Neil Armstrong in 1972. Rumour has it that he actually took a piece of Armstrong tartan to the moon!

A couple of waterfall walks can be found locally. The first is the **Fairy Loup Waterfall** (NY5783) at Byreburn, which can be accessed from the east bank of the Esk between Byreburnfoot and Byreburnside. The second is a little further to the east, **Penton Linns Waterfall** (NY3774). From Canonbie take the B6357 towards Newcastleton and at Harelaw take the Penton turning. The falls start at the bridge over Liddel Water, which also marks the Scotland–England border.

14 BENTPATH, WESTERKIRK & GLENDINNING

The B709 runs northwest from Langholm and offers splendid views to the hills to the northeast. The hamlet of **Bentpath** (NY312902) is prettily arranged on either side of a bridge across the River Esk and overlooked by Westerkirk Parish Church on the hillside opposite. The surrounding hills and lanes are those that were known to **Thomas Telford**, who was born a few miles up the single-track road at **Glendinning** (NY299969), where a cairn on the hillside has been erected in his memory. It's an isolated spot and you can't help but wonder how a young lad from such a remote backwater was able leave such a mark on the world.

Part of Telford's legacy stands in the form of **Westerkirk Library** (westerkirkparishlibrary.org) on the main road out of Bentpath, in front of which is a stone monument to the man himself. The library was founded in 1791 and is the oldest one still in use in Scotland. Telford left £1,000 towards its maintenance and today it holds over 8,000 books and records going back 200 years. Anyone can visit but opening times are extremely limited and borrowing of books is restricted to those who live in the parishes of Westerkirk and the surrounding villages.

NORTH ESKDALE

From Bentpath to Eskdalemuir the countryside is dotted with traces of ancient camps, notably **Castle O'er** (NY243928) and **Bessie's Hill**, two Iron Age ring forts that are linked by a six-mile walk. The **Eskdale Prehistoric Trail** takes in these and seven other sites (out of the 60 sites of archaeological importance in the area); marked with signposts, it can be driven or cycled but the sites themselves are accessed on foot.

15 ESKDALEMUIR

Approaching the hamlet of Eskdalemuir from Langholm, look out for two sets of stone circles on the left down towards the river, first the **Girdle Stanes**, dating back perhaps as far as 4000BC, and then the smaller **Loupin Stanes** (NY256966) from around 2500BC, from where there is a delightful view northwards.

Eskdalemuir stands 600ft above sea level in an exposed valley of the White Esk and was the location in days past of the curious Handfasting Fair. Originating from the late 14th century, this was an annual event at which local lads and lassies would clasp hands as a sign that they wished to embark on a year's trial marriage. At the fair the following year, if they still wished to marry, the appropriate ceremony would be arranged. However, if either of the partners had changed their mind, then he or she could walk away with no obligation, unless children were involved, in which case they went with the unsatisfied party. The practice died out in the 18th century but was only formally proscribed by an Act of Parliament in 1940.

Eskdalemuir today is known chiefly as the location of the Kagyu Samye Ling Monastery. There's also a community 'hub' (check out what events are planned at eskdalemuir.com) and café (see opposite).

16 Kagyu Samye Ling Tibetan Monastery

DG13 0QL NT246002 013873 73232 samyeling.org temple: 06.00–21.00 daily; tea room & shop: 09.30–12.20 & 13.30–16.00 daily, except Wed morning

For those not in the know, Samye Ling presents perhaps the biggest surprise in Dumfries and Galloway when the monastery's tall golden stupa comes into sight among the hills. Established in 1967, this was the first Tibetan Buddhist centre in the West.

Nothing quite prepares you for your first sight of the main temple; there is little hint of it from the road, even though you know it's there. Inside it's a riot of colour: pristine and primary reds, yellows, golds, blues and greens. Every morning 1,000 small water bowls are filled and every afternoon they are emptied and dried. Standing watching from the back of the temple, the silence is broken only by the sharp ring of glass on glass as the bowls are stacked by two volunteers in the half-light of the late afternoon, not a word spoken between them. Visitors are welcome to look in, but please remove shoes and be quiet, especially if there is a class in progress.

Visitors are welcome to stroll around the peace garden and grounds at any time of the day. The Tibetan Tea Rooms serves many tasty treats while the shop offers both local and Nepalese items.

FOOD & DRINK

Eskdalemuir Community Hub and Café The Old School, DG13 0QJ ✆ 013873 73760 eskdalemuir.com. A welcoming and spacious community hub and café in the old school, with the menu chalked up on the old roller blackboard, a toasty wood-burning stove, and a fine array of solar panels out the back. Everything from morning coffee to themed bistro evenings is offered in the café, and events are held in the same building.

The Tibetan Tea Rooms Kagyu Samye Ling Tibetan Monastery, DG13 0QL ✆ 013873 73758 samyeling.org. Pause for a relaxing break with a difference amid traditional décor with brightly coloured Tibetan rugs lining the benches. Teas, coffees, snacks and fuller vegetarian meals are served in a peaceful atmosphere of good karma.

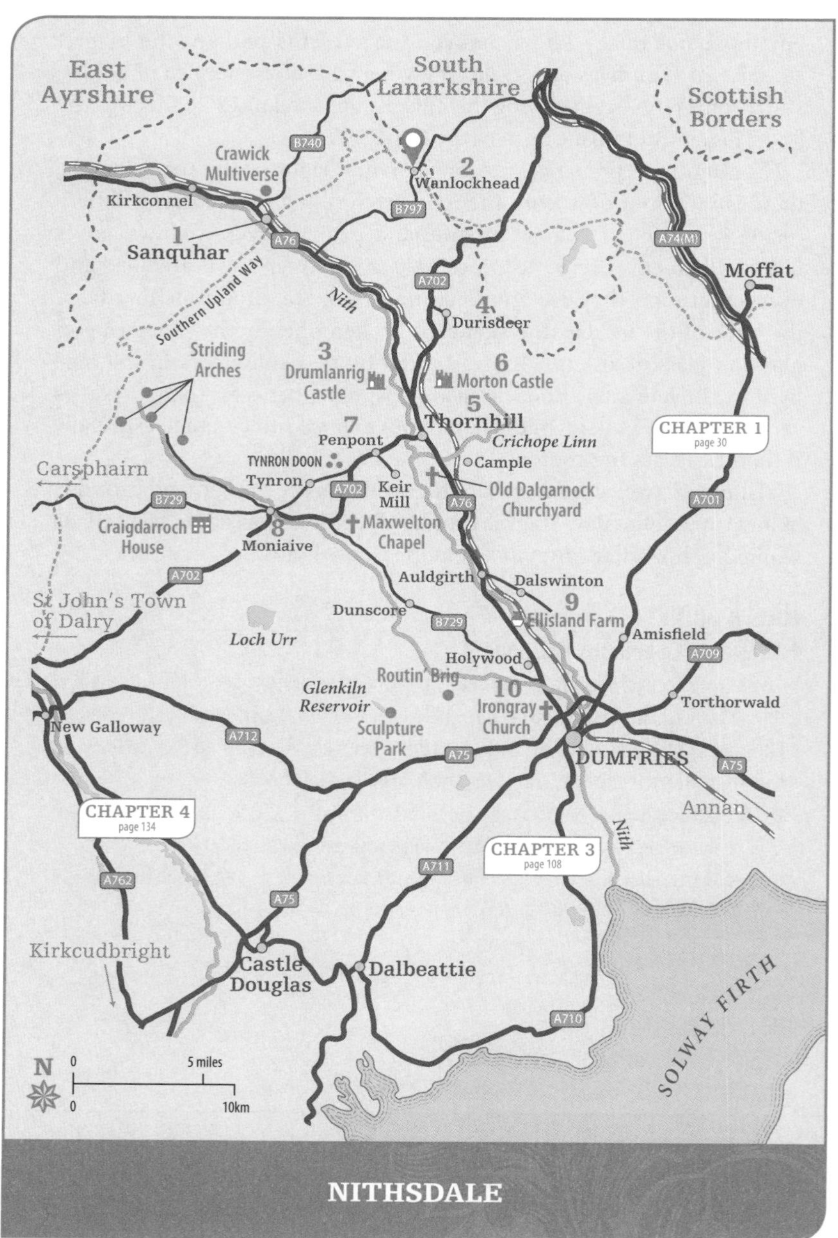
East Ayrshire
South Lanarkshire
Scottish Borders
Crawick Multiverse
Kirkconnel
1 Sanquhar
2 Wanlockhead
Southern Upland Way
Nith
4 Durisdeer
Moffat
3 Drumlanrig Castle
6 Morton Castle
5 Thornhill
Striding Arches
7 Penpont
Crichope Linn
Cample
CHAPTER 1 page 30
TYNRON DOON
Tynron
Keir Mill
Old Dalgarnock Churchyard
Carsphairn
Craigdarroch House
8 Moniaive
Maxwelton Chapel
Auldgirth
Dalswinton
St John's Town of Dalry
Dunscore
9 Ellisland Farm
Amisfield
Loch Urr
Holywood
Routin' Brig
Glenkiln Reservoir
10 Irongray Church
Torthorwald
Sculpture Park
New Galloway
DUMFRIES
Annan
CHAPTER 4 page 134
CHAPTER 3 page 108
Kirkcudbright
Castle Douglas
Dalbeattie
SOLWAY FIRTH
5 miles
10km
NITHSDALE

2
NITHSDALE

Nithsdale cuts a narrow swathe down the landscape, with the river valley broadening out as you head south towards Dumfries and the Nith Estuary. The area is bordered by East Ayrshire and South Lanarkshire to the north, the Glenkens area of Dumfries and Galloway to the west, and Annandale to the east. The River Nith, long known for its excellent salmon and trout fishing, is the longest of the rivers of the Dumfriesshire Dales, running 65 miles from its source in the Carsphairn Hills of East Ayrshire down to the Solway, passing the key towns of **Sanquhar**, **Thornhill** and **Dumfries** en route. The rail line follows the course of the river for much of the way, with stations at Kirkconnel, Sanquhar and Dumfries.

The joy of Nithsdale is in the drama of the valleys and gorges of the Nith, the hills to the west and east, and the magnificence of the passes to the northeast that form two of the main access routes to the area and which are generally regarded as the grandest of the 'southern highlands'. Both Mennock and Dalveen offer breathtaking and moody scenery with high hills dropping sharply to the valleys below. Resplendent in the sun, atmospheric when shrouded in mist, majestic in snow... no matter the season, these landscapes are memorable. At the top of the Dalveen, the River Clyde rises as not much more than a puddle at the start of its journey to Glasgow. Keep an eye open for wildlife and birds of prey around here; we had a terrific view of a short-eared owl on one trip.

The area is strongly associated with Robert Burns. Afton Water, captured by Burns in his eponymous poem, rises just outside the Dumfries and Galloway boundary in East Ayrshire and joins the Nith at New Cumnock. Burns lived in Nithsdale and travelled its length and breadth during his time as an exciseman, before moving in his final years to Dumfries. While at Ellisland Farm (page 104) he was at his most productive in terms of his body of work.

To keep chapters to a manageable size and for ease of exploration, this chapter includes all of Upper and Mid Nithsdale, but only the upper part of Lower Nithsdale. Dumfries itself and the Nith estuary are covered separately in *Chapter 3*.

GETTING AROUND

North–south (or vice versa) is the predominant travel direction in Nithsdale. The busy A76 from Ayrshire follows the Nith Valley all the way down to Dumfries at the river's estuary. The other main A road, the A702, strikes out westwards from the small town of Thornhill, passing through numerous pretty villages, heading for the Glenkens (page 139).

PUBLIC TRANSPORT

Both ends of the Nith Valley benefit from having an accessible **train service**, something that much of the region doesn't enjoy. **Scotrail** (🖱 scotrail.co.uk) runs a frequent service throughout the day Monday to Saturday (but only a couple of services on Sunday), which takes in Dumfries, Sanquhar and Kirkconnel along its Newcastle to Glasgow route.

The Nithsdale **bus services** tend to follow the north–south A76, which means that Thornhill and Sanquhar don't fare too badly, with services such as the 236 and 246 operated by Stagecoach West Scotland/ Houstons (although return tickets issued by one operator might not be accepted by another on the same route – always check when buying). Moniaive is mainly served (via Thornhill) by the infrequent 202 and 212 services (Mon–Sat only), operated by James Robertson and Houstons. Wanlockhead is served Monday to Saturday by the 221 Stagecoach West

TOURIST INFORMATION

There are no VisitScotland information centres in the area covered by this chapter.

In the north of the area, **Kirkconnel Parish Heritage Society** (40a Main St, DG4 6NB ✆ 01659 660002) carries a fascinating range of local information, from leaflets about the area to Valuation Rolls from 1862 onwards and historic photographs. Staff at **A'The Airts** in Sanquhar (see box, page 82) are also happy to help and offer a range of local information.

Both are also part of **Discover Upper Nithsdale** (🖱 uppernithsdale.com f). If visiting Thornhill, you may want to check out the town website, 🖱 visitthornhill.co.uk.

Scotland and Brownriggs from Kirkconnel and Sanquhar, which is handy for taking a day trip up into the hills or if you want to walk part of the linear Southern Upland Way from Wanlockhead back to Sanquhar; just make sure you don't miss the last bus back.

There are also various infrequent services that run around the area once a month or on alternate weeks, such as the Cairn Valley Community Transport between Castle Douglas and Moniaive. Local public transport information is provided by South West of Scotland Transport Partnership (swestrans.org.uk), or Traveline (0871 200 22 33 traveline.info).

CYCLING

There are plenty of small quiet lanes and tracks criss-crossing the Nith Valley, which make for pleasant, if sometimes quite hilly, cycling. Consulting the OS map for the area soon reveals numerous options for routes between the key towns and villages that avoid the busier trunk roads. The **Kirkpatrick Macmillan Trail** (bikemap.net, search for 'Thornhill') was developed in 1990 to mark the 150th anniversary of the invention of the pedal bicycle at the Nithsdale hamlet of Keir Mill and runs from just north of Dumfries up to Keir Mill itself. To work the legs a little harder, the trip to Wanlockhead has one steep route up along the B797, taking in the beautiful Mennock Pass. You will work up a sweat arriving, but can enjoy freewheeling down on your return. Dumfries and Galloway Council's free walking and cycling downloads are available from dumgal.gov.uk (look under 'Leisure' and then 'Outdoor Access and Paths').

CYCLE HIRE

Rik's Bike Shed Drumlanrig Castle, Thornhill DG3 4AQ 01848 330080. Bike hire, and Rik himself is usually on hand to advise on a range of circular trails around the Drumlanrig Estate that are suitable for all abilities.

WALKING

The **Southern Upland Way** and **Enterkin Pass** are two of the more famous linear routes that offer fine upland walking, with glorious views to match. The bus service between Sanquhar and Wanlockhead offers the chance to complete a 7½-mile section of the Southern Upland Way and return by bus.

Not all walking in the area has to be quite as strenuous though; the views from the valley bottoms, along the River Nith and tributaries such as Mennock Water, are a joy. We often randomly pick from any number of village churches at which to stop off and have our picnics (you're pretty much guaranteed a bench in a kirkyard). Alternatively, simply wander around the streets of Sanquhar, Thornhill or Moniaive, stopping for a spot of shopping or tea and a tray bake. Dumfries and Galloway Council's free walking and cycling downloads are available from dumgal.gov.uk (look under 'Leisure' and then 'Outdoor Access and Paths').

UPPER NITHSDALE

Entering Upper Nithsdale from East Ayrshire, slag heaps testify to the coal mining days of the past, an industry that sustained Kirkconnel and Sanquhar for many years, and which more recently has lent itself to the development of an environmental arts attraction for the region in the form of a regenerated former open-cast coal mine site at the **Crawick Multiverse** project (page 85).

In the northern reaches the valley is broad, with the Nith flowing first on one side of the road and then the other, teasing you onwards. Access to Upper Nithsdale from the north is either on the main A76 from East Ayrshire, or on the B740 from South Lanarkshire. The latter is a particularly attractive route, a scenic drive through the **Lowther Hills**.

Kirkconnel, Upper Nithsdale's most northerly town, is said to be the burial place of St Conal, a shepherd's son who in the 6th century was taken by St Kentigern to the monastery at Hoddom in neighbouring Annandale (page 54) to be prepared for the priesthood. Conal later returned to his home where he administered to his flock, preaching in a church at the foot of Kirkland Hill to the north and baptising converts in the nearby well, where an outdoor service is still held once a year. In the 18th century the **church** was moved closer to the developing town, to the site where it now stands at the northern end of the main street. Next to the gate a sign tells the story of local man **Alexander Anderson**, who in the 19th century worked first as a surfaceman with the new Glasgow and Southwestern Railway before becoming known for his poetry in the Scots tongue.

Kirkconnel is a convenient starting point for walking the hills of Upper Nithsdale amid grand scenery, with scarcely a soul to be seen.

1 SANQUHAR & AROUND

Blackaddie Country House Hotel (page 260)

The royal burgh of Sanquhar was once a mining town and historic wool centre and is today a handy stopping point on the **Southern Upland Way**, with a population of just over 2,000. Crawick Water courses its way down through the hills, flowing into the Nith on the edge of town to the north, while Euchan Water tumbles down the **Euchan Falls** before joining from the southwest. **Crawick Mill** was the first large-scale mill in Upper Nithsdale, capitalising on the burgeoning wool trade in the early 19th century. From here carpets known for their quality and durability were sent out around the world; even today, this small town still has an industry presence thanks to Sanquhar Tile Services, a subsidiary of Shaw, North America's largest carpet tile manufacturer.

Wool was the mainstay of the local economy until the development of the coal industry in the late 19th century, and the First Statistical Account of Scotland shows that in 1793 the sheep to human ratio here was 10:1. By the 19th century Sanquhar's sheep fair was one of the country's most important, notable also for the fact that it was a 'character market' in which stock wasn't actually shown but was traded on the character and reputation of the dealer. Sanquhar knitwear (see box, page 82) has been produced since at least the start of the 17th century and these days is known the world over for its intricate, two-colour designs.

Sanquhar's name is believed to come from 'Saen Caer' meaning 'old fort', thought to be taken from the old Roman fort just north of town. It is one of Scotland's oldest burghs having been made a royal burgh in 1598 by James VI. In the 17th century the town became a centre for the Covenanters when **Reverend Richard Cameron** rode in along with his brother and a handful of supporters and affixed a paper to the town cross that was read aloud and in which he renounced his allegiance to Charles II. This was the first **Sanquhar Declaration** and it cost Cameron his life. The king declared war on him and around a month later Cameron and his men were surprised and killed at the **Battle of Airds Moss** in Ayrshire. Cameron's name lived on, though, for in 1689 it was adopted by **The Cameronians**, a regiment that lasted 279 years until the defence cuts of the 1960s.

A second declaration followed five years after Cameron's on the same spot, this time by **Reverend James Renwick** who had attached himself to the Cameronian sect and in effect picked up where Cameron left off.

SANQUHAR KNITWEAR AT A' THE AIRTS

Yvonne Barber is manager of A' the Airts Community Arts and Crafts Centre. We are grateful to her for providing the following text.

Since the 17th century, Sanquhar has been the home of the world-famous Sanquhar Pattern, a fiendishly intricate knitting pattern known for its distinctive and stunning geometrical designs.

The Sanquhar Pattern is in fact not one pattern but a variety of patterns. Some of the first designs are said to have originated in the 17th and 18th centuries, although no exact date can be given. A pattern comprises two often contrasting colours, creating a geometric design, and a large number of these 'patterns' are based on a grid of 11x11 (the number of stitches in a square). The most popular Sanquhar pattern is called the Duke, which was named after the Duke of Buccleuch (examples of it, and all the designs, can be seen in A' the Airts; see below).

Exports of Sanquhar textiles reached their peak during the Victorian era. Knitted gloves and other garments from the region were especially sought after for their quality and unique designs. However, this was a cottage industry and most, if not all, of the textiles were produced at home by locals to subsidise their income. Despite modernisation, the influence of the Sanquhar pattern knitting tradition was so great that it carried on through the generations.

Today the Sanquhar Pattern is thriving and has become global, attracting visitors from as far afield as Japan and the USA to see the town where it all began. Thousands of knitters worldwide make garments and textiles with the pattern.

In 2014, the Sanquhar Pattern Designs initiative was set up to revive the cottage industry and safeguard the local tradition, producing original knitwear from Sanquhar. Today visitors can meet the knitters (Tue–Thu) who are based in the building next door to A' the Airts.

This second declaration was also to come at the ultimate cost and in 1688 Renwick was captured in Edinburgh and hanged at the age of just 26.

There's something creative stirring in Sanquhar these days, from the **Sanquhar Arts Festival** (spring) and **Festival of Folklore** (September) to an innovative mix of projects helping to stimulate interest in the town. **A' The Airts** café and arts centre (page 85) is the town's hub, driving initiatives such as **Sanquhar Pattern Designs** ('From Fleece to Fashion'), helping to reinvigorate and keep relevant the unique art of Sanquhar knitting (see box, above). It also stocks a good range of gift items that draw on local talent, including Sanquhar knitwear, and runs a wide range of events and activities. Come on the right day and you'll find a group of specialists knitting by both hand and machine. Classes are run, too, if you want to have a go. The centre also runs a wide range of events, including films, poetry and photography for adults, as well as crafts, writing, art and performance for kids.

Also up this end of town – in Sanquhar's self-styled 'Cultural Quarter' – are the **Merz and Zip art spaces** (merz.gallery), the former in the old abattoir on St Mary's Street, the latter in the old lemonade factory on Queen's Road. Conceptual artist David Rushton has been behind this development, creating artists' residency spaces, renovating caravans for short stays (ideal for walkers and cyclists) and establishing a small museum to display his extraordinary model art. The range, application and enthusiasm of David's creative input is fun, quirky and inspirational.

A walk down High Street takes in the history of the town. The striking **Tolbooth** at the northern end was designed by renowned architect William Adam and bears its pleasing symmetry proudly thanks to the sweep of the double staircase up the front exterior, black railings (a later addition) adorned in summer with colourful hanging baskets. The Tolbooth was at one time used as a jail, by all accounts one of the most insecure in Scotland: detainees would regularly break out of an evening to spend the night at home, before returning in the morning, and one man went home for blankets because he was cold!

Inside the Tolbooth is the local **museum** (High St, DG4 6BN dumgal.gov.uk then search 'Sanquhar Tolbooth' Apr–Sep Tue–Sun, closed for lunch) with a good audio-visual introduction to Sanquhar and Upper Nithsdale and displays on many aspects of local life, including Sanquhar knitwear. Midge and Flea, Pheasant's Eye, Fleur de Lys and Rose and Trellis patterns are all shown, and if you fancy a scarf, gloves or any other items for yourself, orders are taken at A' The Airts next door.

Robert Burns is remembered in the town. He was a regular visitor to Sanquhar as he carried out his duties as an exciseman, and he named the town 'Black Joan' in his ballad 'Five Carlins' (Carlin meaning old woman) in which the five Dumfriesshire boroughs are personified as five women, each giving their opinion as to who should be their parliamentary representative at Westminster. Burns was admitted as an honorary burgess of Sanquhar in 1794 and the town today has its own Burns Club known, of course, as The Black Joan. Incidentally, the other boroughs named by Burns were Dumfries ('Maggy, by the banks o'Nith, a dame wi' pride eneugh'), Lochmaben ('Marjory o' the mony lochs, A carlin auld and teugh'), Annan ('blinkin' Bess of Annandale, That dwelt near Solway-side') and Kirkcudbright ('whiskey Jean, that took her gill in Galloway sae wide').

Continue down the main street with its brightly painted houses and neat gardens. Look out for information plaques (some a little weathered) on the walls and in the entranceways to the old closes that run between the houses. Just beyond A' The Airts café and arts centre (page 82), on the left-hand side, is the **post office**, believed to be the oldest in the world, in continuous operation since 1712 (spot the date above the door). A little further along stands the stark granite obelisk of the **Cameron Monument**, marking the spot (more or less) of the town cross, where Cameron and Renwick pinned their papers and made their declarations.

Sanquhar Castle (⚲ NS785093) has stood a sad ruin (now fenced off) for well over 300 years at the southern end of town, set off to one side in a defensive position at the top of a steep bank that runs down to the river plain. Built originally in the 11th century, the estate was bought by Sir William Douglas, the first Duke of Queensberry, in 1639. Despite going on to build Drumlanrig (page 91), his favourite home always remained the castle at Sanquhar.

Heading south from Sanquhar, the single-track road along the southern side of the Nith follows the line of the hill and offers views back across the river to town and the castle. Rejoining the main road, just past the turning to Wanlockhead, a **picnic area** on the banks of the Nith is a pleasant spot to stop for a moment. Dippers might be spotted in the water and you can walk alongside the river. Toilets can also be found here. Immediately after this, take a look at the **bridge** over the Nith. There are pleasant views up and down the river, birds flitting around (we spotted a green sandpiper here) and a curious story attached. In the stone wall of the bridge can be seen some **grooves**, which according to the plaque on the wall were made around 1870 by a runaway horse that was startled by a passing train and leapt on to the wall before plunging to its death in the Nith below. Also noted is that 'the grooves were perpetuated… as a warning to disobedient youth of future generations'!

The single-track road across the bridge climbs up into the hills. This is a good access point for the splendid scenery of Upper Nithsdale. The road follows Burnsands Burn for a short distance before climbing and passing farmhouses and old stone buildings – communities of just three or four homes with terrific vistas back down the valley. The road runs through mixed deciduous woodland of chestnut, beech, alder and oak.

Take your pick of the lanes to follow, but if you head for Penpont (page 96) there are views across the village as you follow Penpont Burn down to the bottom of the valley.

Crawick Multiverse

NS775115 crawickmultiverse.co.uk accessible daily, site staffed & visitor facilities roughly May–Oct, check website for exact times & entry charges

Immediately north of Sanquhar, the work of renowned architect and landscape designer **Charles Jencks** (1939–2019) can be viewed in all its glory at the impressive Crawick Multiverse, a major land-restoration project that was completed in 2015. Jencks lived a little further down Nithsdale (page 104), and the astrological and cosmological themes that characterise his own garden, and much of his work generally, are strongly in evidence here. The site occupies 55 acres and the scale of the work is striking. Virtually all of the materials used in its creation have come from the site itself, including many hundreds of boulders that were unearthed in the early stages, some of which are now used to line the North–South Path, a 450yd walkway oriented precisely on a north–south axis. Other features include an amphitheatre that can hold 5,000 people and which uses the shapes and forms of a total eclipse, two galaxy mounds, Andromeda and Milky Way at 82ft and 49ft respectively, water-filled lagoons, and scalloped cliffs with Comet Walk above. For 360° views the Belvedere offers a great vantage point, complete with a hand constructed from boulders that points to the North Star. A path around the site connects the four ecologies of grassland, mountains, a water gorge and a desert.

Crawick Multiverse has echoes of both Stonehenge and Glastonbury Tor but is very much a work of our time and of its own location, a unique part of the Dumfries and Galloway landscape.

FOOD & DRINK

A' The Airts 8–12 High St, DG4 6BL 01659 50514 atheairts.org.uk Tue–Sat. 'A vibrant wee arts centre in the heart of Upper Nithsdale', as it describes itself. A great spot to sit and watch the goings-on of the high street and enjoy the enticing selection of sandwiches, soups, cakes and other baked goods.

Blackaddie Country House Hotel Blackaddie Rd, DG4 6JJ 01659 50270 blackaddiehotel.co.uk. Chef Ian McAndrew bought the hotel in 2007 and since then has been wowing diners (and reviewers) with his talents. McAndrew trained with Anton

Mosimann and has been ranked alongside David Adlard, Alastair Little and Gary Rhodes. Bookings are essential for the small, intimate dining room. Dishes are all locally sourced as far as possible and McAndrew grows many of his own ingredients in the two-acre grounds of the hotel on the banks of the Nith.

Oasis Restaurant Nithsdale Hotel, 1 High St, DG4 6DJ ✆ 01659 501333 ⊙ most eves & w/ends. Ideal for dinner for two or larger groups, or simply for an early evening drink. Homemade soup, roasts, Caledonian chicken with haggis, salmon with asparagus and chocolate fudge cake could all feature.

2 WANLOCKHEAD

The Wanlockhead Inn (page 260)

Between Sanquhar and Thornhill, the B797 heads off to the northeast, up the Mennock Pass to Wanlockhead, Scotland's highest village at 1,531ft (and location of Scotland's highest pub and micro-brewery, too). This is a dramatic route, with steep hills on either side creating a narrow pass all the way up to the top. Sheep roam freely (mind your speed if driving), gulleys drop down, and scree slopes plummet to Mennock Water, the course of which is followed by the road for much of the trip. Pictures of the pass have been mistaken for Glencoe and it comes as a surprise to many that Scotland's highest village should be here and not further north in the Highlands. The pass is a popular spot with wild campers in the summer and gold panners can also often be seen here. Alas, at times piles of rubbish left by a small minority and scarred patches from open fires are a blight on an otherwise pristine setting.

For the energetic, there are walks aplenty to be enjoyed from the village, while the really determined can cycle up and freewheel back down again. A popular but lengthy walk from Wanlockhead takes in the Enterkin Pass, described by Daniel Defoe in his *A Tour Thro' the Whole Island of Great Britain* (1726) as 'a precipice horrible and terrifying'. It was also famously the location of a 1684 Covenanter ambush of Dragoons.

Robert Burns was a visitor to Wanlockhead in 1789, at which time he commissioned the blacksmith to make spiked shoes for his horse, Pegasus. In payment he wrote a poem, 'Pegasus at Wanlockhead'. Pegasus is now commemorated, cast in lead, atop the column on the central roundabout at Thornhill (page 94).

The village itself hunkers down, a scattering of houses randomly arranged, some nestling into the lee of the hills, others more exposed to the breezes that whistle through. It's an appealing place, a welcoming

THE HILLTOP HERBALIST

Victoria Chanin is a qualified herbalist living in Wanlockhead. She can be contacted via her Facebook page: The Hilltop Herbalist.

Am I the highest herbalist in Scotland? Such a question tends to be misunderstood, but I have been the Hilltop Herbalist up in the Lowther Hills, first in Leadhills, and now in Wanlockhead for nine years.

It isn't the most obvious choice of residence for a herbalist, with its windswept hills and lack of hedgerows. For foraging, I descend the winding road down the majestic Mennock Pass into Dumfries and Galloway's more verdant lowlands. Even before we leave the pass there is bounty in Mennock Wood, a glorious assembly of Scottish woodland species, with hazel, hawthorn, blackthorn and wild rose at its edges, and oak, scots pine, larch, ash and many more within its path-free interior.

A boggy stretch of grassland runs alongside the burn, filled with meadowsweet and valerian, two of my favourite medicinal plants, flowering together from the end of June and into July, a froth of creamy flowerlets fizzing up from meadowsweet and a subtle pinkish-purple haze from valerian. The scent lifts the spirits, its most immediate healing action.

Back in my hilltop home, the near silence, clean cut of the air and the scoop of the hills across the wide skies more than make up for the lack of foraging opportunities. Leaves and flowers are dried, berries are turned into syrups; herbs, vinegars and honey become an oxymel. The making of potions is a meditative experience and I welcome the quiet space to create.

It isn't all solitude and wilderness of course. There are patients to see, classes to run in the community hall, workshops to organise and traditional herbal knowledge to be passed on in the spirit of Nicholas Culpeper. There are craft fairs and festivals, and there's all manner of sociable fun to be had as a herbalist sharing the joy of plants in Dumfries and Galloway.

sight after the austere surroundings of the drive up. There's plenty to see and do here, not just in Wanlockhead but also in the neighbouring village of Leadhills over the border in South Lanarkshire. Gold was mined here 400 years ago and can still be found today, but the opening of lead mines in the 17th century is the real reason for the village's existence. A community of lead miners once lived here, extracting lead and gold from the surrounding hills in mines owned by the Duke of Buccleuch. Silver, too, was produced, as a by-product of smelting galena (lead ore). Employment and the allure of untold wealth brought in prospectors and workers alike, swelling the population to such an extent that by 1916 the local school had 125 pupils. With the closure of

High above Wanlockhead

Explorer map 329; start: Museum of Lead Mining (accessible by bus 221) NS874129; 5 miles; moderate

Beginning any walk in Wanlockhead offers the leg-saving bonus of already starting from a lofty position; this means every step upwards opens ever-growing vistas of hills, moorland and valleys. It also has the added bonus of a difficult refreshment choice upon your return – tea room at the mining museum, or the village inn complete with micro-brewery?

This is a simple route on hard-surfaced tracks and grass-hill paths, with some steeper sections, but best not attempted in adverse weather as the saddle above the Enterkin Pass when heading over to East Mount Lowther can be very windy. Haggis, our little terrier, sometimes struggles to keep upright when crossing.

From the end of the **1 Museum of Lead Mining** car park, climb the steps then continue to the road, where you cross and join the marked Southern Upland Way. Continue past the houses and start to climb uphill across open moorland with the hills ahead dominated by the masts and distinctive 'golf ball' radar. While on the moorland, look and listen out for grouse, raven and short-eared owls.

Cross a wooden bridge and follow the path until it meets the tarmac service road, turn right, following the road around the bend, and join the grass path found at the end of the **2 crash barrier**. After a short distance this will once again join the tarmac road; here, you can either turn right and follow the road until you come to **3** the **track** on your right signed 'Core Path Inglestone Farm' (NS885109), or climb to the 'golf ball'. For this latter option, go straight over the road and continue uphill along the Southern Upland Way – when ready, turn around and follow the service road back down to point 3.

the mines, the numbers dwindled and by 1943 had dropped to just 35, though they increased again with evacuees during the war.

Most of the various points of interest in Wanlockhead come under the umbrella of the **Museum of Lead Mining** (ML12 6UT 01659 74387 leadminingmuseum.co.uk 1st week Apr–last week Sep 11.00–16.30 daily, check website for exact dates) and are run by an efficient team of locals. The museum itself is set in a hollow in the hills at the lower end of the village and you can opt to buy either a ticket that covers all

Turn right (or left, if you have been up to the 'golf ball') and follow the track down to the saddle (the low point between the two hills). Look off to your left at the Enterkin Pass, which Daniel Defoe in *A Tour Thro' the Whole Island of Great Britain* (1726) described as: 'Enterkin, the frightfullest pass, and most dangerous that I met with, between that and Penmenmuir in North Wales'.

Keeping the fence close to your left, ascend East Mount Lowther (Auchenlone). This is the steepest section of the walk, but it eventually plateaus out as you approach the summit and the **4 locator post** (NS878100; erected in 1944). Take a moment to enjoy the views, which on a clear day take in the length of the Nith Valley from Sanquhar to your right, all the way down to the Solway Firth to your left and the hills of the Lake District beyond.

Retrace your steps back to the saddle and take the path off to the left passing under the **5 pylons**. Keep following the path, cross a burn and rejoin the tarmac, then retrace your outbound route back to Wanlockhead.

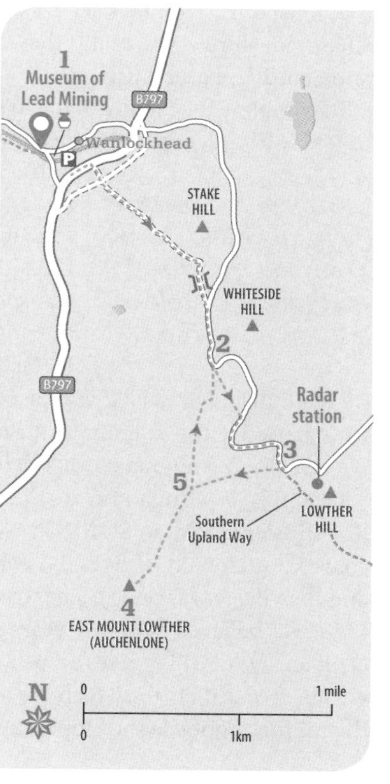

four attractions or separate tickets for individual ones. As well as the museum, you can walk into one of the actual **mines**, look round two **miners' cottages** depicting life from the mid 18th to early 20th centuries, and visit the **miners' library**, the second-oldest subscription library in Europe after the one at Leadhills (page 90). Also here is Historic Environment Scotland's **Beam Engine**, a unique piece of hydraulic pumping equipment that is the only remaining water-bucket engine to be seen in a mine in the country.

There is much to interest and entertain here and, either on its own or combined with a walk in the surrounding hills, a visit to Wanlockhead makes for a good day's outing for all the family. And, of course, there's always a spot of gold panning to have a go at (tickets available from the museum). Wanlockhead has hosted the World Gold Panning Championships – yes, really, they exist – and regularly hosts the British and Scottish championships.

To complete the picture of life in the hills, carry on from Wanlockhead to **Leadhills**, a couple of miles down the road and just over the border into South Lankarkshire, where you'll find a narrow-gauge railway built by famous engineer Robert MacAlpine in 1902, during the days when lead had to be transported across the hills to Elvanfoot in the northwest, from where it was carried on to Leith Docks in Edinburgh. The railway (leadhillsrailway.co.uk seasonally at w/ends, check online) today runs between the stations at Leadhills and Glengonnar, just outside Wanlockhead, and makes for a delightful sojourn.

"To complete the picture of life in the hills, carry on from Wanlockhead to Leadhills, a couple of miles down the road."

Leadhills is also home to the **oldest subscription library** in the British Isles (15 Main St, ML12 6XP 01659 74369 leadhillslibrary.co.uk seasonally at w/ends) and the **highest golf course in Britain**, and the village was once home to one John Taylor who, when he died in 1770, was believed to be 137 years old. His story is told on a board at the cemetery, where his grave can be found. A heritage trail runs around the village, free leaflets for which are available from a dispenser attached to the railings opposite the Hopetoun Arms Hotel.

FOOD & DRINK

Hopetoun Arms 37 Main St, Leadhills ML12 6XP 01659 74234 hopetounarms.co.uk. Occupies an 18th-century shooting lodge and was commented on by Dorothy Wordsworth while writing about her travels through the area with her brother and Samuel Coleridge in 1803. Offering everything from snacks to hearty fare, coffees to whiskies in front of the fire, it's a welcoming spot.

Museum of Lead Mining Wanlockhead ML12 6UT 01659 74387 leadminingmuseum.co.uk. Serves teas, coffees, cakes, soups, scones, sandwiches and daily specials, and there are some interesting historical photographs and documents on the walls to browse with your brew.

The Wanlockhead Inn Garden Dyke, ML12 6UZ ✆ 01659 74535 ⊘ wanlockheadinn.co.uk ⊙ Tue–Sun. Scotland's highest pub offers lunches and evening meals. The inn stands on the site of what used to be the Duke of Buccleuch's hunting lodge and, if you ask, convivial landlord James McKelvey will show you a picture of what it used to look like. His son Dean started up and runs the Lola Rose Brewery on the same site – Scotland's highest micro-brewery, producing the aptly named 1531 beer with the cracking strapline of 'Beer with Altitude'!

MID NITHSDALE

Mid Nithsdale is home to some of the area's most striking scenery, especially as you head west towards the neighbouring Glenkens area. Here, too, are charming villages and an attractive estate town, **Thornhill**, closely associated with one of the finest stately homes in Britain, **Drumlanrig Castle**. Also connected with Drumlanrig, at **Durisdeer**, is one of the area's most striking churches and a marble memorial that gives even the best Greek edifices a run for their money. A sense of community and culture pervades, both across the area and also within the individual villages, and there is a thriving arts scene encompassing music and literature in particular. Even just the thought of heading over this way fills us with gleeful anticipation; there is always something going on and the scenery and changing light always reveal new views.

3 DRUMLANRIG CASTLE

Thornhill DG3 4AQ ⚲ NX852993 ⊘ drumlanrigcastle.co.uk ⊙ castle: summer, limited times (check website); estate grounds & tea room: Apr/Easter–Sep daily, check website for exact dates

No visit to this part of the world is complete without spending time at Drumlanrig, arguably the jewel in Dumfriesshire's crown and notable not least for the distinctive pink hue of the sandstone from which it is built. In some respects Drumlanrig is something of an anomaly: called a castle, it is actually more of a house (a mansion house, true, but a house nonetheless). The broad façade that greets visitors on the approach up the drive is actually the back, not the front; and despite its mighty appearance, it is not as large as it first appears (though it is by no means small – with 120 rooms, they say there is a window for every day of the year) – for it is actually four L-shaped tower houses joined together around a central courtyard, each of which has its own circular staircase within its tower. (It was only in later years, as lady's dresses became larger and moving up and down the old staircases became more problematic, that the main staircase within the building was added.) One other oddity is that the elegant external staircase by which the house is entered, with sweeping stairs rising up both sides of the building, is not quite symmetrical. If you look at the house from a distance and count the ground floor arches that flank the staircase on either side, you'll see that they don't quite match in number: they are out by half an arch.

Drumlanrig's history is not without its quirks either. Completed in 1689 for the first Duke of Buccleuch, he moved in but spent only one night here. The story goes that the duke was unwell and, despite calling for his servants, the place was so big that no-one heard him and nothing could happen in a hurry. Off he went the next morning back to his small castle at Sanquhar, never to sleep here again.

Drumlanrig today is one of the homes of Richard Scott, tenth Duke of Buccleuch and 12th of Queensberry, one of Europe's largest private landowners and one of only five people in the UK to hold two separate dukedoms. There are 14 rooms open to the public, although visitors can only enter as part of a tour. As you would expect, the rooms are sumptuous and filled with priceless works of art and furniture, including paintings by Van Dyck, Holbein and Rembrandt, and a tapestry that was worked on by Mary, Queen of Scots. You can also see where part of the *Outlander* series was filmed. Family stories abound, including that of the irresponsible fourth duke who brought the estate to its knees through profligate spending, but who was succeeded by his son, the much shrewder fifth duke who married – of necessity, one might imagine, but apparently for love – one of the richest women in Europe.

"As you would expect, the rooms are sumptuous and filled with priceless works of art and furniture."

There is an enormous amount to see and do here, not just in touring the house but also exploring some of the 45 acres of formal gardens (not to mention the 100,000 acres of the estate). The stables have been converted and house a visitor centre and independent shops, and there's a tea room in the original kitchen in the castle itself. If you want to explore further afield, bike hire is available from Rik's Bike Shed next to the shops (page 79), and there are plenty of walks around the grounds.

4 DURISDEER

NS894038

Tucked away in the lee of the Lowthers on a road that goes nowhere, few spots are more peaceful than Durisdeer. Aside from its delightful setting, what makes Durisdeer so remarkable (and yet comparatively unknown) is its church, shaded by mature sycamore trees and positioned beside a collection of pretty cottages and a war memorial.

A **church** is first mentioned here in the 13th century, but the present one was built in stages and dates from 1695 to 1720. That it is out of proportion with its petite village surroundings tells something of its importance, for Durisdeer was the parish kirkton for nearby Drumlanrig. The church is an arresting combination of Presbyterian and Baroque, the former in the solid X-plan layout with its central pulpit, galleries and box pews with central communion tables, the latter in the exceptional baldacchino in the Queensberry burial vault to the rear. Carved in 1695, it is known simply as the '**Durisdeer marbles**' and has been accurately described as a 'riot of swagged fabric, garlands of flowers, urns, barley-sugar columns, cherubs, skulls and pediments, all in gleaming white marble'. It is a sight to behold, a monument not just to James, second Duke of Queensberry and his duchess, Mary, but also to late Baroque ostentation and extravagance.

"Aside from its delightful setting, what makes Durisdeer so remarkable (and yet comparatively unknown) is its church."

Beneath the monument lies the burial vault of the Douglas family, among whom is the third duke, whose wife Catherine ('Kitty'), much courted in literary circles, was a friend of Alexander Pope. Something of an eccentric beauty, she was renowned for the grand parties at her London home and gained notoriety for being expelled from the court of George II for taking up the cause of John Gay, who had been refused a licence for *Polly*, the sequel to his immensely successful *Beggar's Opera*. She is buried here at Durisdeer having died in 1777 after a brief illness caused, according to Horace Walpole, by eating too many cherries.

There are some fine funerary monuments in the graveyard, including a sombre memorial to Daniel McMichael, Covenanter, who was shot dead in 1685.

You may wish to plan a visit to Durisdeer on a Sunday, to tie in with the offer of afternoon teas in the church (Jul–Sep; check scotlandschurchestrust.org.uk for exact dates & more information).

5 THORNHILL & AROUND

🏠 **Buccleuch & Queensberry Arms Hotel** (page 260), **Nithbank Country Estate** (page 260), **Trigony House Hotel** (page 260)

Smart, tidy and compact, Thornhill is an exemplary estate town that's clearly comfortable in its own skin. As one guidebook writer of old commented, it's a place that displays a blend 'of dignity and humility – dignity of ducal spaciousness and the humility of well-trained, well-planned obedient streets in which doorways and windows are as regularly spaced as buttons on a waistcoat'. Its poise is, of course, thanks to its long relationship with nearby Drumlanrig and the earls of Queensberry, the third of which founded the town in 1664 as a Burgh of Barony. Their influence is explicit, notably in the **Mercat Cross** at the very centre of town, on top of which slender column is a lead figure of **Pegasus** 👆, the emblem of the dukes of Queensberry, which is cast in lead mined in the hills of nearby Wanlockhead and Leadhills (page 86). There may have been a Roman settlement here, but the town in its present layout dates from 1714, when it was a staging post on the new road from Dumfries to Glasgow.

The main attraction of Thornhill is its sheer pleasant browsability. It's a place to come for lunch or afternoon tea and a wander around the shops. Old favourite **Thomas Tosh** (19 East Morton St, DG3 5LZ ✆ 01848 331553 ⊘ thomastosh.com) offers one of Dumfries and Galloway's finest ranges of gifts and homeware (and has a good café too; see opposite), while the **Moniaive Chocolatier** (55 Drumlanrig St, DG3 5LY ✆ 01848 200000 ⊘ tartanchocolate.co.uk) is in prime position at the cross and is choc-full (pun intended) of exquisite handmade confectionary. An extensive range of Oriental furniture and lamps can be found in the old church at **Zitan** on Townhead Street. With a butcher, baker, two small supermarkets and a popular hotel in the centre of town, Thornhill also makes a good base for self-caterers.

On East Morton Street stands a memorial to **Joseph Thomson**, Africa explorer, who was born in 1858 in nearby Penpont (page 96) and who is buried in the cemetery further up the street.

A short distance outside Thornhill, at the village of Cample (📍 NX898940), **Cample Line** (Cample Mill, DG3 5HD ✆ 01848 331000 ⊘ campleline.org.uk ⏲ check website) is an innovative gallery in a disused mill by a railway viaduct. Set up in 2016 by Tina Fiske, art historian and former lecturer at the University of Glasgow, it's gaining a reputation as a cutting-edge contemporary art centre.

FOOD & DRINK

Buccleuch and Queensberry Arms Hotel 112 Drumlanrig St, DG3 5LU ✆ 01848 323101 ⊕ bqahotel.com. Come first for a drink in the comfortable and cosy bar, then eat in the AA-rosette restaurant, which makes good use of local ingredients. Bar snacks are also available. Restaurant reservations are recommended for Friday and Saturday nights and for Sunday lunch.

Drumlanrig Café & Restaurant 53–54 Drumlanrig St, DG3 5LJ ✆ 01848 330317. Offers everything from breakfasts to pizzas, as well as teas, coffees and sandwiches throughout the day at reasonable prices. Perfect for a relaxed bite to eat.

Thomas Tosh 19 East Morton St, DG3 5LZ ✆ 01848 331553 ⊕ thomastosh.com. Fun and friendly, housed in an impressive former parish hall building, with a great selection of teas, coffees, soups, sandwiches and cakes in one half of the building, and an exceedingly good gift shop in the other. Vegan, gluten-free and veggie options offered, coffee and tea are fair trade, and beer and wine are served also. Events and workshops are also held here; check website for details.

Trigony House Hotel Closeburn DG3 5EZ ✆ 01848 331211 ⊕ trigonyhotel.co.uk. Just south of Thornhill, Trigony House Hotel this hotel is open to non-residents for lunch, afternoon teas (by reservation only) and dinner. Its seasonally changing menu and unfussy, classic approach to food are regularly reviewed positively by the press.

6 Morton Castle

NX891992; year-round daily; Historic Environment Scotland

Northeast of Thornhill, ruined and isolated Morton Castle stands in one of the most tranquil and romantic locations of any castle in Scotland. (Technically, it's a rare example of a hall house rather than a castle.) It's believed to have been here since at least the 14th century and was a stronghold of the Douglases. However, as part of the negotiations to return the captured David II in 1357, one of the conditions stipulated by the English was that Morton, along with various other castles, be destroyed. If the weather is warm, this is a great spot for a picnic, sitting on the hill overlooking the artificial loch that surrounds one half of the site. It's also a good place to bring kids, with heritage and nature trails to follow.

Crichope Linn

NX910955

Almost due east of Thornhill, off a small back road between Gatelawbridge and Closeburnmill, a path takes off into the woods signposted for Beattock. About half a mile along this path in the bottom of the valley are the gorge and rapids of Crichope Linn, an impressive waterway that has carved its channel through the rocks over the centuries. Nature lovers have been coming here for a long time, there's some rather neat Victorian graffiti chiselled out of the rocks, and it's believed that Burns may have added his signature, too. In summer this is a lush and beautiful place, but take note and take care, the path is very narrow and in parts almost eroded completely, and it follows a course that at times runs high above the water. It is far from the easiest of walks, not suitable for children while in its present state, and you may also wish to keep dogs on a lead. We advise caution: attempt it at your own risk.

Old Dalgarnock Churchyard

NX876936

Nothing remains of the village that once stood at Dalgarnock except its churchyard, sitting in isolation at the end of a driveable dirt track south of Thornhill. Follow the sign for Kirkbog Farm and, when you reach it, continue through the farmyard, past the cottages on the right and down the track straight ahead. Here in a beautiful setting with tall beech trees framing the cemetery gate is one of the most peaceful and poignant churchyards we have visited. Aside from its location and the echoes of the village it once served, it is notable for a monument to the Nithsdale Martyrs and the grave of the persecuted Covenanter James Harkness. If the weather is clement, pack a picnic and relax awhile here, soaking up the silence.

PENPONT, MONIAIVE & THE WEST

There's an otherworldly feeling about the villages and landscape of the western part of Mid Nithsdale. It's almost Tolkienesque, as if part of the 'Shire', a sense reinforced by the place names themselves: Penpont, Moniaive (pronounced Mon-ee-ive), the water and glen of the Scaur (pronounced Score), *Striding Arches*, Tynron (pronounced Tin-ron) and Tynron Doon… This is an area where the mobile library still does the rounds and community spirit is strong.

7 Penpont & around

Scaurbridge House (page 260)

Crossing the Nith Bridge on the A702 as you head west from Thornhill, look out for the ancient cross in a field on the left, the only **Dark Age**

cross in the region that's still in its original position, a late 9th- or early 10th-century Celtic shaft richly decorated on all sides. A little further on, take note of the beehive-like cairn on top of a small hill in a field to your right. This is one of several works by, and references to, the renowned sculptor and Penpont resident **Andy Goldsworthy** (see box, below) that punctuate this part of Nithsdale.

Penpont was built originally to house families displaced by new farming methods. The **Penpont Heritage Centre** (Marrburn Rd, DG3 4BL NX847947 01848 330700 (answerphone) penpontheritage.co.uk Jul–Aug 14.00–16.00 Sat, may vary annually so check website) occupies a 19th-century cottage that was the birthplace in 1858 of the Africa explorer, **Joseph Thomson**, who subsequently lent his name to Thomson's gazelle.

Head south out of the village, towards Keir, and there's a lovely view of Penpont Church up to your left. In the other direction, for an escape into the impressive surrounding countryside, follow Scaur Water up **Scaur Glen** or, alternatively, take a circular route following Penpont Burn up Marrburn Road and loop around to come down Scaur Glen. The roads are narrow but the views are breathtaking.

ANDY GOLDSWORTHY OBE: COLLABORATING WITH NATURE

Andy Goldsworthy moved to Dumfries and Galloway in 1985, first to Langholm and then to Penpont. Many of his pieces are characterised by their ephemeral and transient state; he likes to work outside with nature, making use of anything he can lay his hands on – literally. 'I need the contact and shock of hand on materials' he says. Those materials consist of ice, leaves, rock, clay, petals, twigs, quarried stone, flowers, mud, thorns and pinecones – to name just a few. Once created, the work is left to weather and allowed to decay, during which time Goldsworthy photographs it in its various states. Thus the decaying work is as relevant as the freshly made one.

Some works, such as a 'rain shadow' in a slate quarry made by lying on his back, arms outstretched during a short burst of rain, are fleeting, disappearing as quickly as they were created. Others have greater longevity, such as the strikingly dramatic *Striding Arches* (page 101) in the hills near Goldsworthy's home. 'It's the landscape around my home that is most important to me, and it is to that landscape that I keep returning, and which is the place that I can learn most about nature and my relationship with it,' he said in an interview with the BBC. All of his works are innovative, intense and uniquely personal.

At **Courthall Smithy** in 1839 in Keir Mill (⚲ NX855935) south of Penpont, blacksmith Kirkpatrick Macmillan invented the bicycle. The smithy is a private house now, but it sits by the road with a plaque on its gable wall. A replica of Macmillan's bike can be seen in the lower level of the Loreburne Shopping Centre in Dumfries, while the man himself is buried in Keir churchyard.

Head west from Penpont, passing the **Harbro Country Store** (⏲ daily except Sun; good for country clothing) and you reach **Tynron**, a picture-perfect village in a hollow of the Shinnel Water, clustered around a now sadly deconsecrated church with gargoyles and chimneys and the graves of a number of Covenanters. From Tynron, there's a rewarding but taxing four-mile circular walk to the mighty **Tynron Doon** (⚲ NX819939). Conspicuously sited on the summit of a steep-sided spur of Auchengibbert Hill, it was first occupied during the Iron Age and it's easy to see why it was chosen as a strong defensive position.

The landscape around here is exquisite and worth exploring just for the sake of it, to revel in the hills, the views and the peace. Strike off down a random road of your choice and see where it takes you. Continue over to Moniaive and you'll be met with a panorama across the hills and views down to the village itself; turn around and come back the way you came for a vista northeast towards Durisdeer (page 93), Wanlockhead (page 86) and the Lowthers.

8 Moniaive & around

Auchencheyne B&B (page 260) **Three Glens House** (page 260)

Much has been written about Moniaive over the years, and not without reason. This charming village has a strong community ethos and an enthusiasm and energy about it that puts more populous places to shame. Indeed, Moniaive's strapline is (justifiably) 'Expect the Unexpected'. With a much-celebrated and lively **festival scene**, especially – but not restricted to – music, and with a national, if not international, reputation, it was once described by *The Times* as 'one of the coolest villages in Britain'. A wide range of events is scheduled through the year (140 in one recent year) and could include anything from a poetry reading to a Folk Festival, Bluegrass Michaelmass Festival, Beer Festival or even a Comic Festival (local resident Alan Grant wrote *Judge Dredd* from the start and was the first non-American to write *Batman* for DC Comics). For up-to-the-minute details check out the excellent moniaive.org.uk (or Moniaive & Glencairn Area What's Going On?). Alternatively, pop into the Craigdarroch Arms Hotel in the centre of the village, which is very much at the heart of the community in every sense. And, if you're lucky, you might bump into indefatigable community stalwart Sue Grant, whose constant focus and determination has been something of a catalyst in driving Moniaive's development forward.

Moniaive lays claim to celebrity residents and visitors: artists, poets, writers and many from the music industry, most notably today Alex Kapranos of the band Franz Ferdinand, who has made this his Scottish home. (Kapranos bought the house of James Paterson, one of the group of artists known as the Glasgow Boys; see box, page 182.) Historically, Anna Laurie, subject of one of the most famous of Scottish songs 'Annie Laurie' (also known as 'Maxwelton Braes'), lived in nearby Craigdarroch House (page 100), while author Rumer Godden, famous for her children's stories and *Black Narcissus*, spent the final years of her life here (see box, below).

RUMER GODDEN – A LITERARY LIFE

We are grateful to Moniaive resident Jane Murray-Flutter, Rumer Godden's daughter, for contributing the following text about her mother.

Rumer Godden (1907–98) was a poet, broadcaster and screenwriter, and she wrote over 60 books in her lifetime, which were translated into many languages. Several of her books were turned into films.

Born in Sussex, Godden went out to India as a young child and she spent the best part of her life in either India or Britain. She always said that when she was in one country she was homesick for the other. The family lived on the banks of the Brahmaputra River in West Bengal and this is where her well-known novel *The River* (1946) is set. As a young woman she trained as a dancer and this is the theme of *Thursday's Children* (1984) and other ballet novels.

India was always her first love and is the setting for her most famous novel, *Black Narcissus* (1939). Her other novels – such as *In This House of Brede* (1969) – cover religion and also children, including *An Episode of Sparrows* (1955) and *The Diddakoi* (1972; winner of the Whitbread Award Children's category). She always wrote books for children, such as *The Dolls' House* (1947), between novels as she said it was very good discipline.

Godden lived in many houses but mainly in Lamb House in Rye, Sussex, which was once owned by Henry James. She married twice and had two daughters. In old age she moved to Dumfriesshire, to a house just outside Moniaive, to be near her daughter. She enjoyed the peace of the hills, the company of her Pekingese, and writing in her study overlooking the Dalwhat River, and she liked to explore and walk in the glens.

Take a stroll down the high street to soak up some of the village atmosphere and pass **The George Hotel**, one of the oldest inns in Scotland where Covenanters gathered in the Killing Times (page 24). Continue along past **Watson's**, the excellent general store with its lovely old-style shop front (plus coffee machine and small lounge area), to the **village cross**, erected in 1638, and the Tower House (now private) next to it, built in 1865 for the local school master. Further along, **Cottage Row** is a beautifully preserved row of traditional cottages, beyond which is **Kilneiss House**, built as a wedding present for James Paterson. At the end of the street, on a hillside overlooking the village, is a monument to **James Renwick**, who was born in Moniaive and became famous for the second Sanquhar Declaration in 1685 (page 81).

Moniaive sits at the confluence of **Dalwhat**, **Cairn**, **Craigdarroch** and **Castlefairn** waters. A short circular walk of 1¼ miles along the embankments takes in all four. Head out from Chapel Street, just past the school, and follow a loop to arrive back a little further along the same street.

In the **John Corrie Wildlife Garden** in Bottom Park at the southern end of the village, plants that were common around 100 years ago are being grown. The concept and garden take their inspiration from a local naturalist who in 1910 published *The Annals of Glencairn*, a history of the parish that detailed all the plants and animals of the day. Also here is the **Moniaive Geodial**, a curiosity made from rocks from the mountaintops, river valleys, quarries and rolling hillsides of Dumfries and Galloway. There's granite from Criffel, sandstone from the area around Thornhill and Dumfries, and slate from the Dalwhat, Shinnel and Scaur valleys. A noticeboard gives full details.

"The Moniaive Geodial, a curiosity made from rocks from the mountain-tops, river valleys, quarries and rolling hillsides."

Beyond Moniaive, a couple of miles along the B729 in a gorgeous setting surrounded by hills, lies **Craigdarroch** (NS741909), Anna Laurie's home (private, but open by appointment as part of the Historic Houses organisation 01848 200202 historichouses.org). Anna herself lived from 1682 to 1764 and came originally from nearby **Maxwelton House** (also known as Glencairn Castle, not open to the public but there is a good view of it from the B729) which lies a short distance southeast of Moniaive and Kirkland. Quaint **Maxwelton Chapel** (NX825895), built in 1869, lies east of the house in its own grounds, serene and inviting on a rise above a pond with views to the hills.

Northwest of Moniaive (seven miles, but feels a lot further), up a small road that follows the course of Dalwhat Water, ***Striding Arches*** (NX700973 stridingarches.com) is no easy jaunt but it's worth the effort to experience this remote art installation by renowned landscape artist Andy Goldsworthy (see box, page 97). Wend your way up from the village, continuing on where the road turns into a gravel forestry track. Just as your nerve starts to falter and you convince yourself that you must have taken a wrong turn, you arrive at a small parking area and interpretation boards. **Byre Arch**, the first of a series of red sandstone self-supporting arches, each around 12ft-high with a span of 21ft, consists of an old barn with an arch passing through the gable wall. If you're feeling energetic, venture further up into the hills to see the arches at Colt Hill, Benbrach and Bail Hill, all left to the elements to weather and frame the surrounding countryside.

Head directly west from Moniaive on the B729 and the 15-mile drive across the moors to Carsphairn in the Glenkens (page 140) can feel considerably longer (the road is single track and potholed in places). The countryside is stunning and the views are vast and impressive, especially to the oft-snow-covered summits in the distance. This is also grand walking country.

Southeast of Moniaive the A702 strikes out through the hills and over the moors to St John's Town of Dalry in the Glenkens area (page 141).

FOOD & DRINK

Craigdarroch Arms High St, DG3 4HN 01848 200205 craigdarrocharmshotel.co.uk. Serves reasonably priced pub fare, is much loved for its live music, and has accommodation on site. Owner Tim O'Sullivan offers a warm welcome. 'We had someone who came for two weeks from Australia, but six weeks later was still here!' says Tim.

Piccola Italia High St, DG3 4HN 01848 200400 eves only. Long-standing and popular Italian in the heart of Moniaive, consistently favourably reviewed.

LOWER NITHSDALE

Rolling hills, wooded valleys and country lanes that meander through leafy dells characterise Lower Nithsdale. For an area which abuts the region's main town, Dumfries, it can come as something of a surprise to discover these bucolic charms in such close proximity to an urban centre. The A76 follows the course of the Nith here as it does for much of Nithsdale, and the heavy lorries and traffic can be off-putting, but stick to the minor roads to either side and you could be in a different world.

Away from the A76 this is good cycling country: many of the smaller roads run along the bottom of the valleys and avoid particularly steep gradients, and with so few cars on the road it is a pleasure to rely on pedal power. A couple of fine options are the previously mentioned **Kirkpatrick Macmillan Trail** from Dumfries to Penpont via Dunscore (page 79) and Dumfries out to Duncow windmill, partly using the **Caledonian Cycleway**.

Broadly speaking, Lower Nithsdale in the context of this guide is the area from Amisfield to the northeast of Dumfries, up to Auldgirth to the north and then out to the Glenkiln Reservoir to the west. Dumfries and the Nith estuary (ie: points south of the A75), both of which are also classed as Nithsdale, are covered in the next chapter.

All of the places mentioned in this section lie to the north and west of Dumfries, with the exception of the village of **Torthorwald** (⚲ NY034784), immediately to the east, where the ruined 14th- to 15th-century **Torthorwald Castle** stands. However, Torthorwald's main point of interest is actually **Cruck Cottage** (Shieldhill Rd, DG1 3PS cruckcottage.com), a rare surviving example of a building type that was common in Dumfriesshire and southern Scotland from medieval times through to the early 19th century. The construction consists of oak 'crucks' or trunks as the main support in a traditional A-frame, with a roof of tie-beams and branch rafters, laid with heather turf and thatched with rye straw. The cottage had been almost derelict when it was gifted by the owner to Solway Heritage in 1990, after which a major restoration was undertaken. The detailed work in maintaining it is impressive and a real testament to the craftsmen involved and the continued support of the Cruck Cottage Heritage Association. The cottage is kept locked but a list of local key holders is displayed.

AULDGIRTH TO DUMFRIES, EAST OF THE NITH

Auldgirth Inn (page 260)

The village of Auldgirth on the banks of the Nith marks the upper limit of Lower Nithsdale, where the quiet road from Kirkton meets the rather busier A76 from Dumfries. There's a pub here with architectural roots in the days of pilgrimage (see below) and, on the other side of the Nith, a characterful Czech café (page 104).

Dalswinton

Heading south of Auldgirth on the east side of the Nith for a couple of miles brings you to the unpretentious estate village of Dalswinton, a row of painted cottages on either side of the road. The surrounding Dalswinton Estate was once home to the Comyns, one of the most powerful families in the country in medieval times, one of whom (John III, Red Comyn), was famously slain by Robert the Bruce in Dumfries in 1306.

Dalswinton House (dalswintonestate.co.uk) was commissioned in the late 18th century by Patrick Miller, who created an artificial loch in the grounds, on which he launched the world's first steamboat in 1788. He was also the landlord and friend of Robert Burns, who took on the farm at Ellisland (page 104). The house itself is private but a walk through the grounds, accessed just beyond the church makes for a pleasant diversion. There is also a holiday let here in the Mews, and fishing for trout and salmon.

A little further on from the village stands one of the area's most intriguing buildings. With its bell-cote, spire and red corrugated iron walls and roof, **Dalswinton Barony Church** (NX942850) looks far more New England than Scotland and comes as something of a surprise. Built in 1881, it's a good example of a 'tin church', of which many were made for use both at home and in the colonies overseas. This was perhaps the original and most ambitious flat-pack assembly ever seen, well before IKEA got involved, for churches were manufactured in kit form and then shipped to the point of order. Inside, the walls are clad in timber pine and the floor and pews are also of pine. Many such churches have either disappeared altogether or are no longer in use, but occasional services are still held here.

FOOD & DRINK

Auldgirth Inn Auldgirth DG2 0XG 01387 740250 auldgirthinn.co.uk. Local lad Rob McAleese took over in 2017, refurbished in 2018 and has earned two AA rosettes for the quality of the food, much of it locally sourced. Low lighting, charcoals and greys make for an atmospheric dining room, complete with a meat-filled dry ageing unit.

The Hamans Auldgirth DG2 0RZ ✆ 01387 740627 **f**. Viktor's roadside café makes for a different option, with its eye-catching interior in the style of a Bohemian café and menu of homemade Czech recipes such as *bramborak* (potato crêpe) and beef goulash soup. Sandwiches and burgers are also available, plus traditional Bohemian and Moravian cake, and old favourites such as Victoria sponge and scones.

AULDGIRTH TO DUMFRIES, WEST OF THE NITH

Friar's Carse (page 260)

Approaching Dumfries from Auldgirth, the connections with Burns grow ever stronger, first at **Friar's Carse** (see box, opposite); then **Ellisland Farm**, where he lived from 1788 to 1791; and then in Dumfries itself, to where he moved from Ellisland and where he died (see box, page 112).

A mile or so south of Ellisland, on a small road off to the left, **Leslie and Baggot** (leslieandbaggott.com) have a fine stock of antiques and paintings for sale from their country house (also associated with Burns), while further down the same road lies **Portrack House** (Holywood DG2 0RW NX939829), which was the home of the American architect and landscape designer Charles Jencks. The garden, known as '**The Garden of Cosmic Speculation**', is open one day a year as part of Scotland's Gardens (scotlandsgardens.org).

A couple of miles further on from Portrack, where the minor road rejoins the main A76, is **Holywood**, now virtually a suburb of Dumfries. To the east of the A76 is the late 18th-century church, now private but with access allowed to the graveyard. The bell in the tower is said to be the oldest in Scotland, though alas it is no longer rung. To the west of the A76, in a nondescript field, stand the **Twelve Apostles**. At around 290ft in diameter, it's notable as the largest stone circle in Scotland, dating from the 3rd or 2nd millennium BC. Access to the field can be gained via a stile over the fence on a minor road off the B729.

9 Ellisland Farm

Holywood Rd, Auldgirth DG2 0RP NX929838 ✆ 01387 740426 ellislandfarm.co.uk
6 Jan–30 Nov 10.00–17.00 Mon–Wed & Sat, 1 Apr–30 Sep also 14.00–17.00 Sun; last entry 16.00

Burns was offered a choice of three farms by Patrick Miller of Dalswinton (page 103) and this was the one he opted for, describing it as 'the poet's choice'. It has often been said that he made a poor farmer but that there was something about the surroundings of Ellisland that brought him poetic inspiration, and, for any visitors today with an ounce of romance in their souls, it's easy to see why. Sitting on the banks of the Nith, the charm of the setting could easily outweigh any misgivings about the stony, infertile ground and its suitability as a farm.

Burns moved to Ellisland at the age of 29. By then his poetry had earned him both fame and money, but he was far from wealthy, having already given half of his earnings to his brother to stave off poverty. Farming Ellisland proved useless and it was while living here that Burns became an exciseman, taking up a position in 1789 in which he was responsible for checking taxes in the ten parishes of Upper Nithsdale. The work was exhausting, often requiring long rides of 30 to 40 miles per day, so in 1790 he took up a new excise role based in Dumfries, to where he moved shortly after.

Whitewashed cottages around a central courtyard are evocative of a bygone era at Ellisland. Four rooms in the house in which Burns lived are

LITERARY SHENANIGANS AT ELLISLAND & FRIAR'S CARSE

While living at Ellisland, Burns was a regular visitor to nearby Friar's Carse (now a hotel; page 260), which belonged to Robert Riddell of Glenriddell. Riddell actually had a folly built in the garden at Friar's Carse, called The Hermitage, which is still there today. Burns scratched a poem on one of its windows, using a diamond, and the window itself is now on display at Ellisland.

During one visit to Friar's Carse, Burns was introduced to Captain Francis Grose who, at the time, was on his second tour of the country, compiling his *Antiquities of Scotland* (a book that has proven invaluable in researching this one). Burns suggested to Grose that he should include the ruinous kirk at Alloway, the village in Ayrshire in which he was born. Grose agreed on condition that Burns supply an account of the witchcraft stones associated with the ruin. This Burns duly did, sending a prose tale that he then followed up with a rhyming version, *Tam o' Shanter*, which Grose printed. It is said that Burns wrote it in one day while pacing back and forth along the banks of the Nith at Ellisland. Visitors today can follow in his footsteps and take a stroll along the 'Tam o' Shanter Path'.

Alas, Burns's friendship with Riddell ended on a sour note and spawned a series of events which, via one John Gribbell of Philadelphia, concluded with two of Burns's original manuscripts forming the most significant items in the Burns collection of the National Library of Scotland in Edinburgh. Ask at Ellisland for the full story.

open to the public: two – the kitchen and the 'spence' (Scots for parlour, the room in which Burns wrote) – have 18th-century furnishings, while Burns' bedroom is used as a pop-up café and the original entrance hall is a shop and reception. The kitchen includes the oven that Burns ordered from the Carrron Ironworks, while his spence contains a number of his original manuscripts, including *The Whistle*, written just down the road at Friar's Carse (see box, page 105).

"His spence contains a number of his original manuscripts, including The Whistle, *written just down the road."*

The wider site includes stable, byres, an orchard and riverside walks, plus displays of farming equipment and even the outside dry toilet used by Burns. There's also a very good audio-visual presentation and a collection of fun limited editions of the Robert Bryden 1896 etchings illustrating some of Burns's best-known work, including *The De'ils Awa' Wi' the Exciseman, Tam o'Shanter* and *The Haggis*.

SOUTHWEST FROM AULDGIRTH

Barnsoul Caravan Park (page 260), **Red Squirrel Campsite** (page 260)

On a road between the main A76 and the village of Dunscore, the **Allanton Peace Sanctuary** (DG2 0RY) is the European home of May Peace Prevail on Earth International, founded in 1955 by the Japanese teacher, philosopher and poet Masahisa Goi. The house – which is available for group bookings and workshops – is set in 18 acres of grounds to which all are welcome. In addition to a Wildlife Woodland Walk, at the heart of the grounds is the Peace Pole Henge, a double circle of 204 Peace Poles representing every country in the world, each of them named.

The appealing village of **Dunscore** sits on a hill with fine views to the north from the parish church of 1823. The area has many associations with the Covenanters and is scattered with communion stones and hillside graves from that time. In the church itself, the **Dunscore Heritage Centre** (dunscoreheritage.org spring–autumn noon–16.00 Sun, otherwise make contact via the website) commemorates **Jane Haining**, who was born here and who was the only Scots woman to die in Auschwitz.

Just outside Dunscore is the **Farmersfield Rest-home for Elderly Donkeys** (07852 447076 farmersfield.org.uk;), a small, family-run charity that welcomes visitors, but by prior appointment only. (Please do not turn up without calling ahead first.)

From Dunscore head west to explore the countryside, myriad hills and burns that make this a delightful area simply to meander around and soak up the scenery. To the west, you could follow the **Glenesslin Burn** on a single-track road up to **Loch Urr** and **Mid Nithsdale**. To the northeast, travel through Dalgonar and up to the quirkily named **Glenmidge**, a lovely spot in a hollow in the hills that we are assured doesn't live up to its name (at least, no more so than any other area) and which offers good camping (page 260).

Alternatively head south to **Irongray** on the southern side of Cluden Water, then west to the locally known beauty spot of **Routin' Brig** (📍 NX886797), where the high-arched bridge surrounded by native woodland crosses the Cairn Water as it tumbles over rocks and drops down the gorge to a pool at the bottom. When the water is low it's a great spot for a paddle. Around four miles further to the southwest lies **Glenkiln Reservoir**, established in 1951. This was at one time, not so long ago, the site of a number of world-class sculptures dotted among the hills, including works by Henry Moore, Jacob Epstein and Auguste Rodin. Alas, in 2013 one of the Moores, worth an estimated £3 million, was stolen. As a result, all of the sculptures have been removed except Moore's *Glenkiln Cross*. You may also spot his *Reclining Figure*, but on closer inspection will discover that, sadly, it's a replica made of fibreglass. Its setting, however, remains memorable.

10 Irongray Church

Irongray's splendid sandstone and cream-painted church occupies a beautiful setting surrounded by hills. The church was built in 1803 and in the graveyard is the tomb chest of Helen Walker, on whom Sir Walter Scott based Jeanie Deans in *The Heart of Midlothian* (1818). Having refused to lie to save her sister from a charge of infanticide, she walked to London to petition the Duke of Argyll for a reprieve. The inscription on the tomb is written by Scott. At the entrance to the church grounds note the protruding stones over the wall, in-built steps worn smooth in the shape of a shoe from centuries of use.

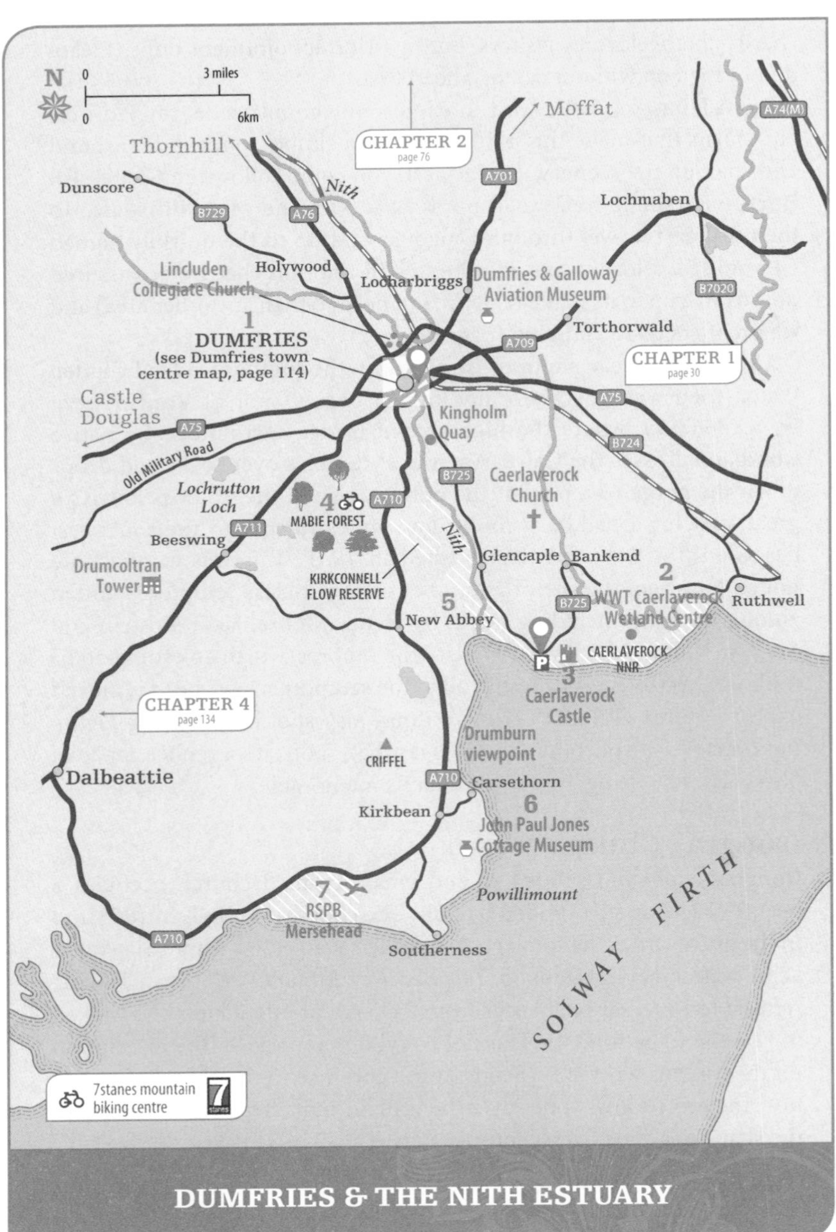

DUMFRIES & THE NITH ESTUARY

3 DUMFRIES & THE NITH ESTUARY

At the southern end of the Nith, just before river broadens to estuary, lies Dumfries, southwest Scotland's main town. It's a historic place with a wealth of interest, some fine buildings, riverside parks, and several significant Burns attractions. It's also home to a major literary attraction with strong connections to J M Barrie and *Peter Pan* – Moat Brae, Scotland's National Centre for Children's Literature and Storytelling, a great place for children and adults alike. Each year Dumfries hosts one of Scotland's premier winter music festivals, the **Big Burns Supper** (bigburnssupper.com), to coincide with the bard's birthday on 25 January, with a wide-ranging programme of everything from folk music to burlesque.

South of Dumfries the river divides the landscape in two, with the flatter wetlands of an internationally important bird reserve on the eastern side and the looming form of **Criffel**, one of the most prominent hills in southern Scotland, dominating the west. The eastern strip is enchanting, a place of ever-changing light and colours, mudflats and saltmarshes, where ships from far-flung places once docked and to where enormous colonies of birds – **barnacle geese**, in particular – now return each year. To the west lies a historic abbey, one of the most romantic in Scotland's history, a 7stanes biking forest also known for its butterflies and, towards the southernmost reach, a quaint waterside village with a fine pub.

GETTING AROUND

The main trunk road, the A75, passes around the north of Dumfries linking the Carlisle to Glasgow A74(M) motorway over in the east to the towns of Castle Douglas, Newton Stewart and Stranraer in western Dumfries and Galloway. As the A75 passes the town numerous other

TOURIST INFORMATION

VisitScotland Information Centre Dumfries 64 Whitesands, Dumfries DG1 2RS 01387 253862 visitdumfriesandgalloway.co.uk Apr–Oct 09.00–17.00 Mon–Sat, 10.00–16.00 Sun; Nov–Mar 09.30–16.30 Mon–Sat, 10.00–15.00 Sun

main roads radiate off northwards to places such as Lockerbie and Moffat, and further afield to Kilmarnock. The town and surrounding roads generally flow freely, although, as with any main town, it is best to avoid rush hour. The Dumfries traffic on the A75 is also noticeably heavier, particularly with haulage lorries, a couple of hours or so after a ferry has come into Cairnryan on the west coast.

Dumfries itself is a compact town and not too difficult to navigate. Parking in the town, at the council-owned sites, is free, but you need to display a disc (free from local shops and council offices) and to observe the time limits. Once in the centre all the town's main sites and attractions are within easy walking distance of each other.

PUBLIC TRANSPORT

Scotrail runs a frequent **train service** throughout the day from Monday to Saturday, but only a couple of Sunday services, along its Newcastle (via Carlisle) to Glasgow route, which stops at Dumfries.

Many of the local and regional **bus services** use Dumfries as their main start/end point. The key routes for sites and attractions along the Nith estuary are the 6a for Caerlaverock operated by Stagecoach West Scotland/DGC Buses, and the 372 to New Abbey by Houstons Coaches.

Local public transport information is provided by South West of Scotland Transport Partnership (swestrans.org.uk), or alternatively Traveline (0871 200 2233 traveline.info).

CYCLING

Dumfries has a traffic-free cycle network that connects many of the main places in town. Cyclists should head for The Frothy Bike Co on Whitesands (page 120).

The country lanes either side of Dumfries and along the west and east flanks of the Nith estuary offer surprisingly different scenery. The west route, starting at Dock Park or Whitesands, leaves Dumfries using the

National Cycle Route 7 (NCR7; sustrans.org.uk) taking in lochs at Lochfoot and Beeswing, Mabie Forest, the attractions of New Abbey and the National Nature Reserve at Kirkconnell Flow. The eastern route, also leaving Dumfries on the NCR7, offers fine estuary views across to the granite dome of Criffel, historical and wildlife attractions at Caerlaverock, and the drama of the tidal bore at Glencaple. For thrill seekers, the **7stanes** mountain biking centre at Mabie Forest (7stanesmountainbiking.com/mabie) has trails for all abilities, from graded routes for novices to the 'Dark Side' trail.

A PDF showcasing the key routes in the area can be found at gosmartdumfries.co.uk.

WALKING

Walking around Dumfries and the Nith estuary offers choices of such variety that you can be high up in the hills in the morning, on a riverside or forest walk at lunchtime, and then exploring the old streets of Dumfries in the afternoon. An ascent of Criffel from New Abbey is the obvious choice for an easily accessible hill walk, but be warned that, although it's only 1,866ft, it's a relatively strenuous and challenging climb starting almost from sea level. The views from the top, however, are superb. Also popular is the walk from Castle Corner to Caerlaverock on the eastern side of the Nith (see box, page 127).

A Criffel walk is available in our book *Galloway: 40 Coast and Country Walks*, while Caerlaverock is covered in the companion book *The Dumfriesshire Dales: 40 Favourite Walks*, both published by Moffat-based Pocket Mountains.

Dumfries and Galloway Council produces a fine selection of free walking and cycling downloads, available from dumgal.gov.uk (look under 'Leisure' and then 'Outdoor Access and Paths').

1 DUMFRIES

20 Castle Street (page 260), **Glenaldor House** (page 261)

Southern Scotland's largest town straddles the Nith where it twists and turns in its final approach to the Solway a few miles further south. We find Dumfries an eminently likeable place offering a mix of history and everyday functionality, and its rakish charm is supported by deep-rooted local pride. Compact and easy to walk around, it has a population of

BURNS IN DUMFRIES

After living at Ellisland (page 104), Robert Burns moved into Dumfries while still working as an exciseman and here he spent the final years of his short life. The town is replete with references to the poet and there is a **Burns Trail**, which links all the relevant points of interest (a leaflet is available from the visitor information centre), many of which are also covered by the walk on page 115. Burns first lived in a flat in the 'wee vennel' as it was known, or Bank Street, before moving to his house in Mill Street (now Burns Street). A **Burns statue** stands prominently at the top of the high street and in addition to the Burns Trail there is a **Burns Walk** along the Nith, from Dumfries to Dalscone, passing the confluence with Cluden Water at Lincluden (page 121).

Along the high street, the **Hole in the Wa'** was one of Burns's regular drinking haunts, though his favourite was the **Globe Inn** at 56 High Street (globeinndumfries.co.uk; page 120), where, in addition to having a drink or a meal, you can now tour the building (booking required) to see various rooms as they were in Burns' time, including the bedroom in which he slept (and, one assumes, had his passionate affair with Anna Park, the landlady's niece). His fireside chair is also there and tradition has it that, if you want to sit in it, you have to recite a line or two of Burns' work. Get practising!

Near to The Globe is the **Midsteeple**, where in July 1796 Burns's body lay in state before the funeral procession to St Michael's Kirk (page 119).

Burns Tours of Dumfries are offered by Bobby Jess (burnstoursdumfries.co.uk) and can also be booked through the VisitScotland information centre (see box, page 110).

just under 44,000 (at the last census) and, while it may not be a major tourist centre in the way of Edinburgh or Glasgow, it is not without its sights and attractions and comfortably offers enough to keep visitors occupied for a few days, especially anyone with an interest in Burns. It is also the location of the oldest working theatre in Scotland and the 'home' of *Peter Pan*, for it was at Moat Brae that J M Barrie dreamed up Neverland. The building is now open to the public after a multi-million-pound refurbishment.

There's always something going on in Dumfries, so if you're minded to take in an event or two while here, it's worth popping into the **Midsteeple Box Office** (High St, DG1 2BH 01337 253383 dgboxoffice.co.uk), which sells tickets for all local venues.

Dumfries has long been known as '**Queen of the South**', a name that is attributed to one David Dunbar, a local poet who, while standing in the general election of 1857, described the town as such in one of his

WILDLIFE & WILD LANDSCAPES

Travelling around the region you will be met by an ongoing succession of memorable views encompassing a broad range of habitats. The diversity of wildlife is what attracts many visitors and includes both common and rare species.

1 The Grey Mare's Tail is the fifth-highest waterfall in the UK.

BRIAN MORRELL/WWT CAERLAVEROCK WETLAND CENTRE

2 Geese fill the dawn sky at WWT Caerlaverock Wetland Centre. 3 Wild goats roam in Galloway Forest Park's Wild Goat Park on the Queen's Way. 4 Red deer can be spotted in Dumfries and Galloway's wild landscapes. 5 Distinctive Burnswark Hill has a rich Roman history and offers superb views from its flat top.

KEITH K/S

JAN HOLM/S

TRIMONTIUM TRUST

ALAN IRVING

6 The peaceful waters of Loch Ken. 7 Red kites are an increasingly familiar sight, especially in the Stewartry. 8 Lonely Loch Enoch on the ascent of Merrick, the region's highest peak. 9 The region is a good place to see the rare natterjack toad. 10 Superb views along the Solway, approaching the summit of Screel.

DG/DF (SLOW BRITAIN)

DOUBLECLIX/S

DG/DF (SLOW BRITAIN)

CREATIVE NATURE MEDIA/S

STEPHANIE ANN PHOTOGRAPHY

1

CASTLES & GARDENS

An impressive legacy of fortified buildings and glorious gardens punctuates the Dumfries and Galloway landscape, some – such as Drumlanrig – combine history and horticulture, others – such as Craigieburn and Glenwhan – are an explicit statement of one person's passion. Taking time to explore them unearths the stories of characters past and present, not least the garden owners, some of whom you might bump into during a visit.

2

HEARTLAND ARTS/S

3

PRODUCTION STAR/S

4

LOGAN BOTANIC GARDEN

TARGYN PLEIADES/S

1 Magnificent views to the Mull of Galloway from Glenwhan Gardens. 2 MacLellan's Castle in Kirkcudbright. 3 Although built in the mid 16th century, by 1700 Dunskey Castle was a ruin. 4 Logan Botanic Garden boasts an astonishing array of southern hemisphere plants. 5 The medieval stronghold of curious, triangular Caerlaverock Castle. 6 Escape to isolated Morton Castle among the hills of mid Nithsdale. 7 Lawns, formal gardens, mixed shrub and herbaceous borders are all found in the gardens at Drumlanrig Castle. 8 Himalayan influences are much in evidence at Craigieburn Gardens – and not just in the planting.

6

7

8

MARTEN LAGENDIJK/S

CRAIGIEBURN GARDENS

BINSON CALFORT/S

STOCKSOLUTIONS/S

TOWNS AND VILLAGES

Community spirit is strong throughout the region and is often reflected in the appearance of well-kept towns and villages. Nowhere is very big, which means that wherever you go it doesn't take long before you find your way around and get talking to the locals.

1 The Devorgilla Bridge across the Nith in Dumfries dates from the first half of the 17th century. 2 Moffat is known partly for its toffee, available from many places, including the irresistible Moffat Toffee Shop on the High Street.

DG/DF (SLOW BRITAIN)

COURTESY OF PETE ROBINSON

COLIN TENNANT PHOTOGRAPHY

RODNEY HUTCHINSON/S

3 Oysters galore at the hugely popular Stranraer Oyster Festival. **4** Wigtown, Scotland's National Book Town, sits peacefully above Wig Bay, an estuary with large areas of salt marsh and mud flats, and the largest Local Nature Reserve in Britain. **5** It comes as a surprise to many that this region and not the north of Scotland is home to Scotland's highest village, Wanlockhead. **6** Village pubs like this one – the Clachan Inn in St John's Town of Dalry – occupy a treasured place at the heart of local communities. **7** The region's regular farmers' markets are a great way to sample local food and drink and get to know local people. **8** Arts and Crafts-style cottages line the road at Parton, on the banks of the River Dee.

THE CLACHAN INN

DG/DF (SLOW BRITAIN)

PETER NORMAN/WWW.WILDSEASONS.CO.UK

DG/DF (SLOW BRITAIN)

EWAN CHESSER/S

GALLOWAYWILDFOODS.COM

RURAL LIFE

Centuries of agriculture have shaped the landscape across the region, from well-grazed pastureland to drystone dykes. A Slower, more rural way of life continues to be the norm; for many, this is one of the chief attractions of living here.

1 Nestled in the beautiful hills and moorland of Upper Eskdale lies the village of Eskdalemuir. 2 Successful foraging is an art form, one to be learned with the region's resident forager. 3 Belted Galloway cows are fondly known as 'Belties'. 4 Langholm's Common Riding is the oldest in Dumfries and Galloway.

DG/DF (SLOW BRITAIN)

addresses. It stuck and is today not only synonymous with the town, but also with the local football club. The club's unofficial nickname is the 'Doonhamers', which in turn is generally synonymous with folk from Dumfries. Its origins lie in the 19th century, when many people worked away from home, especially the railway workers who were based in Glasgow and talked about going 'doon hame' ('down home'). One particularly notable doonhamer of recent years is Adam Wiles, better known as DJ Calvin Harris.

History has been made in Dumfries, for it was here that Robert the Bruce famously slew his rival, the Red Comyn, in Greyfriars Kirk in 1306 (the exact spot is long since gone and is now the site of a branch of Greggs), thus blazing the trail to Scottish independence at Bannockburn eight years later. The town's motto, 'A Loreburn' from its coat of arms, dates from those early years when Dumfries was a frequent place of conflict due to its proximity to the Scotland–England border and was regularly subjected to attack. 'A Lore Burn' would ring out the shout, 'to the muddy stream', summoning arms to the town's weakest point on its eastern edge. Today you'll come across the modern spelling, Loreburn, frequently: it's the name of the shopping centre, primary school, housing association… you can't miss it.

The river has been central – both literally and metaphorically – to Dumfries's development and is today still crossed by the massively buttressed Auld Brig, commonly referred to as the **Devorgilla Bridge** after Lady Devorgilla's (see box, page 131) original structure of the 13th century. This was the main link to the kingdom of Galloway, whose lands started immediately west of the Nith. Sitting on the frontier of Scotland's wild southwest, Dumfries was a place where pilgrims stopped on their way to Whithorn (page 211). Partly for them did the good Devorgilla build Greyfriars Monastery on the Dumfries side, where now stands today's Greyfriars Kirk (St Bride's Anglican Church).

Dumfries was a thriving port from the late 17th century right through to the mid 20th century, mostly with local coastal trade in crops and livestock. In the 18th century the town established links with the British colonies in North America and shipping increased, and by 1740 so much tobacco was being imported from Virginia that Dumfries became known as the 'Scottish Liverpool'. John Paul Jones, the 'Father of the American Navy', was born just south of Dumfries (page 132) at the wide mouth of the Nith and it was from here that he sailed to America.

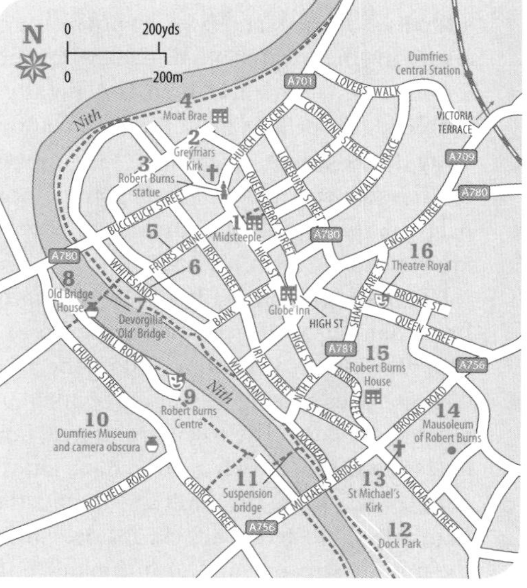

In conjunction with the developing port, Dumfries became one of the most important market towns in southwest Scotland and was on the droving route from the far west (page 226), with great herds of cattle being brought by boat from Ireland and then across Galloway on foot, before continuing, still on foot, to the major cattle markets in the south. At **Midsteeple** on the high street a sign gives the droving distances; it's notable that Glasgow and Edinburgh are closer than Portpatrick on the west coast, and it's particularly sobering to see just how far cattle had to be walked to market: Huntingdon 272 miles and London 330 miles.

Dumfries became a busy mill town in the 18th and 19th centuries. The suspension bridge across the Nith was built in 1875 to help workers – mostly girls – reach the tweed mills on the far side of the river. It is said that 1,200 girls used to cross this bridge each day on their way to work, often stopping to stamp their feet all at the same time to hear the noise and feel the bridge sway.

The arrival of the railway in the 19th century marked the start of the decline of the port, but by the early 20th century the town reinvented itself as a centre for car manufacturing with the opening of the Arrol-Johnston factory in July 1913. Known as 'The Rubber Works', the factory was part of a company that became the largest car manufacturer in Scotland.

In more recent years Dumfries has become home to a burgeoning and pioneering range of academic institutions and businesses at the Crichton campus on the southern edge of town, east of the Nith. The universities of the West of Scotland and Glasgow both have departments here, as does the Open University, and around 80 businesses and third-sector organisations are based here, including the Crichton Carbon Centre and the Solway Centre for Environment and Culture. The Crichton's splendid grounds are open to all and make for a delightful leafy retreat.

A TOUR OF THE TOWN ON FOOT

Walking the town is by far the best way to get to know it and, given its comparatively small size, it's possible to follow an easy route that takes in the main sights.

1 Midsteeple on the pedestrianised High Street or **2 Greyfriars Kirk** (officially known as St Bride's Anglican Church) on Church Crescent make for good starting points. The present church dates only from 1868 but stands close to where Devorgilla's Greyfriars Convent stood, before the high altar of which Robert the Bruce slew the Red Comyn in 1306. This was also the site of Maxwell's Castle, more of a fortified town house than a castle and one of the many homes of the Maxwell family. It was bought by the townsfolk who pulled it down in 1720, following which the New Church was built in 1727. That, too, was eventually demolished and replaced by the present church.

"The present church dates only from 1868 but stands close to where Devorgilla's Greyfriars Convent stood."

Opposite the entrance to Greyfriars stands a **3 statue of Robert Burns**, executed in Carrara marble from a model by Scottish sculptor Amelia Paton Hill, who is believed to have been the first woman sculptor to have a sculpture exhibited in a public space. The statue is a strong work showing Burns seated with a dog at his feet and was unveiled in 1882 by Archibald Primrose who went on to become one of the country's least-remembered prime ministers (1894–95).

Standing with your back to Greyfriars, turn left along Church Crescent, pass Anderson Kilts and then turn left again up Irving Street to reach **4 Moat Brae** at the top corner (where it becomes George Street). Scotland's National Centre for Children's Literature and Storytelling (page 116) was around ten years in the making and offers a stimulating mix of literary history, exhibitions, period house and architectural interest, and of course the garden in which J M Barrie invented Neverland.

Moat Brae was designed and built in 1822–23 by local architect Walter Newall, who was also responsible for many of the buildings in the surrounding streets, some of which you will pass as you carry on down George Street and then continue left along Castle Street.

At the traffic lights, cross straight over, pass the Burns statue on the left and then turn right down **5 Friars Vennel** to **6 Whitesands** on the east bank of the river. This was left as orchards and grazing until

THE HOME OF NEVERLAND

We are grateful to Dr Simon Davidson, Moat Brae's Director, for his contribution below.

In the northwest corner of central Dumfries, tucked into the bend of the Nith, lies **Moat Brae**, a Grade B listed building described as a 'five-bay, four-storey Greek revival town house'. It was designed by Scottish architect Walter Newall, who came from nearby New Abbey and was the area's leading architect from the 1820s until his retirement. Newall also designed the Assembly Rooms on George Street (more or less opposite Moat Brae) and remodelled the observatory, which is now the museum and camera obscura (page 118). The house's slightly strange name comes from the medieval Maxwell Castle or 'Motte', which was built in 1300, just around the corner on the site of the present Greyfriars Kirk.

Moat Brae was built in 1823 for a local (merchant) solicitor and Postmaster General but in 1865 was bought by the Gordon family. Their son Stewart attended Dumfries Academy, where J M Barrie, the author of *Peter Pan* came to school in 1873 at the age of 13 from his family home in Kirriemuir, north of Dundee. The Barrie family were great believers in education and not only did Dumfries Academy have a particularly good reputation, but Barrie's eldest brother, Alexander, was inspector of schools for Dumfriesshire.

Barrie and Stewart Gordon became instant friends and from the outset Gordon, who called himself 'Dare Devil Dick', called Barrie 'Sixteen String Jack'. 'He asked me if I would join the pirate crew,' wrote Barrie in later years. Together the boys played in the garden at Moat Brae and it was here that Neverland was invented. Barrie later wrote 'I think the five years or so that I spent here were probably the happiest of my life, for indeed I have loved this place'. On being awarded the Freedom of the Burgh of Dumfries in 1924 he reflected that 'when the shades of night began to fall, certain young mathematicians shed their triangles, crept up walls and down trees, and became pirates in a sort of Odyssey that was long afterwards to become the play of *Peter Pan*. For our escapades in a certain Dumfries garden, which is enchanted land to me, were certainly the genesis of that nefarious work.'

From 1914 up until 1997 Moat Brae was operating as a nursing home, after which it was left empty and fell into a state of disrepair. Although designated for demolition, the building was eventually acquired by the Peter Pan Moat Brae Trust in 2009 and, after a ten year, multi-million-pound fundraising project supported by the National Lottery Heritage Fund and Creative Scotland (among others), Moat Brae opened on 1 June 2019 as **Scotland's National Centre for Children's Literature and** the 18th century, when the first line of buildings was erected. The river is broad here and runs fast over the weir when the water's high. In autumn, if the conditions are right, you can see salmon leaping.

Storytelling (George St, DG1 2EA 01387 255549 peterpanmoatbrae.org 11.00–17.00 Mon–Sat (closed Mon term time), 10.00–16.00 Sun; check online in advance as hours may change).

It didn't take long for this new, innovative attraction to be noticed and by the end of the year Moat Brae had been voted one of *Time* magazine's Top 50 Coolest Places in the World for Kids 2019. Visitors can expect a visceral connection with the 1870s world of a teenage J M Barrie and an inspiring voyage through the birthplace of *Peter Pan*. The idyllic Neverland garden flanks the River Nith and an array of unusual trees and plants charts a route around its foreboding pirate ship, enchanting mermaid's lagoon and adorable Wendy house. There are hidden trails of stone-carved crocodiles to be found and you can try and spot artist Aliisa Hyslop's ghostly floating sculptures that depict the dancing and playing Lost Boys.

The building itself, far from being a museum, is a place of inspiration, with full audio-visual interpretation that takes you through Barrie's time in Dumfries (1873–77) via talking portraits, interactive games and storytelling chairs. The gracious ground-floor rooms have been restored to an 1870s style (the entrance hall's cupola is particularly impressive) and the house is frequently redecorated to suit the season (Christmas is wonderful!). Seasonal touring exhibitions are staged in the first-floor gallery, while on the attic floor you can try and catch Peter Pan's shadow in the Darling's Nursery, from where you can also crawl through Nanna's kennel to the play theatre with its costumes and scripts. Numerous reading rooms with listening stations, book burrows and snugs are dotted around the house, and there are hidden gems everywhere, from secret books with torch-revealed characters to key holes through which you can spy on an entire fairy house. In the basement, true to the *Peter Pan* story, is the Home Under the Ground, with cinema screen, sound system and campfire log cushions.

Families can easily spend all day at Moat Brae because when the children have burnt out, they can curl up with a good book while the parents chill out in the café.

The centre is no stranger to celebrity and has a star-studded audiobook of *Peter Pan* containing the voices of its patron Joanna Lumley, along with Jennifer Saunders, David Walliams, Kit Harington and Michael Morpurgo among others. However, behind the glitz and glamour, there is a mission afoot. As Simon Davidson explains: 'We have a simple but important vision, which is to create a world where reading and storytelling are an integral part of growing up'.

Where the buses stop, look out for the **'DIY Statue' plinth**: hop up and stand on the indented feet plates, it's your opportunity to be a Dumfries 'Local Hero'!

The **7 Devorgilla 'Old' Bridge** is an impressive span and offers pleasant views up and down the river from its midpoint. On a calm, sunny day the bridge reflects in the Nith below just before it cascades down the weir. Sandmartins skim the water, feeding on the wing; willows on the west bank trail lazily; ducks squabble and seagulls swoop. At the far side of the bridge is the **8 Old Bridge House** (Mill Rd, DG7 2BE ⏲ Easter/1 Apr–Sep daily), which claims to be the oldest house in Dumfries, with parts of it dating from 1620 when they rebuilt the bridge with houses at either end. Although small, it's worth a visit for its well-presented information boards about the history of Dumfries, of the bridges and of the house itself.

Leaving the museum, turn left and walk along the river to the **9 Robert Burns Centre** (Mill Rd, DG2 7BE ✆ 01387 264808 ⊘ rbcft.co.uk ⏲ summer Tue–Sat; Sept–May Mon–Sat), housed in an old mill building. In addition to telling the story of the connections between Robert Burns and Dumfries, the centre also houses an intricate scale model of Dumfries in the 1790s, the time that Burns was here, plus a bookshop, café (page 120) and popular small **Film Theatre**.

From the centre, walk up Millbrae and then climb up through the gardens to **10 Dumfries Museum and camera obscura** ☛ (The Observatory, Rotchell Rd, DG2 7SW ✆ 01387 253374 f ⏲ all year, reduced hours out of season; free entry to museum, small charge for the camera obscura), the region's largest museum with an extensive collection on local history and prehistory, including the fossil footprints discovered by Dr Henry Duncan at Corncockle Quarry (page 65).

The camera obscura started out as a means of studying the sun but quickly became a tourist attraction. Even now the view on a clear day offers a surprising degree of detail and if the sun is out and the sky clear you might even be able to spot the northern mountains of the Lake District, 30 miles to the south. Do note, though, that the camera obscura doesn't work on a wet day, so choose the time of your visit according to the weather report.

From the museum, head back down to the river and continue along to cross the **11 suspension bridge**, turning right on the other side to make your way along to the junction. Cross straight over here to enter **12 Dock Park**, a pleasant leafy spot to linger on the banks of the Nith. A wander along the riverside and back through the park passes a *Titanic* memorial commemorating one of the fated ship's stewards and a band member who came from this area. There's also a nod to Burns, with some of his words inscribed in the ground at the bandstand, and there are views across to the extraordinary Rosefield Mills building of 1885, once Dumfries's largest tweed mill, with the arches of its frontage calling to mind (for the more imaginative among us) the Doge's Palace in Venice. Now standing empty, it is in the hands of Dumfries Historic Buildings Trust who are raising funds for its restoration.

Returning to the junction from the park, turn right to reach **13 St Michael's Kirk**, which stands on the site of a much older 12th-century church. Here in the churchyard is **14 the mausoleum of Robert Burns**, with his wife Jean Amour buried next to him. Burns was initially buried in a different plot but in 1815 his remains were moved to a vault under the mausoleum, which was erected to his memory. A plan at the entrance to the graveyard shows the location of his original resting place, as well as the location of the graves of his contemporaries.

From here it's only a couple of minutes' walk to **15 Robert Burns House** on Burns Street (🖰 dumgal.gov.uk, then search 'Robert Burns House' ⏲ Apr–Sep daily; Oct–Mar Tue–Sat, check hours online), in

A FEW SHOPS ALONG THE WAY

We're not big shoppers but we do have a few favourites – independents one and all.

20 Castle Street 20 Castle St, DG1 1DR ☏ 07712 130204 f. Well-chosen and interesting selection of antique, vintage and contemporary furniture, artworks, gifts and beautiful items for the home.

The Dumfries Larder 170–172 High St, DG1 2BA ☏ 01387 268410 f. Offers a range of food and drink from around the region and specialises in cheese.

TB Watson Ltd 11 English St, DG1 2BU ☏ 01387 256601 🖰 drambusters.com. Established in 1909, the company has been through several incarnations but now specialises in wines and spirits, with a vast range of whiskies. The shop's neatly named website is very good and has a selection of over 500 whiskies.

The Yellow Door 16-22 Queen St, DG1 2JF ☏ 01387 259338 f. Gallery/exhibition space, bringing a run-down Victorian building back into use, with changing exhibitions featuring lots of local artists and crafts people, and a programme of events.

which the poet and his wife lived from 1793 until his death in 1796, although Jean continued living there until her death in 1834. The house was bought in 1851 by their son Colonel William Burns and placed in the hands of trustees. The four rooms that make up the house are open to the public and contain a range of period furniture, portraits and personal items.

Turn right out of Robert Burns House and continue down the road to the junction with Shakespeare Street, appropriately named for up to the right is the **16 Theatre Royal**, built in 1792 and now the oldest working theatre in Scotland. From here it's a short stroll back down to Whitesands and the river, or alternatively turn up the high street to take in some more Burns sights (see box, page 112).

FOOD & DRINK

As you'd expect in a town of this size, there are venues and flavours for every occasion.

The Douglas Arms 75 Friars Vennel, DG1 2RQ daytime & eves. Known locally as the Dougie; cosy bar with open fire and a good range of beers; often has live music.

The Frothy Bike Co. 77–78 Whitesands, DG1 2RX 01387 248770 thefrothybikeco.com daytime only. You don't have to be a cyclist to get a kick out of Ross Anderson and Lucy Ryvar's bike shop cum café, a bright open space with views across the Nith to the park. Interesting and tasty food – healthy breakfasts and lunches – and a relaxed, slightly hip atmosphere. This is no greasy spoon: bacon is notable by its absence; instead there's homemade soup, halloumi, a superfood salad, baked sweet potato and a Buddha Bowl (wild rice, homemade kimchi and veg, sesame seeds and lime). The smoothies go down well, too.

The Globe Inn 56 High St, DG1 2JA 01387 323010 globeinndumfries.co.uk daytime & eves; see ad, 4th colour section. Robert Burns's favourite drinking spot has recently been refurbished and offers an atmospheric restaurant for lunch and dinner: smoked venison sandwich with truffle mayonnaise, pulled Galloway brisket in a BBQ marinade, and passionfruit delice could all feature on the menu. Whisky lovers will be in their element with 242 to choose from.

Home Rugmans Hall, 92 Whitesands, DG1 2RX 07896 355074 Home restaurant eves only. (Relocation is planned, check the Facebook page.) A Mediterranean-, European- and Scottish-influenced menu with vegetarian, vegan and gluten-free options. The choice is interesting and the quality top notch. One of the region's best restaurants.

The Jaggy Thistle Bistro Robert Burns Centre, Mill Rd, DG2 7BE 01387 320102 daytime only. Café by day, bistro by evening; perfect for lunch or afternoon tea outside overlooking the river on a sunny day, or for a hot dog to take into a movie.

Moat Brae George St, DG1 1EA ✆ 01387 255549 peterpanmoatbrae.org ⊙ daytime only. Delightfully bright café overlooking the Neverland Garden in Scotland's National Centre for Children's Literature and Storytelling (see box, page 116). Teas, coffees, cakes, scones, soups, sandwiches and daily specials.

Mrs Green's Tea Lounge 16 Queensberry St, DG1 1EX ✆ 01387 814268 ⊙ daytime only. Their description of themselves on their Facebook page says it all: 'emporium of delicious food and all manner of cakey loveliness'.

Pizzeria il Fiume Dock Park, DG1 2RY ✆ 01387 265154 pizza-pasta.co.uk ⊙ eves only. A family-run Italian restaurant (complete with wood-fired oven) that's been going for over 40 years, specialising in pizza, pasta, chargrilled steaks and seafood.

The Stove 100 High St, DG1 2BJ ✆ 01387 252435 thestove.org ⊙ daytime only. Community-based arts organisation with a popular café at the heart of the high street. Good coffee and food, great space, worthwhile ethos.

The Usual Place Academy St, DG1 1BZ ✆ 01387 253485 theusualplace.org ⊙ daytime only. Innovative and award-winning café occupying a former church that provides opportunities for young people with additional needs. Breakfast, lunch and afternoon teas. From porridge to ploughman's; toast to teacakes.

Your Sweet Home 42 Brooke St, DG1 2JL ✆ 07871 387107 ⊙ daytime only. Tucked away down a residential street a few minutes' walk from the high street, Mirka Dratwinska's cute tea room and café is a wee gem of a place. Sandwiches and healthy homemade soups are available for lunch – the latter might include anything from a dish from Mirka's native Poland such as cream of tomato with rice to Hungarian *bogracz* (goulash soup). The real speciality here, though, is cake, which comes in all shapes and sizes. The warm apple and cinnamon is mouth-wateringly good.

BEYOND THE TOWN CENTRE

Lying just north of Dumfries centre, in a peaceful setting on the banks of Cluden Water (but rather swallowed by the surrounding housing estate) where it joins the Nith, are the remains of **Lincluden Collegiate Church** (NY966779 ⊙ Apr–Sep 09.30–17.30 daily, last entry 17.00; Oct–Mar 10.00–16.00 daily, last entry 15.30; Historic Environment Scotland). Originally an earthenwork castle, or motte, stood on this naturally defensive site, which was gifted to a house of Benedictine nuns who founded a convent here in 1164. What remains are the ruins of the original chapel and adjoining domestic quarters, worth a visit for their history and architecture (the choir is one of the finest examples of Gothic architecture in Scotland). In the 14th century the nuns were turfed out by Archibald the Grim, Lord of Galloway, who had his sights set on what he saw as a nobler cause: himself, his family and his descendants, prayers for whom were to be said by the priests who replaced the nuns. To achieve his aim, Archibald persuaded the pope to effect the change on the basis that the nuns were running a house of questionable morals, diverting the resources afforded to them to dress their daughters 'born in incest' in the best clothes.

From (or to) Lincluden there is access to the riverside path on the west bank of Cluden Water and the Nith. Robert Burns used to walk here on the east side, on a path that now runs from central Dumfries to Dalscone a little further on, and the route is still known as **Burns Walk**. It was here in 1794 that he wrote the revised version of *Ca the Yowes tae the Knowes* ('Call the Ewes to the Knolls'), one of his most haunting songs, with its reference to Cluden Water.

If driving to Lincluden, access is off the A76 Kilmarnock road to your right as you head away from Dumfries. One oddity to keep an eye open for is the **Lincluden Rhinoceros**, a model of a rhinoceros and baby that sits atop what looks like a storage container. In days past this was an art installation on top of a bus stop. When the bus stop was removed, there was such an outcry over the loss of the rhinoceros that it was reinstalled in its present location.

To the northeast of the centre, ten to 15 minutes' walk away, is **Gracefield Arts Centre** (28 Edinburgh Rd, DG1 1JQ ⏲ varying hours for exhibitions, café & craft shop Tue–Sat, check website for details), home to an impressive collection of between 600 and 700 Scottish paintings from 1700 onwards, including pieces by the Glasgow Boys (see box, page 182) and Elizabeth Blackadder, a selection of which are on display at any one time. There are also two temporary exhibition spaces, a shop and café (⏲ Tue–Sat), all set in pleasant grounds in which further works are on display, including a sculpture by Andy Goldsworthy (see box, page 97).

"The Lincluden Rhinoceros is a model of a rhinoceros and baby that sits atop what looks like a storage container."

Further out of town to the northeast, flying and plane enthusiasts head for the **Dumfries and Galloway Aviation Museum** (Heathhall Industrial Estate, Heathhall DG1 3PH NY000785 01387 251623 dumfriesaviationmuseum.com ⏲ seasonal on selected days), accessible by bike from Dumfries using the Caledonian Cycle Route or the regular No 2 bus service from the town centre (with a ten- to

15-minute walk). Even if planes aren't your thing, there's a wealth of historical detail here about Dumfries and Galloway during the war which makes for fascinating reading and combines well with a visit to the Devil's Porridge (page 59) to build up a picture of wartime life in the region.

East of town on the road that runs down the eastern side of the Nith estuary is **Castledykes Park**, once the site of Dumfries Castle and now a landscaped hillside retreat with pleasant tree-shaded grounds and a sunken garden with an imposing statue of Robert the Bruce. It's a good spot to let the kids run around.

FOOD & DRINK

Casa Mia 53 Nunholm Rd, DG1 1JW ✆ 01387 269619 www.casamiadumfries.co.uk ⏲ lunch & dinner. In a peaceful setting, this is an old Dumfries favourite offering a smart but relaxed dining experience and a Mediterranean- and Scottish-inspired menu. Booking recommended.

Easterbrook Bistro The Crichton, Bankend Rd, DG1 4TL ✆ 01387 702500 easterbrookbistro.co.uk ⏲ brunch, lunch, afternoon tea & dinner. Bar, restaurant, pool and spa (and beauty treatments, too) in a delightful setting on the Crichton campus, south of the town centre.

Hubbub Gracefield Arts Centre, 28 Edinburgh Rd, DG1 1JQ ✆ 01387 262084 ⏲ 10.00–15.30 Tue–Sat. A good option if you want to combine a meal with a gallery visit. Wholesome soups, sandwiches, cakes and scones.

Kilnford Barns Farm Shop and Restaurant Kilnford Barns, The Glen, DG2 8PT ✆ 01387 253087 kilnford.co.uk ⏲ daily. Located on the western edge of Dumfries. The Rome family have farmed around Kilnford for over 300 years and, in transforming their derelict barns into a shop and restaurant, have continued a tradition of supplying local food that started generations ago. It's a good place for kids, too, with a nature trail, bird hide and wildlife pond, and an outdoor play area.

NITH ESTUARY: EAST SIDE

From Dumfries centre it doesn't take long to reach a different world down the east side of the Nith, an agricultural area that feels rural virtually from the instant you cross the town boundary. This short stretch of countryside, no more than ten or so miles, links to the southern end of Annandale and with its quiet outlook across the Nith estuary stands in notable contrast to the life of the town on its doorstep.

Views to Criffel and the merse (saltmarsh) on the west side of the Nith abound, with plenty of opportunities for birdwatching and retreating into the quiet, gentle landscape.

Immediately south of Dumfries, **Kingholm Quay** was originally part of the town's port. It's a quiet spot now with a popular local pub (see below). Downstream another three or four miles lies **Glencaple**, where a row of cottages strung out along the waterside makes for an attractive setting and an enticing café/restaurant (see below) awaits on the quayside. The views of and across the Nith estuary to Criffel and Kirkconnell Merse are superb and many an hour can be whiled away on the riverbanks watching birds, enjoying the ever-changing light and keeping an eye open for otters. Come at the right time and you'll also catch the **tidal bore** as it sweeps up the Nith. Glencaple's history as a port is commemorated in the novel and attractive oak boat benches that line the road south of the café, on which words and pictures have been created out of flattened nail heads. One bench notes the fact that 'Enough tea leaves were landed here to make 14 million cups of tea'!

FOOD & DRINK

The Boathouse Quayside, Glencaple DG1 4RE ✆ 01387 770673 theboathouseglencaple.com. Has a splendid setting on the quay, with great views up and down the Nith and across the water to Criffel. Operates as a café daily – serving more than your average café fare – and as a restaurant with a mouthwatering menu on Friday and Saturday evenings. Extremely popular, booking recommended. Gluten-free, vegan and vegetarian options available.

The Swan Kingholm Quay, DG1 4SU ✆ 01387 253756 theswandumfries.co.uk. In a pleasant waterside setting, open from lunchtime onwards, offering a sizeable and varied menu with several vegetarian options. Lots of tables but can be very busy at weekends.

CAERLAVEROCK

Wildfowl and Wetlands Trust Caerlaverock (page 261)

The Caerlaverock Estate, owned by the Lords Herries of Terregles, covers 5,200 acres on the east side of the Nith, encompasses the villages of Glencaple (see above) and Bankend, and includes several farms which incorporate arable land, permanent pasture, wetlands and woodlands. The estate also includes part of the Caerlaverock National Nature Reserve managed by Scottish Natural Heritage, part of which is in turn managed by the Wildfowl and Wetlands Trust (WWT). For visitors, the main attractions are walking and wildlife watching, and visiting the splendid **Caerlaverock Castle**, dating from the 13th century and now in the care of Historic Environment Scotland. Details of the area can be found on the Caerlaverock Community Association website caerlaverock.org.uk and the Caerlaverock Estate Facebook page, as well as the websites of the WWT and Historic Environment Scotland, and from Scotland's National Nature Reserves.

Caerlaverock Church (NY025692) stands on its own at the end of a lane, through a farm, off the Bankend Road, 1½ miles east of Glencaple. It's notable as the burial place of Robert Paterson, immortalised by Sir Walter Scott as **Old Mortality** (page 145), who spent his later years wandering southern Scotland carving gravestones to mark the burial sites of Covenanters.

Caerlaverock National Nature Reserve

nnr-scotland.org.uk

Covering almost 20,000 acres, Caerlaverock National Nature Reserve is a vast flat expanse of sand, sea, mud and merse (saltmarsh) stretching almost ten miles along the Solway Coast south of Dumfries. Around 85% of the area is made up of tidal flats and mudbanks that disappear at high tide. This is a haven for wildlife of all sorts, from birds to the rare natterjack toad and the even more obscure tadpole shrimp, a freshwater crustacean that has existed for over 200 million years and which, until its discovery at Caerlaverock in 1994, was thought to exist in only one location in the UK. The name Caerlaverock is derived from the old Scots for a skylark – a laverock – thus Caerlaverock is either 'castle of the lark' or 'lark's nest'. No surprise then that every year there are over 300 pairs of skylarks here.

"This is a haven for wildlife of all sorts, from birds to the natterjack toad and the even more obscure tadpole shrimp."

This is a truly special place. Unlike many other firths, the **Solway Firth** remains in a largely natural state, undisturbed for the main and, for the birds that return year after year, a vast natural larder on the saltmarshes and mudflats. Local farmers subscribe to the ethos of the area, too, providing safe grazing for geese in their fields, with any costs incurred being met by the Solway Goose Management Scheme managed by Scottish Natural Heritage.

Visitors can access both the nature reserve generally, which is free of charge, and the WWT reserve, for which either membership is required or an admission fee is charged for non-members. Travelling south down the estuary from Dumfries, once past Glencaple there are one or two waterside benches where it's possible to stop off, but the main parking area for the nature reserve is at Castle Corner (see box, opposite) roughly halfway between Glencaple and the turning for Caerlaverock Castle. From here there are walks into the reserve, where a good hide is located with views across the flatlands to the Solway. It's a peaceful spot and a great area simply to wander the paths.

2 WWT Caerlaverock Wetland Centre

Eastpark Farm, DG1 4RS NY051656 01387 770200 wwt.org.uk 10.00–17.00 daily except 25 Dec, last entry 16.00

Caerlaverock Wetland Centre lies at the end of a lane a short distance on from the turning to Caerlaverock Castle and was the second WWT centre to be opened by Sir Peter Scott after Slimbridge in Gloucestershire. The centre occupies what were the outbuildings of Eastpark Farm and WWT manages the saltmarsh part of the larger nature reserve: 1,500 acres of mainly saltmarsh and goose grazing fields. It's an international place, with connections around the world. In winter the Icelandic and Norwegian flags are flown, the former for the whooper swans and the latter for the barnacle geese, for it is to the Solway coast each year that the entire population – all 40,000 of them – returns from Svalbard, around 10,000 of which are usually to be found in the WWT reserve. Several bird hides offer good vantage points, and the Sir Peter Scott Observatory is an impressive state-of-the-art facility at the whooper swan pond, complete with touchscreen swan database, very funky swan wallpaper that reproduces in exact detail the markings and identification tags of a number of swans, and an audio system that facilitates commentated feedings each day during the season (late autumn and winter).

WWT Caerlaverock is, in our view, one of the absolute highlights of Dumfries and Galloway. If you have an ounce of interest in wildlife, or simply in being outdoors in a beautiful place, you could easily lose yourself for a day – or longer – here. And kids will love it, too. There are family events throughout the year, balance beams and stepping stones, pond dipping in the summer, and a tower to be climbed that offers terrific views over the wetlands and that houses what are believed to be the largest binoculars in Scotland (not yet restored, but they're working on raising the funds for it). There are trails to be followed and nests to be spotted, evening events and occasional walks accompanied by rangers. And when it all gets too much, you can always retreat to the Cathan Coffee Shop in the visitor centre.

Caerlaverock Castle & wetlands

OS Explorer 322; start: Castle Corner NY018652; accessible by bus from Dumfries; 5 miles; easy to moderate, some inclines & boggy bits.

This walk offers sweeping views of the Solway Firth with mile upon mile of wetlands, a fine castle ruin, remains of an Iron Age fort, and year-round wildlife highlights.

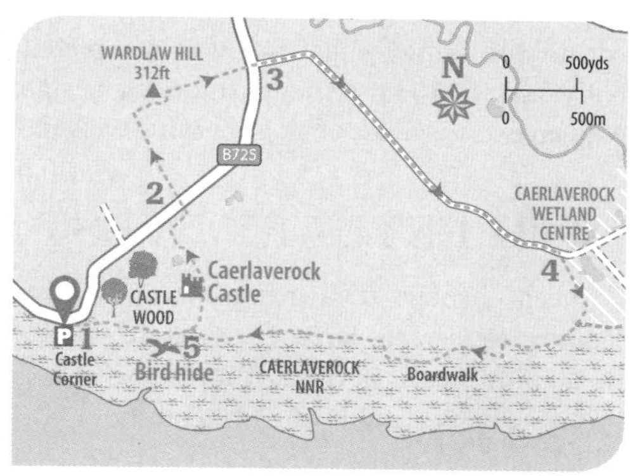

From **1 Castle Corner** follow the footpath right, passing through the gnarled oaks of Castle Wood, where in summer you'll see beautiful Scotch argus butterflies. Once you reach a couple of cottages, the path becomes a track, and soon arrives at the impressive triangular Caerlaverock Castle (page 128).

Leave the castle by the main gate and, at the **2 junction** with the road, go straight over and follow the footpath up Wardlaw Hill. It might only stand at 312ft but, with few high points on the estuary, it provides far-reaching views across the Solway Firth and to Cumbria beyond. Pass around the right side of the hill, taking the footpath to descend through a field and down to the road.

Go straight across the **3 road** and follow the lane down to WWT Caerlaverock Wetland Centre (just under 2 miles away), where a tea room, information centre and fine nature reserve await (see opposite).

From **4 the WWT**, take the often-boggy track to the right immediately before the entrance to the centre and then continue through a gate on the right. The path runs between two fences across fields before reaching the Flooders boardwalk, which passes through the reeds.

Keep following the boardwalk along the merse to the **5 nonagonal** (nine-sided with equal sides and angles) **bird hide** and turn left to soon rejoin the woodland path and return to the start.

3 Caerlaverock Castle

Glencaple DG1 4RU NY025656 Apr–Sep 09.30–17.30 daily, last entry 17.00; Oct–Mar 10.00–16.00 daily, last entry 15.30; closed 25–26 Dec, 1–2 Jan; Historic Environment Scotland; free to members

Next door to WWT Caerlaverock stands the distinctive, red-pink sandstone Caerlaverock Castle, which can be reached by a one-mile waterside path from the wetlands centre or by car. Another great place for kids, this is a castle as you imagine castles should be, with moat, bridge, rooms to run through, towers to climb, and intriguing corners to explore. What's more, it boasts an unusual design as it is triangular, believed to be built on a triangular piece of rock.

Of all the additions and alterations to the castle, perhaps the most impressive is the **Nithsdale Lodging**, an ornately embellished range within the castle walls that was completed by Robert, first Earl of Nithsdale, in 1634. It's an extraordinary sight, a Renaissance frontage with an extravagance of stone carving within the confines of this fortress.

NITH ESTUARY: WEST SIDE

To keep chapters to a manageable size, we have stretched the 'Nith Estuary' to reach as far as Crocketford to the west on the main A75 and then south as far as the RSPB reserve at Mersehead. Strictly speaking this area comes under the old county of Kirkcudbrightshire, much of which equates with the Stewartry (page 134). However, access is easy from Dumfries and it also brings a more rounded view of the Nith estuary as a whole. It's an area of much scenic variety and interest, with a history that incorporates a couple of crannogs at Lochrutton and Milton Loch (although there is little to be seen), the Old Military Road that was previously the main route west, the birthplace of the 'Father of the American Navy', and arguably the most romantic abbey ruin in the country. Cycling is popular, notably at Mabie Forest, part of the 7stanes scheme, and so too is walking, not least to the top of Criffel, only just under 1,900ft high but one of the most prominent hills in Scotland.

WEST OF DUMFRIES

Between the A75 to Crocketford and A711 to Dalbeattie runs the **Old Military Road**, marked as such on OS maps and featured in many cycle routes in this area. **Crannogs** have been identified at **Lochrutton Loch** just south of Lochfield and **Milton Loch** between Crocketford and Milton. The former was excavated in 1901 and the latter in 1953 after being revealed while the level of the loch was lowered. Finds from both are now held at Dumfries Museum (page 118). At nearby **Crocketford**, also known as Nine Mile Bar as it is exactly halfway between Dumfries and Castle Douglas, are local amenities, including a shop and post office, and the convenient watering hole and restaurant of the Galloway Arms Hotel. Curiously, Crocketford owes its existence to the arrival in the late 18th century of the strange sect known as the Buchanites, at the centre of which was one Mrs Elspeth Buchan, who claimed to be immortal but whose death in 1791 disproved her.

"One Mrs Elspeth Buchan, who claimed to be immortal but whose death in 1791 disproved her."

South of Milton off a quiet back road is **Drumcoltran Tower** (NX869684 year-round; free; Historic Environment Scotland), a fine example of a 16th-century tower house, the traditional home of the Scottish landowner. Once owned by the Maxwell family who held the lairdship of Caerlaverock (see opposite) and Threave (page 156) castles and many other estates in the region, today it stands on private farm land, but there is access from the road up a fenced pathway. Generally quiet and relatively undiscovered, much can still be seen of how life here would have been lived. Kids will particularly enjoy climbing up the stairs all the way to the top, where you can get out on to the roof for views of the surrounding area.

Northeast of Drumcoltran lies **Beeswing**, a small village notable for its name. Originally called Lochend (in reference to nearby Loch Arthur), in the 19th century the local inn was purchased by a racehorse owner who renamed the village in honour of the eponymous British thoroughbred racehorse who won 51 out of 63 races between 1835 and 1842. Next to the village is the very popular **Loch Arthur Camphill Community Creamery and Farmshop** (NX899688).

FOOD & DRINK

Loch Arthur Camphill Community Creamery and Farmshop Beeswing DG2 8JQ 01387 259669 locharthur.org.uk Mon–Sat. Sells all manner of organic goodies and serves delicious teas, coffees and fuller meals from a purpose-built, light and airy shop and restaurant. The outdoor tables are particularly sheltered on a sunny day. Always popular. One of our favourites.

4 MABIE FOREST

A few miles south of Dumfries on the road to New Abbey lies Mabie Forest (NX949712), a Forestry and Land Scotland site and one of the 7stanes biking centres (page 15). Mabie is also one of only three reserves that come under the care of Butterfly Conservation Scotland, and 20 of Scotland's 32 butterfly species can be found here, including the scarce pearl-bordered fritillary (*Boloria euphrosyne*). There's plenty to see and do, with **walking** and **biking trails** to suit all abilities, picnic tables, a children's adventure playground, and lots of wildlife. There's also a hide at Lochaber Loch. During one visit in May we spotted several pearl-bordered fritillary as well as various day-flying moths, plus the big hairy black and ginger caterpillar (commonly known as 'woolly bears') of the night-flying garden tiger moth (*Arctia caja*). We also came across a surprisingly tame roe deer. There are some fine trees, too. Although this is managed land, it's not just plantation, but also mixed woodland, which includes a sizeable sequoia and a wide range of trees that provide a more variable habitat.

The main car park (pay parking) at Mabie is accessed from the A710 between Dumfries and New Abbey. Note that there is a sign into Mabie Farm Park just before the turning into Mabie Forest (which shares an entrance with the Mabie House Hotel), but there is no vehicle access to the forest from the farm park.

5 NEW ABBEY

Romantic souls will be in their element at New Abbey, a small village that nuzzles up to the northern shoulder of Criffel where it drops to the flat plain of the western side of the Nith. Quaint and historic, its neat rows of houses sit within what would have been the grounds of the Cistercian New Abbey itself, founded in 1273 and so-called to distinguish it from the then 120-year-old Dundrennan Abbey (page 189). The abbey is now known by the much lovelier name of **Sweetheart Abbey** (Apr–Sep 09.30–17.30 daily, last entry 17.00; Oct–Mar 10.00–16.00 daily except Thu & Fri, last entry 15.30; closed 25–26 Dec, 1–2 Jan; Historic Environment Scotland; free to members) thanks to the good Lady Devorgilla (see box, opposite). When her beloved husband died, she not only founded the abbey but also had his heart embalmed in a casket that she carried with her wherever she went until it was buried here with her on her death in 1290. The monks subsequently rechristened the abbey

LADY DEVORGILLA

Few women are as well remembered in Dumfries and Galloway as Devorgilla, Lady of Galloway. Born in 1210, at the age of 13 she was married to John, Baron de Balliol of Barnard Castle in Durham, who in 1263 founded Balliol College in Oxford. Devorgilla was educated, intelligent and took an active role in public life, founding Greyfriars Convent in Dumfries as well as endowing Balliol College after her husband's death with enough money to ensure its future. With John Balliol she became one of the largest landowners in Europe, and on his death she founded and built the abbey at New Abbey (see opposite), south of Dumfries, in his memory. She was descended on her mother's side from the kings of Scotland, and her son John was briefly king, albeit known as 'toom tabbard' or 'puppet king' to Edward I. Her grandson, John's son Edward Balliol, was also king, while another grandson was John III Comyn, 'Red Comyn', who was murdered by Robert the Bruce in 1306.

dulce cor, meaning 'sweet heart'. A good portion of the abbey can still be seen today. The nave, at 112ft long, is particularly impressive with its parade of pillars and arches.

Following restoration, the water-powered **New Abbey Corn Mill** (⏲ Apr–Sep 09.30–17.30 daily, last entry 17.00; Oct–Mar 10.00–16.00 daily except Thu & Fri, last entry 15.30; closed 25–26 Dec, 1–2 Jan; Historic Environment Scotland; free to members) at the opposite end of the main street is now in full working order (demonstrations in summer only). The neat whitewashed buildings are picturesquely positioned next to a duck pond and contain all the fixtures and fittings as they were left over half a century ago.

FOOD & DRINK

Abbey Cottage Tearoom 26 Main St, DG2 8BY ☎ 01387 850377 🖱 abbeycottagetearoom.com. A convenient stop right next to Sweetheart Abbey, with a gift shop attached.

NEW ABBEY TO MERSEHEAD

The coastal road south from New Abbey, at the foot of Criffel, offers heavenly views of the Nith estuary, with a good stopping place at **Drumburn viewpoint** (⚲ NX980618) looking out to where the Nith meets the Solway. From here you can see to Wardlaw Wood, site of the Roman fort above Caerlaverock on the other side of the Nith, and south across Carse Sands to Carsethorn. Immediately south is **Drummains Reedbed**, part of the Solway Site of Special Scientific Interest (SSSI) and

Special Area of Conservation, managed by the Scottish Wildlife Trust. The coastal reedbed, saltmarsh and mudflats support wildfowl and waders and are good places to spot sedge warbler and reed bunting. The access path is roughly one mile north of Kirkbean on the A710; park on the grassy verge.

At **Kirkbean** the village church is noted primarily as the burial place of the father of John Paul Jones (see below). Kirkbean developed as an estate village for nearby Arbigland House and if you're visiting the area you may want to dip into the excellent website of the Kirkbean Parish Heritage Society (kirkbean.org), which offers a wealth of information.

Head out to the coast from Kirkbean, a mile or so northeast, to **Carsethorn**, a picture-postcard village with a row of cottages strung along the waterfront and a popular pub (see below). It was once a historic port, and during the late 18th and early 19th centuries there were frequent sailings from here to the American and Australian colonies.

FOOD & DRINK

Steamboat Inn Carsethorn DG2 8DS 01387 880631 thesteamboatinn.co.uk. A great waterfront location combined with thoroughly good and filling meals from local produce, especially – and appropriately – fish. Can be busy.

6 Arbigland & the John Paul Jones Cottage Museum

NX987572 www.jpj.demon.co.uk Apr–Sep 10.30–17.00

A mile or so southeast from Kirkbean in the grounds of Arbigland Estate is the John Paul Jones Cottage Museum, the birthplace on 6 July 1747 of the man who was to become a naval hero of the American Revolution and who is regarded as the 'Father of the American Navy'. Born the son of an Arbigland worker, his birth name was simply John Paul, but he changed it to John Jones, and subsequently to John Paul Jones, after killing the ringleader of a mutiny in the West Indies in 1773 and fleeing to Virginia. Although he died at the age of just 45, his career was both distinguished and controversial, ranging from his seaman's apprenticeship at the age of 13 (sailing from Whitehaven, on the southern side of the Solway) to championing and fighting for the colonists in the American Revolution. In Britain he became regarded as something of a pirate, a reputation that was only enhanced after his victory in 1779 at Flamborough Head.

Jones died in Paris in 1792 and his body then lay in an alcohol-filled coffin in an unmarked grave for over a century until, under the orders of President Roosevelt, a search was undertaken and it was rediscovered. He was finally laid to rest in 1913 in the chapel at Annapolis Naval Academy on Chesapeake Bay, east of Washington DC.

The cottage is furnished in 1700s style and presents the story of Jones' life through audio headsets and an audio-visual presentation of his most-famous battle at Flamborough Head. There's also a reconstruction of the cabin of his man o' war, *Bonhomme Richard*, and an exhibition gallery and shop.

Arbigland House and Gardens (🖱 arbiglandhouseandgardens.co.uk) are open to the public, the former by appointment for a guided tour of the principle rooms of the 18th-century house, the latter by ticket (Apr–Sep noon–last entry 16.30 daily). Among the gardens' many features are a Broad Walk from the house to the beach, a sunken rose garden and a Japanese garden with a variety of acers and cherries.

A few minutes' walk from the gardens takes you to **Powillimount beach** (parking available), a lovely spot looking straight across the Solway and with views to **Southerness lighthouse**, the oldest in Galloway but sadly long since decommissioned. The rocky beach offers lots of space when the tide is out and if you head along it to the left you'll reach the Thirl Stane natural sandstone arch. Although the name Southerness may seem appropriate for the location, it is actually a corruption of Satterness, derived from Salterness, the saltworks of which were given by Roland, Lord of Galloway, in the 12th century to the monks of Holmcultram (now the village of Abbeytown), on the other side of the Solway in Cumbria.

7 RSPB Mersehead

Mersehead Farm, Southwick DG2 8AH 📍 NX925560 ☎ 01387 780579 🖱 rspb.org.uk
🕒 dawn–dusk daily; visitor centre 10.00–16.00 daily

A couple of miles from Southerness is an extensive wetland and saltmarsh area supporting a range of bird species, including lapwing, reed warbler and, in autumn and winter, pintails and large numbers of barnacle geese. Harbour porpoises, otters and natterjack toads are also found. A small visitor centre by the car park offers information, self-service teas and a cosy viewing area looking out over the merse. Coastal and wetland nature trails, the latter including a couple of hides, are an ideal way to get out into the reserve. Mersehead is a SSSI and Ramsar site.

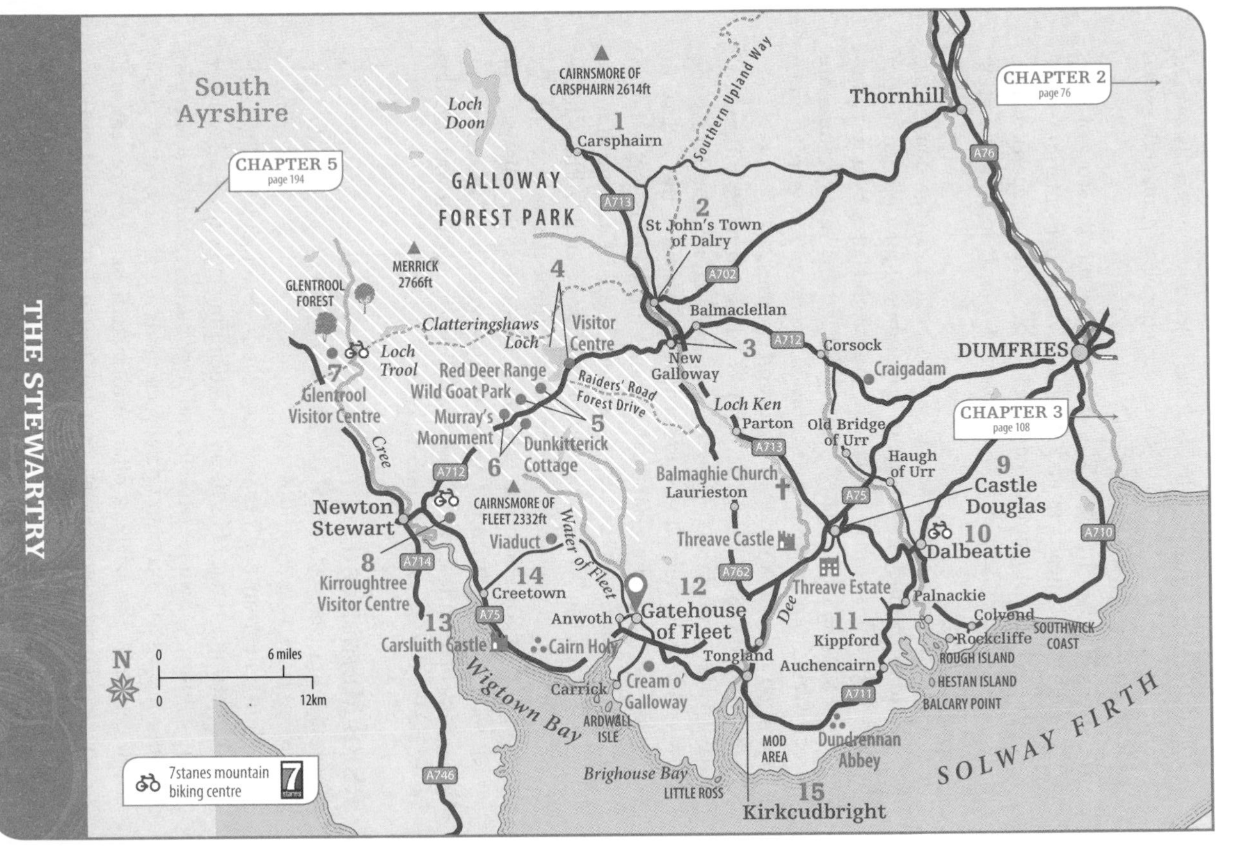
THE STEWARTRY
South Ayrshire
CHAPTER 5 page 194
CHAPTER 2 page 76
CHAPTER 3 page 108
Loch Doon
CAIRNSMORE OF CARSPHAIRN 2614ft
1 Carsphairn
Southern Upland Way
Thornhill
A76
A713
GALLOWAY FOREST PARK
2 St John's Town of Dalry
A702
MERRICK 2766ft
GLENTROOL FOREST
4
Clatteringshaws Loch
Visitor Centre
Balmaclellan
3
New Galloway
A712
Corsock
Craigadam
DUMFRIES
Loch Trool
7 Glentrool Visitor Centre
Red Deer Range
Wild Goat Park
Raiders' Road Forest Drive
5
Murray's Monument
Dunkitterick Cottage
6
Loch Ken
Parton
A713
Old Bridge of Urr
Haugh of Urr
Cree
A712
Balmaghie Church
Laurieston
9 Castle Douglas
A75
CAIRNSMORE OF FLEET 2332ft
Newton Stewart
Threave Castle
10 Dalbeattie
A710
Water of Fleet
Viaduct
8 Kirroughtree Visitor Centre
A714
A762
Threave Estate
14 Creetown
12 Gatehouse of Fleet
Palnackie
Dee
Anwoth
11 Kippford
Colvend
SOUTHWICK COAST
A75
13 Carsluith Castle
Cairn Holy
Rockcliffe
Tongland
ROUGH ISLAND
Auchencairn
N
0 6 miles
0 12km
Wigtown Bay
Carrick
Cream o' Galloway
HESTAN ISLAND
A711
BALCARY POINT
ARDWALL ISLE
MOD AREA
Dundrennan Abbey
SOLWAY FIRTH
7stanes mountain biking centre
A746
Brighouse Bay
LITTLE ROSS
15 Kirkcudbright

4
THE STEWARTRY

Blessed with fine hill and coastal landscapes, replete with history, overflowing with anecdotes and tales of characters past and present, and the location of some of Dumfries and Galloway's most attractive towns – the Stewartry has it all. No wonder that those in the know return to it time and again. It is varied and big, stretching from the north of the wild Glenkens down to the rocky bays of the Kirkcudbright coast, and it would be easy to spend a week in any one of the five different locales into which we have split this chapter, let alone take the time to discover the others.

The name – 'Stewartry' – is a corruption of 'Steward', dating from the 14th century when a steward was appointed by Archibald the Grim, Lord of Galloway, to collect revenues.

The area is the location of the **Galloway Hydroelectric Scheme**, built in the 1930s and consisting of a network of dams and power stations. Much of it falls within the Glenkens, but you will spot the striking Modernist power stations all the way down to the valley of the Dee at Tongland. This is an area with a strong literary heritage, too, the glorious scenery inspiring John Buchan and Dorothy L Sayers to set books here, not to mention local author S R Crockett. And this is the place to come for the **Galloway Kite Trail**, with opportunities to see these impressive birds at close quarters.

A history rich in smuggling characterises the coastal strip. Between Southerness in the east and Fleet Bay in the west there are some 30 bays and coves. This is one of the most stunning stretches of coast in Scotland, yet many parts of it remain relatively undiscovered and it is not unknown to have a beach to yourself. Alternatively, if you prefer wilder places, the Stewartry is also the location of the enormous **Galloway Forest Park**, the country's first Dark Sky Park and a remote and invigorating landscape of moorland and mountains.

TOURIST INFORMATION

There are no VisitScotland information centres in the Stewartry. However, there are several centres run by local communities and staffed by volunteer teams. In addition to the places listed below, there is plenty of information and a good stock of leaflets available from the helpful staff at **The CatStrand Arts Centre** in New Galloway (page 144). There are also three visitor centres in Galloway Forest Park, details of which can be found on pages 149 and 115.

Dalbeattie Visitor Information and Craft Centre 24 High St, Dalbeattie DG5 4AA ✆ 01556 612752 🖱 dalbeattiematters.net 🕒 Apr–late Dec 10.00–16.00 Mon–Sat

Gatehouse of Fleet Tourist Information Centre Mill on the Fleet, High St, Gatehouse of Fleet DG7 2HS ✆ 01557 814099 🖱 millonthefleet.co.uk 🕒 mid-Mar–Oct 10.00–17.00 daily

Heart of Galloway Visitor Centre Market Hill car park, Castle Douglas DG7 1AE ✆ 01556 503918 🖱 castledouglas.info 🕒 Easter–Oct 10.00–17.00 Mon–Sat, winter 10.00–16.00 Mon–Sat

Kirkcudbright Information Centre Harbour Sq, Kirkcudbright DG6 4HY ✆ 01557 330494 🖱 kirkcudbright.town 🕒 Apr–Oct 10.00–17.00 daily, Nov–Mar reduced hours

GETTING AROUND

The Stewartry feels a bit like an area of two halves. The Glenkens to the north is a place of fewer main roads, crossed by the A713 and A712, and dominated by hills and remote moors dotted with small towns and communities. Closer to the coast the main A75 cuts east to west, bypassing Castle Douglas, Kirkcudbright and Gatehouse of Fleet, all of which are worth visiting.

For something a bit different, a classic car can be hired to explore the area from **Kippford Classic Car Hire** (🖱 kippfordclassiccarhire.co.uk); a Triumph Herald convertible, Morris Minor and VW Camper are available.

PUBLIC TRANSPORT

The Stewartry has no train service; the nearest stations are at Dumfries to the east and Stranraer to the west. Given its central location in Dumfries and Galloway, **bus services** offer a better option for criss-crossing the area, with numerous services connecting with the railway stations. The fastest service is the 500/X75 Stranraer to Carlisle, stopping at key points along the main A75. From the east, the 501/502 from Dumfries can drop you at Castle Douglas and further down at Kirkcudbright. From the west, the 431/517 also terminates at Kirkcudbright coming from Gatehouse of Fleet. The 520 runs to key points northwards from Castle Douglas through New Galloway, St Johns Town of Dalry and on into Ayrshire. Local public transport information is provided by South West of Scotland Transport Partnership (swestrans.org.uk), or alternatively Traveline (0871 2002233 traveline.info).

CYCLING

Quiet coastal lanes, upland tracks and mountain biking trails are typical in this area of green farmland, secluded moors and forestry plantation, the latter dotted with native woods. Much of the area is pleasantly rolling, but there are also many more challenging spots for those looking to work the legs a bit harder. There are two world-class **mountain biking centres** at Kirroughtree and Dalbeattie (7stanesmountainbiking.com). Forestry and Land Scotland's Kirroughtree Visitor Centre has **cycle hire** (page 151), along with some of the best technical single track in the country. Dalbeattie, with its coastal setting and smaller hills, has a relaxed feel but is not without rocky outcrops and fine views. See Dumfries and Galloway Council's Core Paths pages on their website for downloadable cycle routes (info.dumgal.gov.uk/mapviewers/pathsmap.aspx.

Many sections of the Southern Upland Way make for excellent mountain biking, particularly the forest tracks and single-track roads; however, the unsurfaced sections over grassy hillsides can be too boggy to cycle. Further details can be found at southernuplandway.gov.uk/explore/cycling.

CYCLE HIRE

The Break Pad Kirroughtree Visitor Centre, DG8 7BE 01671 401303 thebreakpad.com Apr–Oct daily; Nov–Mar Wed–Sun. Claims to have the largest bike fleet in Dumfries and Galloway, and hires out road and mountain bikes.

Gorsebank Cycle Hire Greenhill Farm, A710 Coast Rd, Dalbeattie DG5 4QT 01556 610174 gorsebankglamping.co.uk/bike-hire. Located 1½ miles south of Dalbeattie, next to 7stanes cycle trails.

Loch Ken Cycle Hire Galloway Activity Centre, Loch Ken, Parton DG7 3NQ 01644 420626 lochken.co.uk. Located ten miles north of Castle Douglas on the A713.

Studio Velo 26–30 St Andrews St, Castle Douglas DG7 1DE ☎ 01556 503069 ⊕ studiovelo.co.uk. Local lad Gareth Montgomerie opened Studio Velo after giving up his career as a professional cyclist, having competed in the Melbourne and Glasgow Commonwealth Games. His impressive shop combines bikes, clothing and accessories with coffee, a wood-burning stove and lots of advice about cycling the local area. Bikes are available to hire and Gareth will even drop them off and pick them up from your chosen route if you're not able to transport them yourself.

WALKING

The Stewartry is an area of contrasting landscapes offering opportunities to enjoy the outdoors for all abilities. The **Southern Upland Way** (⊕ southernuplandway.gov.uk) passes through the heart of the Glenkens.

GALLOWAY GLENS LANDSCAPE PARTNERSHIP

Launched in 2018, the Galloway Glens Landscape Partnership (5 St Andrew St, Castle Douglas DG7 1DE ⊕ gallowayglens.org) is an ambitious five-year project consisting of an exceptionally broad range of initiatives – 35 in total, ranging from wildlife conservation, observation and habitat creation to day camps for young people and the creation of a Dark Skies Visitor Centre in Kirkcudbright, all under a hugely energetic and upbeat team leader, local lad McNabb Laurie. The area in question incorporates the River Dee and Galloway hydroelectric scheme, which is more or less synonymous with the Stewartry as a whole. All sorts of intriguing projects are on the go, including:

- **Historical mapping:** working with local estate owners to digitise pre-OS (pre-1750) maps on the National Library for Scotland website.
- **Place name research:** studying local place names with a toponymist (place name researcher) from Glasgow University.
- **Drystane dyking:** demonstrations and workshops to help preserve the art.
- **Creating the Glenkens Way** from New Galloway to Carsphairn, which follows the Old Pack Road between Galloway and Ayrshire.
- **Canoe trail:** development of a long-distance canoe trail from St Johns Town of Dalry to Tongland.

Other projects include the restoration of native fish populations, bringing woodland into community management and the creation of a multi-purpose heritage hub for the Glenkens… the list goes on. Visit the website for full details.

This is the longest stretch at 25 strenuous miles and should only be attempted in a day by the very fittest. Pick-up points at Stroanfreggan Bridge and from the valley of the Scaur Water can be used to break this section into more manageable parts.

Down at the coast the short walk from Rockcliffe to Kippford (and back; page 163) is one of the region's most popular. The district also offers walks to interest art lovers or film location buffs, and there are those encompassing an architectural folly or two, and many fine views.

Dumfries and Galloway Council produces a selection of free walking and cycling downloads, available from dumgal.gov.uk (look under 'Leisure' and then 'Outdoor Access and Paths'). For a handy pocket-sized walking guide try our *Galloway: 40 Coast and Country Walks* published by Pocket Mountains (pocketmountains.com).

THE GLENKENS & LOCH KEN

Remote and wild are adjectives often used to describe the Glenkens and local people here and in the neighbouring Nithsdale villages across the moors might be heard referring to themselves wryly as the 'hill tribes'. Occupying the most northerly reaches of the Stewartry, the Glenkens is easy enough to reach while also offering a sense of getting off the beaten track. Outdoor activities are definitely on the cards: walking and cycling, but also, thanks to lovely Loch Ken, all manner of watersports. There is also wildlife and iconic birdlife (most of the Galloway Kite Trail falls within this area) to be spotted, historic castles, quaint villages with local artisans, and tea rooms stuffed with home baking.

The Glenkens lie on the eastern fringe of **Galloway Forest Park** with boundaries more or less defined by the valley of the **River Ken**. It therefore incorporates the string of villages that run down the length of the valley from **Carsphairn** in the north to Parton in the south. **Corsock**, a little further to the east, is also involved in Glenkens community activities, as is **Laurieston** to the west, so both are included in this section.

Further information can be found on the community website theglenkens.org.uk.

NORTH GLENKENS

The far north of the Glenkens, where Dumfries and Galloway meets East Ayrshire, is an area of wide open space, moorland and hills surrounding the ominously named **Loch Doon**, which can be glimpsed to the west from the main A713.

1 Carsphairn

The Galloway Tourist Route to/from Ayr runs down the A713 offering splendid views, leading to Carsphairn (the name means 'alder meadow'). In the 19th century this was a lead mining area: **Woodhead lead mine and village** were located in the hills a couple of miles to the west and the remains of the village can still be visited. Carsphairn was also a Covenanter village and claims its own martyr, **Roger Dunn**, whose tombstone is found near the churchyard gate. It is recorded that he was killed on the night of Carsphairn Fair in June 1869, though some records claim that it was a case of mistaken identity. The church itself has one of the few central communion tables still in use in Scotland.

The village was for a few years the home of **John Loudon McAdam**, the great engineer and road builder, whose family lived just outside Carsphairn at Lagwyne Mansion. The house burned down when McAdam was six, almost taking him with it, after which the family returned to Ayrshire, where he had been born. Despite his Ayrshire connections, McAdam remains associated with Dumfries and Galloway. Not only is there a memorial to him here in the church, but he also died in the region, in Moffat, where he is buried (page 38).

The **Carsphairn Heritage Centre** (DG7 3TQ NX559934 carsphairn.org) lies at the northern end of the village and it is hoped it will reopen again in the near future, having come under community ownership. In the meantime, Carsphairn Heritage Group continues to operate, focusing in particular on the mammoth task of digitising their genealogy and local history records. Further information about the group, and the village in general, can be found on the community website detailed above, while general information can be found on the community noticeboard outside the heritage centre. The **Carsphairn Tea Room** (see opposite) also carries a limited range of information.

In the area around Carsphairn, in the large conifer woodland at **Polmaddy** (about halfway down the A713 towards St John's Town of Dalry; Forestry and Land Scotland), a short walk takes in the site of a ruined farming village abandoned over 200 years ago. It's also possible to do a linear walk from here to Carsphairn – the Bardennoch Trail – which is around four miles (there and back).

FOOD & DRINK

Carsphairn Tea Room & Bistro On the A713 through the village, DG7 3TQ 01644 460568 carsphairntearoom.co.uk. Lindsay and Paul's tea room and shop on Carsphairn's main street won Café of the Year in 2018 in the Dumfries and Galloway Life awards. Breakfasts and lunches are offered, there are monthly themed bistro evenings, the homemade soups and cakes are delicious, and there's even a range of speciality gins.

2 St John's Town of Dalry

There is a choice of roads to reach St John's Town of Dalry from Carsphairn, the main A713 or the smaller B729/B7000, both offering a glimpse of the dams of the hydroelectric scheme (page 135).

The intriguingly named St John's Town of Dalry (often shortened to Dalry, but not to be confused with the Ayrshire town or Edinburgh suburb of the same name) is an attractive Galloway village of painted cottages tumbling down the hill. The village as it appears today has its roots in a late 18th-century medieval hamlet that was developed by the Earl of Galloway. At the top end of the village is a natural stone in the shape of a chair. Legend has it that John the Baptist rested upon it, thus giving the village its name, but the more commonly accepted truth is that the land was owned by the Knights Templar (or, later, the Knights Hospitaller, also known as the Knights of St John) who administered to pilgrims travelling south to the shrine of St Ninian at Whithorn (page 211).

At the foot of the village on a high bank of the Water of Ken stands **Dalry Parish Church**, completed in 1831 and believed to be the third on this site. In the churchyard is the **Gordon Aisle** of 1546, the resting place of the Gordons of Lochinvar, whose seat, Lochinvar Castle, stood on an island in Loch Lochinvar, three miles across the moors to the northeast. (For a trip into the wilds of the surrounding countryside, take the Moniaive road out to lonely Lochinvar.) The castle was lost when the Lochinvar Dam was built and the waters rose. Sir Walter Scott's poem *Marmion* tells the tale of 'Young Lochinvar', a character associated with the 15th-century Sir William Gordon.

St John's Town and the surrounding area have a strong Covenanting history, which is commemorated in the **Covenanter Memorial** (see box, page 142) and the grave of Robert Stewart and John Grierson in the parish church. Stewart and Grierson had been active in freeing Covenanters held in Kirkcudbright Tolbooth (page 185) and had also been involved in the murder of the curate of Carsphairn. They were

THE PENTLAND RISING

The striking **Covenanter Memorial** of 2004 stands in the park at the southern end of the village and is based on the 'Burning Bush' from *Exodus chapter 3*. Donated by one Bill Dunigan, a member of the Scottish Memorials Association, it was decided to erect it here to mark the start of the Pentland Rising, one of the most significant events of the period, which was precipitated by a skirmish in St John's Town in 1666. What started with four Covenanters coming out of the hills in search of a meal turned into an attempt to rescue an old farmer from soldiers, which then escalated with the involvement of Covenanters holding a Conventicle at nearby Balmaclellan (page 145). Rebellion had begun and culminated in 900 Covenanters marching to Edinburgh where, on 28 November at Rullion Green on the edge of the Pentland Hills, they were met by around 3,000 soldiers. Carnage followed with around 100 Covenanters reported killed on the field and a further 300 killed as they tried to escape. Around 120 were taken prisoner and sentenced to death.

marked men, pursued by John Graham of Claverhouse, 1st Viscount Dundee (page 25), who caught and killed them. Their bodies were brought to Dalry for burial.

Dalry is a good spot to linger and explore, with plenty of walks in the surrounding area. The Southern Upland Way passes through the centre of the village and there is an easy three-mile loop along the river and up Mulloch Hill. Slightly to the east is a path to **Holy Linn Waterfall**, a Covenanter's meeting and baptism place, accessed from either the A702 or through mixed deciduous woodland and along the Garple Burn from the B7075 to Balmaclellan.

The **Donald Watson Bird Walk** is a circular loop taking about 1½ hours that is detailed on a leaflet available from The CatStrand in New Galloway (page 144) and online (watsonbirds.org). It was one of the favourite walks of Donald Watson, an internationally renowned wildlife artist and author who made Dalry his home from 1951 until his death in 2005. There is also a leaflet detailing the **Donald Watson Art Trail** (also available from the website), a 47-mile route around the Glenkens that includes many of the locations that provided inspiration for his paintings. A permanent exhibition of Donald Watson's works can be viewed at nearby Balmaclellan (page 145).

The **Glenkens Farmers' Market** is held on the second Saturday of every month throughout the year in Dalry's Town Hall (the red-roofed building in the centre of the village).

FOOD & DRINK

Clachan Inn 8–10 Main St, DG7 3UW ☏ 01644 430241 🖱 theclachaninn.co.uk. Perfectly located at the heart of Dalry and described by the Campaign for Real Ale as 'one of the most attractive pubs in southwest Scotland'. This is a country pub as country pubs ought to be, with a fine range of Scottish real ales, craft beers and malt whiskies, not to mention quality food using local ingredients. Open fires in winter make for a cosy retreat.

3 NEW GALLOWAY & BALMACLELLAN

Cruachan House (page 261) **Nether Ervie** (page 262), **New Galloway Cottages** (page 262)

New Galloway

John Rennie's graceful bridge of finely dressed granite over the Ken sets the tone for New Galloway, a village of undeniable charm that exudes an air of calm country life but is far from inert. In fact, New Galloway has for some time been a village buzzing with creativity thanks to initiatives such as the CatStrand Arts Centre and the Scottish Alternative Games. Recent years have seen New Galloway Community Enterprises secure funding for further development and the opening of a smart new community-owned shop (🖱 newgallowaycommunity.shop) with an enviable range of produce, from fresh veg and quinoa to frozen chips and local produce from suppliers such as Galloway Smokehouse (page 176). Manager Lynsey keeps it all running and, with her colleagues, also looks after the two lovely rental properties in the same building (page 262) and the public self-service laundry out back.

New Galloway lies just two miles outside the eastern edge of **Galloway Forest Park** and is on the **Red Kite Trail**, both factors that help to bring in the visitors. It is Scotland's smallest royal burgh, a status conferred upon it after Sir John Gordon of Lochinvar (page 141) obtained a charter from Charles I in 1629. The village was popularly referred to as the 'New Town of Galloway', which in time has been shortened to today's name. It lies in the parish of Kells and the **parish church** 👆 of 1822 with its battlemented tower stands on a hill above the northern end of the village with delightful views over the surrounding hills and a number of interesting headstones in the graveyard.

In more recent days New Galloway's profile has been considerably raised, partly thanks to actor Sam Heughan – who plays Jamie Fraser in the *Outlander* series based on Diana Gabaldon's novels – who hails from here, and partly because of the **Alternative Games** that are held here on the first Sunday in August. The games first took place in 1977 for the Queen's Jubilee after a local farmer, Mungo Bryson, found an old rusty gird n' cleek when he was tidying the barn. (A gird n' cleek is a metal hoop that is attached to a metal rod via a smaller hoop. The aim is to hold the rod and roll the hoop along the ground; it's much trickier than it sounds.) Recalling childhood games, he began to dream up other pursuits and thus the annual contest was born. It's an alternative to the traditional Highland Games – sports include Tossin' the Sheaf (throwing a sheaf of corn over a high bar with a pitchfork), Hurlin' the Curlin' Stone (like a shot putt), Tug o' War, the official Gird n' Cleek World Championship, Tractor Pull and Snail Racing.

"Recalling childhood games, he began to dream up other pursuits and thus the annual contest was born."

The **CatStrand Arts Centre** (High St, DG7 3RN ✆ 01644 420374 🖱 www.catstrand.com ⏲ Mon–Fri 10.00–17.00, Sat 10.00–16.00, Sun 11.00–16.00) is the village's modern jewel in the crown, housed in the old school. 'Strand' is an old name for a small stream, while 'Cat' was the name of the stream that ran beneath the school. A regular programme of music, drama and films is offered, and there's a shop and café.

FOOD & DRINK

The CatStrand High St, New Galloway DG7 3RN ✆ 01644 420374 🖱 www.catstrand.com. A light and airy café at the back of the arts centre building, offering sandwiches, salads and home baking. Internet access also available.

The Smithy Tea Room and Craft Shop High St, New Galloway DG7 3RN ✆ 01644 420269 🖱 thesmithy-newgalloway.co.uk ⏲ Mar–Oct Wed–Mon. Foodies Margaret and Andrew took over The Smithy after having visited New Galloway for almost 20 years. Their focus on quality local fare combined with a range of menus (kids, vegan, vegetarian, gluten-free), plus an ethos of reducing waste and ethical sourcing earned them the accolade of the Scotland Business Awards' Best New Food Business in 2018. In addition to toasties and sandwiches there are homemade tartlets, a range of staples from ham, egg and chips to pulled pork (Andrew slow roasts the pork for 24 hours himself) and homemade fishcakes. A coffee bar at one end has USB ports and Wi-Fi is also available. Opening hours may vary throughout the year, but they are always closed on Tuesdays (which happily coincides with the day that lunches are offered at New Galloway Town Hall, should you happen to find yourself here). They also run occasional themed evenings – check the website or Facebook page for details.

Balmaclellan

Neighbouring Balmaclellan (meaning 'House of McLellan' [sic]), two miles to the northeast, is smaller than New Galloway and enjoys eye-catching views westwards over the Rhinns of Kells from the war memorial. It is also the location of a permanent exhibition of paintings by renowned wildlife artist and author **Donald Watson** (page 142), housed in **The Old Smiddy** (watsonbirds.org).

Balmaclellan once had links with the monks at Dundrennan (page 189) through sheep farming and is also noted for the memorial in the churchyard to **Robert Paterson** (1715–1801), immortalised as Old Mortality by Sir Walter Scott in his eponymous novel. A stonemason by trade, Paterson spent the last 40 years of his life searching out unmarked graves of the Covenanters and carving their tombstones. He and his wife lived at Balmaclellan (his wife started the school here), but Robert spent much of his time away. He died aged 86 in Bankend, just south of Dumfries, and was buried in the cemetery of the church at Caerlaverock (page 125).

LOCH KEN

Loch Ken stretches southwards for nine miles, fed by the Water of Ken from the north and the River Dee (also known as Black Water of Dee) from the west. Part of the Galloway Hydroelectric Scheme, the loch is a Ramsar area, included in the list of sites on the Ramsar Convention designed to protect wetlands (named after the city of Ramsar in Iran, where the convention was signed in 1971). A section of the loch has also been designated an Environmentally Sensitive Area and the habitats here support internationally important roosting numbers of Greenland white-fronted geese and Icelandic grey geese. The loch is also popular for its watersports.

Kenmure Castle

NX635764

Situated around one mile south of New Galloway, atmospheric Kenmure Castle is one of those forgotten ruins you can't resist exploring. It has connections with John Balliol, husband of the good Lady Devorgilla (see box, page 131) and the Gordons of Lochinvar (page 141), one of whose descendants moved to America in the 10th century, where he acquired in the state of Virginia a plantation house that had been built by the sister of George Washington and her husband. In tribute to his home he renamed it Kenmore.

If you want to explore Kenmure, be warned that much of the building has collapsed and by all accounts more of it may follow. Entrance is at your own risk.

The east side of Loch Ken

Barwhillanty Estate Holiday Cottages (page 261), **Galloway Activity Centre** (page 261) **Loch Ken Holiday Park** (page 262)

In the hills above Crossmichael lies the **Barwhillanty Estate** (barwhillantyestate.co.uk), set in 5,000 acres of gorgeous rolling countryside. Although not generally open to the public, the estate offers two holiday properties and also runs yoga retreats, including sessions in the enchanting and sheltered walled garden.

Courses in all manner of watersports are offered at the **Galloway Activity Centre** (Near Parton, DG7 3NQ NX657735 01644 420626 lochken.co.uk) on the east shore. Alternatively, if you're an experienced hand you can hire equipment for your own use. There's also a café and an interesting range of accommodation.

Waterskiing and wakeboarding are run from Loch Ken Marina a mile or so further south, out of which the **Loch Ken Waterski and Wakeboard School** (Parton DG7 3NF 01644 4670333 lochken) operates. A little way further on, a public slipway offers access to the waters of the loch.

The hamlet of **Parton** was built in 1901 as an estate village for Parton House (now demolished) and consists of a cute row of black-and-white Arts and Crafts-style cottages with a church at one end. It still wears its motto proudly and *Floreat Partona* ('Let Parton Flourish') is proclaimed above the door to the village hall. Parton is home to one of the region's quirkiest listed buildings, the **Parton Privy**, an octagonal building housing the communal toilets for the cottages. Not so long ago one of the loos was still open for viewing, complete with visitors' book! Today the privy stands in a private garden behind the cottages and is not open to the public but can be seen from the road.

In the **churchyard** at Parton is a monument to the physicist **James Clerk Maxwell** who is buried here. His family home, Glenlair, is nearby, near Corsock. Maxwell is credited with one of the most significant discoveries of the modern age, the theory of electromagnetism, and his work received plaudits from many notable scientists, including Albert Einstein. **Glenlair House** (Knockvennie DG7 3DF 01556 650209 glenlair.org.uk) has a small visitor centre dedicated to Maxwell that is open by appointment.

The west side of Loch Ken

At **Glenlochar** the waters of Loch Ken flow southwards as the River Dee. A barrage here controls the flow of water and a bridge crosses the river. **Balmaghie Church** (NX723664 balmaghiekirk.com), dating from 1794, is found about 1½ miles up the west side of the loch on a slight rise, with delightful views up the loch and to Crossmichael on the other side. In the 17th century this was a strong Covenanter area and in the churchyard are the graves of three covenanting martyrs. Also buried here is the novelist **S R Crockett** (1859–1914), who was born in the parish at Duchrae.

Another mile or so beyond the church lies the **RSPB's Ken Dee Marshes reserve** (NX699685 year-round). This is a great place for nature lovers of all ages with an easy-to-follow path running up the side of the loch, passing a goose-viewing platform (best visited Oct–Apr for spotting visiting Greenland white-fronted geese) and a hide, before cutting off through woodland to reach a second, raised hide. Look out for red squirrels, nuthatches, elusive (declining) willow tit and, on the water, ducks and wading birds. In summer you might spot purple hairstreak butterflies. Migrant birds, spring flowers and bats are all here, too. No matter what time of year you come there is likely to be something to see, and the path is dotted the whole way along with informative noticeboards to help identification.

"This is a great place for nature lovers of all ages with an easy-to-follow path running up the side of the Loch."

Further north, the road up to New Galloway runs right along the edge of the loch with several stopping places that offer access to the shore and small lochside beaches.

The endearing village of **Laurieston** to the southwest is known for its **Red Kite Feeding Station** (Bellymack Hill Farm, DG7 2PJ NX688652 01556 670464 bellymackhillfarm.co.uk), where there is daily feeding at 14.00. Laurieston is also home to multi-award-winning photographer Phil McMenemy, who is always happy to welcome visitors to

The Gallery at Laurieston (Woodbank House, DG7 2PW ☎ 01644 450235 🖱 philmcmenemy.smugmug.com ⏲ check before visiting) to view his work and have a natter. His cheery tea room within the gallery is a welcoming space in which to relax surrounded by his pictures and enjoy a selection of cakes and a cuppa. The gallery can be found on the Gatehouse Road, immediately west of the crossroads. Phil's images, printed on a range of materials, including aluminium and wood, can be spotted in various places around the region and are exhibited internationally.

At the northern end of the village, on a rise above the road, stands a **memorial to S R Crockett**. From Laurieston the B795 runs back to Glenlochar, offering a good view of Threave Castle (page 156) to the south along the way. Alternatively, the minor road heading west through Laurieston Forest is a memorable way to approach Gatehouse of Fleet (page 165), with superb views down to Fleet Bay and, on a clear day, beyond to the Isle of Man and the Machars.

GALLOWAY FOREST PARK

Forestry and Land Scotland's website (🖱 forestryandland.gov.scot), details access points, activities, viewpoints, memorials and visitor centres; parking is charged at the visitor centres, but not at the smaller parking areas elsewhere in the forest

At 300 square miles, Galloway Forest Park is Britain's largest. Established in 1947 and sometimes referred to as 'the Highlands of the Lowlands', it encompasses some of the region's most dramatic scenery and the highest peak of the Southern Uplands, Merrick (2,766ft) – part of the range of 'The Awful Hand', so-called because of its resemblance to fingers. No matter what sort of outdoor pursuits you're looking for, there's every chance you will find it here. Notable are the **7stanes mountain biking centres** at Glentrool and Kirroughtree.

The park has a particular reputation as the first **Dark Sky Park** in the UK. With a resident population so small that light pollution is minimal, Galloway has some of the darkest skies in Europe. Over 7,000 stars and planets are visible with the naked eye from here and the nightly show changes constantly as the seasons pass. On the Sky Quality Meter scale, the night sky of the park scores between 21 and 23.6. The scale runs from 0 to 25 and in the middle of a major city the reading would be around 8, while in a photographer's dark room it would be 24. This really is the place to come for some uninterrupted stargazing.

It has to be said that plantation forests *per se* don't usually excite us, but the effort and creative thinking that has gone into Galloway Forest Park is striking. Not only are there three worthwhile **visitor centres** (at Clatteringshaws, Glentrool and Kirroughtree, further details of which are given below and on page 151), but Forestry and Land Scotland is actively involved in developing its assets for local enjoyment, often working in partnership with local community and arts initiatives to enhance the natural environment. **Sculptures** are positioned around the forest, for example, and parts of the forest have also been used for experimental **music and light installations**. Keep an eye on the website to see what is going on when you are here.

For a full daytime experience of the park, head out along the **Raiders' Road Forest Drive** (⏲ walkers & cyclists all year; cars Apr–Oct with small charge), which for most of its way follows an old drove road featured in the book *The Raiders* by local author S R Crockett. This ten-mile track runs through the forest from the west side of Loch Ken to Clatteringshaws, passing Stroan Loch and viaduct along the way. Further along, about halfway, is the **Otter Pool**, a lovely riverside picnic spot (with toilets).

For grand views and an eclectic range of attractions, the A712 from New Galloway to Newton Stewart, known as the **Queen's Road**, makes for a fine leisurely amble. All points of interest, from Clatteringshaws in the east to Murray's Monument in the west, are detailed on OS maps of the area and are covered below.

4 CLATTERINGSHAWS LOCH & VISITOR CENTRE

NX552764 01644 420285 ⏲ Mar–Nov

Overlooking Clatteringshaws Loch, with views on a clear day of Merrick, the visitor centre is good for birdwatching in the summer. It's also a short stroll from here to the site of one of two **Bruce's Stones** (the other is at Glentrool, page 151), a granite stone where Robert the Bruce is said to have rested. The loch was created in 1934 by the construction of a dam across the River Dee to flood adjacent marshland as part of the Galloway Hydroelectric Scheme. The visitor centre offers information and a café, complete with wood-burning stove for cooler days. Look out on the path to Bruce's Stone for the surfboard-like star-gazing plinths set to one side of the trees. Try them out: lie down on them and gaze upwards. Even a bit of daytime sky-watching has its rewards.

5 RED DEER RANGE & WILD GOAT PARK

The **Red Deer Range** (⚲ NX521731 ◷ year-round; tours with rangers Apr–Aug, booking required) is a purpose-built hide from which to view red deer. The best time to see them is between April and October. In autumn listen out for the roar of the stags at the start of the rut.

Up a dirt track on the right-hand side of the road between the deer range and Wild Goat Park is **Black Loch** and **the Eye sculpture**. You can't miss the Eye, a 25ft conical terracotta obelisk, so-called because of a hole that runs through the middle of it at eye height.

Beyond the track to Black Loch, a couple of miles on from the Red Deer Range, wild goats roam on a hillside of craggy rock at the **Wild Goat Park**. Pull in and the chances are they will make their way down pretty quickly to see you in the hope of a snack. Please note that they are now on a diet and, despite any appearances to the contrary, request not to be fed!

6 DUNKITTERICK COTTAGE & MURRAY'S MONUMENT

Next stop after the deer range is **Dunkitterick Cottage**, which is set at the foot of the hills on the left as you head south down the A712. From the parking area a short walk runs along a lovely stretch of the Palnure Burn to the ruin of the cottage that, in the late 1700s, was home to young Alexander Murray (1775–1813) and his six siblings, plus mum Mary, shepherd dad Robert, and the family cattle. Despite his humble beginnings, Murray became a professor of Oriental Languages at Edinburgh University and is now commemorated by the monument in his name, of which there's a grand view from the cottage ruin.

To visit the **monument** itself, continue a little further down the A712 to the parking area (⚲ NX487718). The climb up is short and steep but worth it for the views. The surrounding slopes have been clear-felled in recent years, which means that if you follow the path that loops the hill there are views of the monument from all directions.

A pleasant circular walk of around two miles can be followed from the monument (follow the waymarked red route), detouring to the Grey Mare's Tail Waterfall (not to be confused with three others of the same name on the west coast of the Machars, above Kirkconnel in Nithsdale and east of Moffat; page 43), the Black Loch and the Eye sculpture if you wish, before dropping back down between the goat park and Palnure

Burn. En route, look out for the eerie faces at the old sheepfold, sculpted from stone and set within the walls.

7 GLENTROOL VISITOR CENTRE

NX372786 01671 840302 generally Mar–Nov daily but may be open winter 10.00–15.00 w/ends; check website (page 148)

North of the A712 and towards the west side of the park, Glentrool has been described as the centre of the Galloway Highlands. Access is via the A714 from Newton Stewart, then turn off at Bargrennan to reach the Glentrool Visitor Centre, a welcoming cabin in a lovely spot in the heart of the forest at the Black Linn (falls or pool) on the banks of the Water of Minnoch. In the car park is a nifty sign showing different views of the night sky and from here you can either walk or drive the three-mile forest track to **Bruce's Stone**, set high above Loch Trool with superlative views all round, from where a track up Merrick can be followed. It was from the Glentrool area that Robert the Bruce launched the campaign which culminated in Bannockburn, and it was also in this area that John Buchan set much of *The Thirty Nine Steps.*

8 KIRROUGHTREE VISITOR CENTRE

NX452646 01671 402165 Apr–Oct

At the southern end of the park, Kirroughtree Visitor Centre offers a different experience again. Accessed off the A75 east of Newton Stewart, the centre is big, bright and airy, with information at one end and a café and **bike hire** (page 137) at the other. It was built using local stone and larch, has been designed so that no light escapes into the night sky, and is heated using geothermal energy from deep underground. There's a good kids' section with nature snippets. The surrounding forest offers walks and hides from which to spot red squirrels, and this is a **7stanes** centre, too.

FOOD & DRINK

All three visitor centres offer hearty fare but in very different settings. **Glentrool** is the smallest, more like a log cabin on the banks of the river, while **Clatteringshaws** has a lovely lochside location. Further south, the glass-fronted café at **Kirroughtree Visitor Centre** is larger and is in a new purpose-built chalet-style cabin with outdoor seating on the decking for warm days. Sitting here in the sun feels almost alpine, with views through the trees towards Cairnsmore of Fleet.

House O' Hill Hotel Bargrennan (on the west side of the park) DG8 6RN ✆ 01671 840243. The reasonably priced seasonal menu here consistently finds favour with both locals and visitors, and the food is generally regarded as being among the best in the area.

CASTLE DOUGLAS & THE EAST STEWARTRY

Local food specialities, beaches, a plethora of history and a wonderful rolling landscape characterise this part of the region, much of which lies within the **East Stewartry Coast National Scenic Area**. If you're arriving from the east you may prefer to avoid the A75 and take advantage of the quieter **Old Military Road** of the 18th century, built by General Wade's successor, Major Caulfeild, to assist in the passage of troops to Ireland. Alternatively, a little further south the A711 runs through some pretty country and skirts **Kirkgunzeon**, with its mighty obelisk in the churchyard, almost taller than the church itself.

If coming from the west, you can detour off the A75 up to **Barstobrick** (barstobrick.co.uk) just north of Ringford, where you can walk up to Neilson's Monument, erected in 1883 to commemorate James Beaumont Neilson, who invented the 'hot blast' process of smelting iron. There's a café here and, should the notion take you, an interactive Galloway Faerie Trail to follow.

Hungry travellers might also wish to take note of The Schoolhouse Café (page 165), located on the A75 roadside roughly halfway between Castle Douglas and Gatehouse of Fleet.

9 CASTLE DOUGLAS

Douglas House (page 261) **Gelston Castle Holidays** (page 262), **Orroland Holiday Cottages** (page 262) **Lochside Caravan and Camping** (page 262)

The small market town of Castle Douglas has bucked the trend of recent years and retained its position as a bustling centre at the heart of local, commercial and agricultural life. A volunteer-run **tourist information centre** (page 136) operates from an office in the main public car park at the top of end of town, where there are also local and regional information boards.

Castle Douglas's history is long, as is testified by the **Carlingwark hoard**, a cauldron filled with ancient artefacts that was brought up in 1868 by two men fishing in Carlingwark Loch at the southwest end of town (now a good spot for birdwatching). Dating from the 1st or 2nd century AD, many of the items are exhibited in the National Museum of Scotland in Edinburgh.

The loch was also a good source of shell marl, a lime-rich mud used in agriculture, which prompted one Alexander Gordon of Culvennan to construct, between 1765 and 1789, a 1½-mile canal, known as Carlingwark Lane, northwest out to the River Dee. Marl – and other goods – could then be transported by canal, river and lochs between Castle Douglas and New Galloway. The venture was relatively short-lived, though, and the canal ceased to be operational around 1840. These days its course can still be traced and there is a notion it might become part of a canoe trail as part of the Galloway Glens Landscape Partnership (see box, page 138).

In the Middle Ages Castle Douglas was the domain of the so-called Black Douglases, noble earls and Lords of Galloway whose mighty Threave Castle (page 156) nearby was the main administrative centre

THE DIFFERENCE BETWEEN A KEG & A CASK

Sulwath Brewers Ltd 209 King St, DG7 1DT ☎ 01556 504525 sulwathbrewers.co.uk
Mon–Sat; entrance is down the alleyway between Carlo's restaurant & 215 King St

Having handed over the day-to-day running of the business to his son Allan, convivial, canny and courteous Jim Henderson is usually on hand to welcome visitors to Sulwath Brewers Ltd. 'I blame my mother-in-law for the fact I turned to drink,' he says with a smile. It was while visiting his wife's family in the Malvern Hills that he was smitten by the pubs serving ale made from local hops.

In 1995 he set up Sulwath Brewers, operating from 'cousin Bob's dairy farm' near Southerness. The business soon outgrew the space, so Jim relocated to Castle Douglas, to what had previously been a baker's premises, and since then it has gone from strength to strength (3.5% to 5.5%, to be precise) and now turns out around 8,000 bottles a year.

You can pop in at any time to sample the beer, or to have a pint and a pie (the latter supplied by another Henderson, one of the local butchers).

Tours of the brewery run on Mondays and Fridays at 13.00 and include the main working area – all gleaming steel and malty aromas. Draught and bottled beers are on sale, including gift packs of mixed bottles. Jim is an expert guide, full of facts, figures, terminology and snippets of brewing trivia. And, if like me, you don't know the difference between a keg and a cask before you go in, you will by the time you come out.

until their demise. Despite the association with the Black Douglases, the town was named for and by a Douglas of a different ilk altogether. William Douglas was a pedlar from Penninghame in the Machars, whose fortune was made in what were most likely dubious trades in Virginia before he returned to Scotland to indulge his ego. First he tried, and failed, at Newton Stewart (page 199) before turning his attention eastwards, where he re-christened Carlingwark as Castle Douglas, laid out the town in its current grid pattern, and built himself a somewhat fanciful turreted castle at nearby Gelston. His **mausoleum** (♥ NX758603) is just outside Castle Douglas to the south, a short distance beyond the gates to Threave's gardens. It was built by his nephew who inherited the estate, and is a fitting tribute for a man who has become known for his trademark grandiloquence. A strange, squat bunker with pagoda-like roof, it sits in a woodland clearing and provides eternal shelter for not just Sir William, but 24 other family members, too.

"Castle Douglas enjoys a reputation that is known well beyond the region for its range and quality of local produce."

There has been a **cattle market** in Castle Douglas since 1819 and it still operates today, run by Wallets Marts (walletsmarts.co.uk), the main local employer, at the top end of Queen Street. Come on a Tuesday to see the weekly livestock sale.

In more recent years Castle Douglas has worked hard to establish itself as the **Food Town** of Dumfries and Galloway and now enjoys a reputation that is known – not just locally, but well beyond the region – for its range and quality of local produce. Despite the opening of Tesco, **King Street** is one of the best high streets in the region for independent shops. Down the length of it can be found delicatessens, a wholefood shop with enough loose-leaf teas to satisfy the most discerning connoisseurs, a traditional sweet shop, bakers, a greengrocer, a chocolatier, and not one but three, yes *three*, butchers. Foodies may want to note the **Earth's Crust Bakery** (36–38 St Andrews Street, DG7 1EN 01556 502506 earthscrustbakery.co.uk), where owner Tom van Rooyen not only sells all sorts of belt-busting goodies, but also runs artisan bread courses.

There are also cafés, sandwich bars, new and secondhand book shops, antiques and bric-a-brac shops (browsers should check out Hazel's warehouse at 44 St Andrew Street), gift shops, galleries and art shops, traditional tweedy outfitters, jewellers and craft shops. There's even a traditional clockmaker and, tucked down an alleyway towards the bottom of the street, A D Livingston & Sons, furniture maker, restorer and upholsterer, here for almost 40 years. For a town with a population of around 4,000 people, it's an impressive list. To top it off, Castle Douglas also boasts its own **independent brewery** on the high street (see box, page 153). Full details of all the local shops can be found on the comprehensive website cd-foodtown.org.

FOOD & DRINK

For something a little different and superb cooking, reserve a space at **Craigadam** near Kirkpatrick Durham, a 15-minute drive east of Castle Douglas (page 158).

Carlo's 211 King St, DG7 1DT 01556 503977 carlosrestaurant.co.uk. Described as a 'real' Italian and 'the best Italian in the southwest' by one restaurant reviewer. The restaurant itself is relatively small, the menu not extensive (this is no typical *trattoria*: pizzas don't feature) but the quality and atmosphere are good.

Designs Gallery & Café 179 King St, DG7 1DZ 01556 504552 designsgallery.co.uk. Offers an appealing mix of gallery, gifts, garden and café serving coffees, speciality teas, home-baked organic bread, cakes and sandwiches. Specials and homemade soup are on the menu every day. One of the town's most popular places to eat.

Moore's Fish and Chips 254 King St, DG7 1HA 01556 502347 mooresfishandchips.co.uk. Since June 1977, the Moore family have been serving up haddock, scampi, prawns and a whole lot more besides, including build-your-own pizza. Most of their fish comes from the North Sea and every day their fish buyer visits the fish market at Peterhead, up beyond Aberdeen on the east coast. Moore's regularly wins awards for the best 'chippy' in Scotland.

Mr Pook's Kitchen The Old Bank, 38 King St, DG7 1AD 01556 504000 mrpooks.co.uk. 'Offering you Dumfries and Galloway on a plate' is Mr Pook's aim, working with local suppliers as well as foraging and collecting ingredients. Think crispy duck egg with foraged chanterelles, pink 28-day Angus beef fillet, and dark matter rum baba with salt-baked pineapple. It's all a little pricier than most local restaurants, but there's also a cheaper 'pre-theatre menu' available from Tuesday to Thursday between 17.00 and 18.15.

Street Lights Coffee House and Bistro 187 King St, DG7 1DZ 01556 504222. Has a wide-ranging menu, from haggis panini and bacon rolls to falafel and chargrilled veg, and hummus and halloumi.

THREAVE CASTLE & ESTATE

Threave Castle and Threave Estate are two separate but connected sites. The former, northwest of Castle Douglas, lies on land owned by the National Trust for Scotland but is run by Historic Environment Scotland. The latter, southwest of Castle Douglas, is solely National Trust for Scotland; in fact it's one of their top ten attractions. Both were acquired in 1867 by Liverpool businessman William Gordon and were subsequently passed to the National Trust for Scotland by his grandson in 1948.

On an island in the River Dee stands the forbidding **Threave Castle** (DG7 1TJ NX739623 Apr–Sep 10.00–16.30 daily (last ticket sales 16.15 and last outward sailing 16.30), Oct 10.00–15.30 daily (last outward ticket sales 15.15 and last outward sailing at 15.30); Historic Environment Scotland; free entry for members). 'High, sombre and – despite its ruinous state – magnificent in its attitude of aggressive medieval power' as one guidebook writer of old describes it, it was built in 1369 for Sir Archibald Douglas, Lord of Galloway, commonly known as Archibald the Grim. He died at Threave on Christmas Eve in 1400.

"One of the delights of a visit is its accessibility, or rather its inaccessibility. The only way to reach it is by boat."

Threave Castle was the seat of the 'Black Douglases', who by the mid 15th century had established a stranglehold on power. James II spent much of his reign trying to break the Douglases and in 1455 laid siege to Threave, gaining entry after two months but only after bribing the garrison. Threave was – and is – a formidable structure, with walls almost 100ft high and 10ft thick. Depending on which story you wish to believe, it is said that James II had the enormous cannon, Mons Meg (now at Edinburgh Castle), forged in Castle Douglas for the attack on Threave.

One of the modern-day delights of a visit to Threave Castle is its accessibility, or rather its inaccessibility. The only way to reach it is by rowing boat from the jetty on the banks of the Dee. If the boat isn't there, ring the bell and wait for the boatman to return from the other side.

Threave Estate (DG7 1RX NX755605 0844 493 2245 gardens & visitor centre late Mar–Nov 10.00–17.00 daily, Nov–23 Dec 10.00–16.00 daily; nature reserve year-round; National Trust for Scotland; free entry for members) consists of four areas: the house, gardens, sculpture garden and nature reserve. William Gordon built Threave House towards the top of the gardens with good views. Access to the **house** is by guided tour only; parts of it are now used as flats for students, while the rest has been restored and furnished in 1930s style.

The **gardens** are superb. Even if you're not particularly green-fingered, there's a blackboard in the visitor centre on which helpful notes are written with suggestions of what to look for depending on the time of the year. There are glasshouses, a sculpture garden, nature reserve, a walled garden and various themed garden rooms, including a secret garden, rhododendron garden and a rose terrace. Threave is particularly popular in spring for its specialist and extensive range of daffodils.

Wildlife plays a significant role on the estate. **Ospreys** have been a feature for several years, either passing through or nesting, notably down near Threave Castle on the banks of the Dee. There are five bird hides along the river and marshes. Since 2010, Threave has also been the location of Scotland's first reserve especially for **bats**, with more species found here than anywhere else in Scotland, including the rare whiskered bat.

THE LOWER URR VALLEY

Chipperkyle Country House B&B (page 261), **Craigadam Country House Hotel and B&B** (page 261) **Brockloch Eco-bothy and Treehouse** (page 261)

THE KING'S MOUNT

NX815647

Motte of Urr (page 158) is also known as The King's Mount, a name that has its roots in a far-fetched tale that is nonetheless good for the telling. The story goes that at this site Robert the Bruce fought an English knight and was aided in his battle by the wife of Mark Sprotte, who lived on the motte. Madame Sprotte, seeing that Bruce was in danger, plunged into the affray and brought the knight to his knees. Not wishing to take advantage, Bruce sheathed his sword and the gentlemen retired. Mrs Sprotte then served up a bowl of porridge to Bruce but offered none to the knight, refusing to serve an Englishman in her house. To defuse the situation, Bruce told her that he would grant to her all the land she could cover while he ate his porridge. The lady duly went out and Bruce shared his porridge, with one spoon, with the knight.

As unlikely as the story may seem, it has been noted that the Sprottes held the lands of the motte for 500 years, on condition that a bowl of porridge should be served to any Scots monarch that happened to be in the area. (One observer has commented wryly that perhaps this accounts for the fact that there have been relatively few royal visitors to Galloway.)

The River Urr rises at Loch Urr near Moniaive in Nithsdale and flows for 35 miles down to the Solway at Kippford in the Stewartry. A meander down its lower reaches through the Stewartry makes for a leisurely sojourn.

Kirkpatrick Durham lies slightly to the east of the river and, like many local parishes, has a 19th-century church built by Dumfries architect Walter Newall, who also designed nearby Glenlair (page 147). In the **graveyard** there is a stone to the wife of Covenanter John Neilson of Corsock Castle, who gave refuge to Gabriel Semple, the minister of Kirkpatrick Durham, when he was driven from his church. Semple's preaching at nearby Corsock is said to have been the start of field preachings or Conventicles (page 25). Neilson himself was hanged at the Mercat Cross in Edinburgh.

"One of the most impressive in Scotland, the motte was built in the mid 12th century, destroyed in 1174 and then rebuilt."

A couple of miles south, the River Urr tumbles down the rocks at **Old Bridge of Urr**, where the village nestles in the hollow of the valley. From here it flows southeast to **Haugh of Urr** and on past the eastern edge of the remains of the **Motte of Urr**. One of the most impressive in Scotland, the motte was built in the mid 12th century, destroyed in 1174 and then rebuilt six feet higher. The spacious bailey is ringed by a mighty ditch, about 8ft deep and almost 50ft wide, and the summit is 85ft above the river. This is a real humdinger of a motte, a magnificent earthwork.

FOOD & DRINK

Craigadam Near Kirkpatrick Durham DG7 3HU 01556 650233 craigadam.com. A 15-minute drive east of Castle Douglas, Craigadam is quite special and offers something a little bit different. Celia and Richard Pickup run a country-house-style B&B from their traditional Galloway farmhouse and non-resident guests are welcome to book for dinner, which is taken family-style around the large table in the wood-panelled dining room. Much of the food comes from their own farm or within a few miles of it and the cooking is superb. Celia specialises in game so you might find pheasant, partridge or venison being served, but equally it could be roast duck with raspberry sauce or lamb with garlic and stuffing.

10 Dalbeattie

Dalbeattie has had a tough time over the years but keeps bouncing back. Originally planned in the 1790s, the town came alive when local man

Andrew Newall started quarrying on a small scale. It wasn't until the early 19th century though that the serious business got underway when the **Craignair quarry** came into operation, yielding up its granite which was shipped so far and wide that it became renowned the world over. Stone from here was used in the base of the Eddystone lighthouse and in the construction of Sydney harbour. Ironically, the one project it wasn't used in was the construction of its own bridge across the Urr, which was built from stone brought in from Kirkgunzeon (page 152).

Despite being six miles from the sea, the Urr is tidal as far as Dalbeattie and at that time there was a thriving port just to the west. Ships were walked up the Urr, pulled by horses to deposit their goods and pick up cargo from the busy industrial town. It was a canny operation, an early example of recycling with rags, bones and scrap metal brought in by ship to be transformed by local mills into brown paper, shovels, ploughs and fertiliser. Dalbeattie folk didn't miss a trick and groceries, too, came in by boat, used as ballast. The port today is no longer used and had fallen into disrepair, but thanks to the work of the Dalbeattie Community Initiative various improvements have been made, interpretation boards installed and access opened up.

The **Dalbeattie Heritage Trail** offers two options: a short one of around a mile that sticks to the town centre and a longer one of around three miles that combines the town centre with a walk through some of the surrounding woodland. A leaflet is available from the Dalbeattie Visitor Information and Craft Centre (see box, page 136).

Dalbeattie Museum (81 High St, DG5 4BS ✆ 01556 611657 🖱 dalbeattiemuseum.co.uk ⏲ Apr–Oct 11.00–16.00 Mon–Sat) tells the town's story in fuller detail and is one of those irresistible local museums that is packed with all manner of intriguing artefacts. Tommy Henderson started the museum in 1993 having been inspired by the determined Miss Drew (page 200) from Newton Stewart. There's not much that the volunteer staff don't know about the town and they make terrific hosts for anyone visiting. Exhibits include a collection of artificial glass eyes, a piece of the Enigma machine donated by a Dumfriesshire lady who worked at Bletchley, paintings by local artist Jim Sturgeon, who was known as the 'Galloway Colourist', and a couple of model churches made from icing

"There's not much that the volunteer staff don't know about the town and they make terrific hosts for anyone visiting."

sugar (not for eating, you understand). There are also a number of items relating to Dalbeattie's most famous son, William McMaster Murdoch, First Officer of the *Titanic*.

Vintage car enthusiasts may wish to check out Dalbeattie Men's Shed project (dalbeattiemensshed.co.uk) to rebuild one of Scotland's earliest cars, the Skeoch Utility Car. Originally built in a Dalbeattie workshop by local man James Skeoch, it was first exhibited at the 1921 Scottish Motor Show in Dumfries, around the same time that the Arrol Johnston factory there was in its heyday (page 114) and Dorothée Pullinger was inventing her car at Tongland (see box, page 180). Skeoch ought to have made a mint from his affordable car, priced at just £180, but alas his uninsured workshop burned down several months later and the automobile revolution continued without him.

While in Dalbeattie, pop in to **The Nail Factory** (56 Southwick Rd, DG5 4EW 01556 611686 nailfactory.org.uk Thu–Sun), which was once (200–300 years ago, it is believed) exactly that, but which today provides a sympathetic space for an ongoing programme of exhibitions for up-and-coming artists. On the high street, shops to seek out are a good independent bookshop, Dalbeattie Books (at 65–67), and Red Squirrel for gifts (at 52).

South of town lies **Dalbeattie Forest**, one of the **7stanes mountain biking centres**, from where the six-mile **Colvend Trail** offers a route for both walkers and cyclists to the coastal community of Kippford (page 162).

FOOD & DRINK

The Galloway Soup Company 17 High St, DG5 4AD 01387 780568. Homemade soup, light bites and teas and coffees are offered by Joanne in her bright café. She's a cheery soul committed to working locally, selling locally sourced goodies in her adjoining shop, and mentoring students from Dalbeattie High in an annual food producers' scheme (ask her about it). She also runs gin evenings consisting of gin (of course) and soup (of course) as part of a 3-course buffet.

The Granite Kitchen 62a High St, DG5 4AA 01556 610361. Angela's family-run café is the place to come for afternoon tea, with some of the biggest cakes we've ever seen.

From Dalbeattie to the coast

Kirkennan Estate Holiday Cottages (page 262)

Much of the area around Dalbeattie falls within the parish of **Buittle** (pronounced 'Bittle'), notable for its historic connection with John Balliol.

His wife, Lady Devorgilla (see box, page 131), is said to have financed the building of the now ruined **Buittle Old Church** (NX808598). The ruins of Buittle Castle, just west of Dalbeattie, are in fact now owned by Balliol College, having been gifted to them by Peter Maxwell QC of Munches, a Balliol man.

A couple of miles south of Buittle is the village of **Palnackie**, once home to the very curious (but now discontinued) **World Flounder Tramping Championship**, in which competitors, who numbered in the hundreds, tramped through the mud looking for flounders. At the bottom of the village is the attractive old harbour basin, still working and the subject of many a photograph. The **Old Mill Gallery** (theoldmillgallery.com), on the road running down to the basin, puts on exhibitions and events and there's also a popular pub (page 162) in the centre of the village and a handy community-owned village shop just round the corner on Glen Road.

"At the bottom of the village is the attractive old harbour basin, still working and the subject of many a photograph."

Beyond the village shop, the narrow road offers good views high above the Urr estuary and then passes through Forestry and Land Scotland's **Tornat Wood**, where almost all non-native conifers have been removed as part of a plan to restore this ancient woodland site. Walking trails run through the wood.

Carry on downhill on the road to reach Glen Isle at the bottom: an enchanting spot, little frequented, with superb views across to Kippford, out to Rough Island and beyond to the Lake District.

South of Palnackie is the imposing and unique mid 15th-century **Orchardton Tower** (NX817552 Apr–Sep 09.30–17.30 daily, last entry 17.00; Oct–Mar 10.00–16.00 Mon–Wed & Sat–Sun, last entry 15.30; closed 25–26 Dec & 1–2 Jan; free entry; Historic Environment Scotland;), the only circular laird's tower house built in late medieval Scotland. Much of it is intact and you can climb all the way to the top to enjoy the views (mind your head on the low doorway at the top).

Beyond Orchardton to the south at the end of the peninsula is **Almorness Point**. This private land can be accessed on foot if you leave your car at the parking area at the gate to Almorness House. It's a 4½-mile walk around the point, with superb coastal views and a bay of fine white sand.

FOOD & DRINK

Glenisle Inn Port Rd, Palnackie DG7 1PG ✆ 01556 600429 f. Friendly village local offering good food, from specials to wholesome pub grub. The burgers are always popular. There's a log burner for cooler days, dogs are welcome, and regular quiz and entertainment nights go down well.

THE COLVEND COAST

If Scotland were on the Mediterranean, the Colvend Coast is what it would look like. This stretch of shoreline from south of Dalbeattie eastwards to Mersehead (page 133) is the most developed part of all of Dumfries and Galloway's 200 miles of coastline but, unlike the worst excesses of the Med, here there is very little of the uncontrolled sprawl of modern holiday resorts. For more than 75 years part of this coast has been in the care of the National Trust for Scotland and, despite the relatively high number of visitors, there is still a timeless quality to much of it. I have memories of building sandcastles here over 40 years ago and – notwithstanding rose-tinted glasses and a few more people – not that much has changed.

South of Palnackie the Urr Water broadens out where river meets Solway, with a long thin peninsula to the west, flat and sandy, and a rocky coastline to the east. North of Palnackie, cross the Urr at Dalbeattie and head south again to reach first Kippford and then Rockcliffe, both enchanting coastal villages in their own right, but quite different in feel.

11 Kippford

At the road turning down to Kippford, stop in at **Barnbarroch Pottery** (barnbarroch-pottery.com generally Tue–Sat) where Christine Hester Smith produces striking works from her superb studio. Inspired by everything from artefacts in the British Museum to fables, wildlife, nature and people, she describes her distinctive style as being 'primarily illustrative in nature', which makes perfect sense when you see it. She usually takes part in the annual Spring Fling Festival (page 23), during which visitors can venture beyond the shop to the studio itself.

Kippford harbour was used in the early 18th century to accommodate large ships at the most northerly navigable point of the Urr. A boat-building industry subsequently developed but in time the village became more of a tourist retreat than a centre of industry. Today, it is a busy and popular holiday spot, good as a base (especially in the quieter low season) or for a day visit. The beach at the southern end can look positively tropical when covered in gleaming white shells, and a couple of pubs, a café and a village store can be found on the waterfront. On the hill above the village, between the caravan park and houses, a Community Nature Reserve offers easy walking paths suitable for buggies and wheelchairs.

From the southern end of the waterfront, by the café, the **Jubilee Path** (not part of the Nature Reserve) runs over the hill to Rockcliffe, offering splendid views over the Urr estuary and the Solway, known here where they meet as **Rough Firth**. There are two paths, a lower one and an upper one. Take one in one direction and the other coming back. There's also a detour off the path to the **Mote of Mark** on the summit of a hill above Rockcliffe, from where the views are even better. This early Dark Age fort or citadel is believed to have been the seat of a powerful chieftain in the 5th and 6th centuries before being destroyed by fire in the 7th century. Keep an eye open for adders as they are known to be here and are sometimes seen lying in the sun on a warm day. The route is covered in daffodils and gorse in spring, with wild garlic and bluebells also making an appearance. There's plenty of birdlife (we've spotted the migratory chiffchaff here), gardens are full of rhododendrons and moss-covered walls mark the edge of mixed deciduous woodland.

FOOD & DRINK

The Anchor Hotel Kippford DG5 4LN 01556 620205 anchorhotelkippford.co.uk. Popular with both locals and visitors. There are a mix of staples on offer such as steak and Criffell Ale pie and fish and chips, as well as specialities such as the chef's seafood chowder with prawns, clams, smoked haddock and mussels. Dogs are allowed in the bar and snug, where there's an open fire in winter.

The Ark Craig Roan, Kippford DG5 4LN 01556 620201. Perfectly positioned shop and café on the waterfront, offering a particularly impressive range of cakes.

Rockcliffe

No matter how busy the beach, the small village of Rockcliffe is one of the prettiest in Dumfries and Galloway, and even in the height of season somehow retains its air of gentility. With its rocky bay, Victorian villas and cottages, and lush gardens and lawns, it has an almost exotic atmosphere. Offshore lies **Rough Island** (National Trust for Scotland), a 20-acre bird sanctuary that's home to oystercatchers and ringed plovers.

It can be reached on foot at low tide but do check the tide times before setting out. It is also requested that you avoid the island in May and June to prevent disturbance during the breeding season.

In addition to the Jubilee Path walk (page 163), there is also a four-mile **coastal walk** northeastwards from Rockcliffe to Sandyhills over more challenging terrain, details of which are given on the noticeboard in the parking area at the top of the village. Incidentally, if you drive to Rockcliffe, parking in the official area is advised as space along the waterfront is very limited.

FOOD & DRINK

The Garden Room The Brae, Rockcliffe DG5 4QG ✆ 01556 630402. Rose Vernon moved from Norfolk to her traditional house on the road down into Rockcliffe 30 years ago. She opens the lower floor for refreshments, plus a shop selling a small but very perfectly formed range of antiques, vintage items and local artwork. Teas, coffees and homemade baking are offered (no savouries) with space for one or two people on the sofa inside, but most seating is at outdoor tables in her suntrap of a back garden. It's a pretty spot, and a convenient one too as it's located right next to the public car park. Generally open five days a week (and not necessarily always the same five: check the notice on the gatepost), but it can depend on what else is going on. From the front of the house there is often a selection of cans of drink and home-baked treats on offer, with honesty box for payment.

Southwick Coast

The A710 runs parallel to the coast, passing through the village of **Colvend** with its shop and café, then on to Sandyhills with its popular beach. Various minor roads drop down to the shoreline, which is celebrated here for its many coves, inlets and rock formations with evocative names, such as Gutcher's Isle, Cow's Snout and Gillis Craig. Scottish Wildlife Trust's Southwick Coast reserve lies along the shore between Sandyhills and the RSPB reserve at Mersehead (page 133) and is a particularly captivating spot with wooded cliffs and extensive saltmarsh. It is also, in our experience, somewhere you may well have to yourself, not least because access is tricky. The entrance is off the main road, opposite the junction with the minor road that goes off to Nether Clifton. The only place to park is in the small space at the junction itself, where there is room for one car only.

In the reserve there are superb views from the clifftop and a track descends to the merse, passing through the Needle's Eye, a natural wave-cut arch. A wide range of birds might be spied – yellow hammer, spotted flyctacher, snipe – as well as otter, common lizard and perhaps even adders. Take care on the merse itself as it is criss-crossed by water channels and in summer cattle may be grazing.

GATEHOUSE OF FLEET & THE WEST STEWARTRY

The western end of the Stewartry is dominated by Cairnsmore of Fleet, at 2,332ft the most southerly Graham in Scotland. (A Graham is a peak between 2,000 and 2,499ft, named after Fiona Torbet, née Graham, who published her own list of them in the 1990s.) Cairnsmore lies at the heart of its eponymous National Nature Reserve (see nnr-scotland.org.uk for more information). Travellers are spoiled for choice in this area when it comes to routes, since the two minor roads that cut across the lower slopes of Cairnsmore to Creetown also traverse the Fleet Valley National Scenic Area, designated as such over 20 years ago for its outstanding beauty and to protect it as part of Scotland's heritage. The coast road offers panoramic views to Wigtown Bay.

FOOD & DRINK

The Schoolhouse Café Ringford DG7 2AL 01557 820250 closed Jan & every Weds. Hungry travellers crossing the Stewartry on the main A75 should take note of this popular café, located roughly halfway between the turn-offs to Kirkcudbright and Gatehouse of Fleet. Local artwork and photographs adorn the cheery pink walls and white wainscoting of the old schoolhouse. Pick a table or sink into one of the comfy sofas, cosy up to the wood-burning stove in winter, and tuck into a wholesome meal that might consist of anything from homemade soup and a cheese scone to a Sunday roast, beef or venison casserole, salmon, or perhaps even a traditional Scottish high tea, served from 15.00. Mobile signal is patchy here, but there's good Wi-Fi.

12 GATEHOUSE OF FLEET & AROUND

Cally Palace Hotel (page 261), **The Ship Inn** (page 261) **Sandgreen Caravan Park** (page 262)

There is a pleasing neatness and quietude about Gatehouse that always leaves us feeling content. It may be its wide main street lined with painted cottages, or the fact that even when busy it's still imbued with an air of calm gentility. Or it could just be its setting, cosily enveloped within the

A LASTING LEGACY

No coverage of Gatehouse would be complete without mention of the Murray Usher family, in particular Mrs Elizabeth (Betty) Murray Usher, who died in 1990. I didn't know her personally, but since those early childhood holidays in the area I have always known about her. Such was her standing within the community that anyone who spent any time here could not fail to be aware of her enormous contribution to the development and well-being of not just the town, but of the wider area and its traditions as a whole. Along with The Stewartry Drystane Dyking Committee, she was, for instance, the founder in 1968 of the Drystone Walling Association of Great Britain, which now has 18 branches around the country.

'We do miss her,' said one Gatehouse resident when asked about her and she is remembered with great fondness. Many a story could be (and still is) told by those who knew her, usually accompanied by a wry smile as they recall her tactics to make things happen and get her voice heard. At one time, unsuspecting visitors who were coming for a meeting with her would be offered on their arrival one of the gobstoppers that she kept on her desk.

For the first edition of this guide, Antony Wolffe, a retired architect and long-time resident of Gatehouse, kindly supplied the following few words about her. Sadly Antony himself passed away in 2016. He was himself a remarkable man, having been born in Germany and moved to Britain in 1937. He opened his architect's practice in Gatehouse of Fleet in 1952 and remained there until his death, only retiring in 2012 at the age of 92. He first met Elizabeth Murray Usher in the 1950s and worked with her on a range of projects over 40 years.

hills on the banks of the Fleet. Suffice to say, it is a delightful place to while away a few hours or as a base for exploring the surrounding area. You may wish to make use of the good local website (🖰 gatehouse-of-fleet.co.uk).

The **Murray Arms Hotel** at the top end of town was at one time the original 'gate' house ('gate' comes from 'gait' or road) and also the only house, a staging post on the route west to Portpatrick and Ireland. Gatehouse might have remained like this had it not been for James Murray of Broughton, entrepreneur and grandson of the fifth Earl of Galloway. It was a time of expansion, the Act of Union of 1707 had created opportunities for growth and James's father, Alexander of Broughton, approached William Adam, the leading architect of the day, about building a fine mansion on lands at Gatehouse. Unfortunately, he died before his project came to fruition, but his son James took up the baton, developing not just the

Elizabeth Murray Usher of Broughton and Cally OBE (1904–90) succeeded her father Colonel Frederick Murray-Baillie in 1924 and at the age of 20 she took charge of the Cally Estate in the parishes of Girthon, Anwoth, Borgue and Twynholm, about 40,000 acres in total.

Cally mansion was let and Cushat Wood was the Dower House for her mother, and Betty lived with her until she married Neil Usher in 1929, when they moved to Carstramon. From 1924 until 1990 – for 66 years – Mrs Murray Usher ran the Cally Estate and took a leading part in the local affairs of Gatehouse of Fleet. As Feudal Superior she took special interest in all new developments and long before the post-war planning legislation she exercised control over local building by insisting on slate roofs, white walls, sash and case windows and black chimney pots. She maintained that in the Stewartry, which is granite country with black soil, red tiles and ridges or natural brick walls are foreign and were not to be used in new building. The original layout of the planned burgh has been protected and, by putting surrounding land under a restrictive agreement with the National Trust for Scotland, the original core of the town became an Outstanding Conservation Area.

The powers of the Superior have now been taken over by the Planning Authority, but we can thank Mrs Murray Usher for having made use of these powers for the benefit of the local community. She latterly served on the Fine Arts Commission but had been on the Scottish Economic Development Council and supported the National Trust for Scotland, as well as many local societies and clubs.

She did not waste words but would send a memo with the name of the property or person(s), with a – ? – which was enough to get a response. And for attention she would ring a bell or sing a cock-a-doodle!'

estate but also creating an industrial settlement on the banks of the Fleet. First came a tannery and then breweries, followed by a cotton mill in 1785, the year the village was made a Burgh of Barony. So successful were these endeavours that Gatehouse became known as the 'Glasgow of the south'. However, development faltered in the early 19th century, after which the population declined to around 1,000 people, which is more or less where it has remained ever since.

Despite such fluctuations, James Murray's grand Georgian mansion has survived and today is run by local business McMillan Hotels as the **Cally Palace Hotel** (page 261), sitting in extensive grounds south of the town (the grounds and hotel are now in separate ownership). Within the grounds are a number of points of interest, including **Cally Gardens** (✆ 01557 815228 ⊕ callygardens.co.uk ⊙ Mar–Oct Thu–Sun), specialising in rare and exotic plants with a collection of over 4,000 perennials in its borders, and Forestry and Land Scotland's **Cally Woods** with a selection of easy waymarked trails. There are also a number of curious buildings tucked away: the '**Temple**' of 1779, a battlemented two-storey folly designed to impress passing traffic, and **Cross Cottage**, originally the chapel to the main house and now a holiday cottage available for rent. Just beyond the southern boundary of the grounds lies **Girthon Old Parish Church**, where in the churchyard is the grave of Robert Glover, one of the earliest gardeners at Cally. He died in 1775 and on his tombstone are carved a hoe, rake and spade.

One local Gatehouse resident tells me that when she moved here 52 years ago the town had 16 shops. Today it's a smaller but eclectic selection: a bakery/café, charity shop, a lovely small secondhand bookshop/gallery (The Book and Art Shop, 15 High St), post office-cum-convenience store, antique shop and, down at the bottom end of the high street, the **Mill on the Fleet**. This converted mill building has a visitor information centre and riverside café on the ground floor and on the second floor the splendid **Garvellan Books**, with around 20,000 new and secondhand books in stock.

> *"Cultural life in Gatehouse of Fleet is thriving with a range of artists and writers choosing to make this their home."*

Cultural life in Gatehouse is thriving with a range of artists and writers choosing to make this their home. Writer, poet and artistic director Chrys Salt organises literary events at **The Bakehouse** (44 High St, DG7 2HP ✆ 01557 814175 🖱 thebakehouse.info), which are advertised on posters around the region. Chrys is building on the town's literary heritage, which famously includes John Buchan, who set much of *The Thirty-Nine Steps* in the area, and Dorothy L Sayers, who visited on several occasions and is known to have stayed at the Anwoth Hotel (now The Ship) while writing *Five Red Herrings* in 1930.

Just to the north of Gatehouse on the east side of the Water of Fleet lies **Carstramon Wood**. Some of my earliest childhood memories are from here, the sight and pungent scent of a mass of bluebells flowering in the woods. We used to come on holiday to Culreoch farmhouse at the end of the track through the wood (now private but Culreoch Cottage is available for holiday lets). These 200-year-old woods, managed by Scottish Wildlife Trust, are known for their bluebells (in May) and pollarded oaks, and form one of the largest semi-natural broadleaved woodlands in the area.

FOOD & DRINK

The Crafty Crow Rutherford Hall, High St, Gatehouse of Fleet DG7 2HS ✆ 01557 814000 ⌖ thecraftycrow.co.uk. A café with crafts and gifts in a converted church, where Kerry and Billy offer a vegetarian menu (vegan and gluten-free options). Breakfasts until noon, lunches thereafter, and pizza evenings – eat in or take-away – on Fridays and Saturdays.

Galloway Lodge Preserves Fleetvale DG7 2HP ✆ 01557 814001. Popular with both locals and visitors, plus convenient parking in the public car park next door. Nigel Hesketh's family firm has been producing fine quality marmalade, jams, chutneys, jellies and mustards for over 40 years. Fiona Hesketh is at the helm these days and the company now supplies coffee shops, restaurants and hotels around the UK, as well as running coffee shops of its own. Breakfast and brunch, soup and sandwiches, toasties and jacket potatoes, afternoon teas and even packed lunches (to order) are on offer, with as many locally sourced ingredients as possible: meat from a Castle Douglas butcher, rolls from Kirkcudbright, eggs from the Glenkens.

The Masonic Arms 10 Ann St, Gatehouse of Fleet DG7 2HU ✆ 01557 814335 ⌖ masonicarms.co.uk. A historic gatehouse hostelry run by Sofía and head chef Jimmy and offering a wide-ranging menu using local ingredients wherever possible, including fish from the Galloway Smokehouse (see box, page 176), beers from the Sulwath Brewers (see box, page 153) and ice cream from Cream o' Galloway (page 172). In recent years it's been completely refurbished and a superb conservatory with wood-burning stove added for dining. There's also an outdoor fireplace in the garden. Themed evenings are often held – curry, music, steak, cabaret – check the website for details. Booking advised for evenings and Sunday lunch.

Mill on the Fleet High St, Gatehouse of Fleet DG7 2HS ✆ 01557 814099 ⌖ millonthefleet.co.uk. Good food served throughout the day – light meals, soup, sandwiches and a couple of specials. For tea and scones it's hard to beat the Mill's sunny riverside terrace.

No. 1 Fleet Street The Ship Inn, 1 Fleet St, Gatehouse of Fleet DG7 2HU ✆ 01557 814217 ⌖ theshipinngatehouse.com/restaurant. Located within The Ship Inn, contemporary dining using local produce is offered by chef Calum Harvey and his wife Toni. Open for lunch, afternoon teas (on certain days, 24-hours notice/booking required) and dinners, No. 1 Fleet Street has built a strong reputation for quality. Local king scallops or oxtail ravioli, saddle of local red deer, sauté of monkfish or wild mushroom and artichoke pithivier could feature. A large beer garden running down to the river makes this a popular spot on sunny days.

Cardoness Castle

DG7 2EH ⚲ NX591553 ◷ Apr–Sep 09.30–17.30 daily, last entry 17.00; Historic Environment Scotland; free to members; no link with Cardoness Estate

Cardoness Castle stands prominently just beyond the southwestern end of Gatehouse. Built for the McCullochs in the late 15th century it was lost to the Gordons of Lochinvar (page 141) in the 17th century before being abandoned. The six-storey tower house is roofless but otherwise remarkably intact, complete with murder hole from the guardroom above the entry to help repel unwanted visitors.

"Research suggests that Trusty's Hill could have been a royal site of the Britons who were familiar with Pictish symbols."

Immediately to the north of Cardoness is **Trusty's Hill**, an archaeological site that in recent years has gained much significance. Pictish symbols discovered here were first described in 1794, but it has only been since work undertaken in 2012 that the full importance of the site has been recognised. Archaeologists were puzzled for many years why such symbols were located here, so far away from the northern territories of the Picts. Research suggests

Gatehouse of Fleet to Anwoth

❋ OS Landranger map 83, Explorer map 312; start: Gatehouse of Fleet NX600564; 3 miles (without detours); easy to moderate (some inclines). Note that refreshments are available in Gatehouse (page 169), which is accessible by bus 431/500/X75.

Starting from the main car park in **1 Gatehouse of Fleet**, turn left and follow the road over the River Fleet until it bends left and the sign is pointing right to Anwoth. Here is the first of a number of mini detours that are worth exploring along the way: **Venniehill** is a wildflower meadow offering drifts of common spotted orchids in early summer followed by a stunning display of knapweed and devil's-bit scabious in August. Return to the road and follow the lane, signposted 'Anwoth'. After a short distance the **old brickworks** is on your right, now a small nature reserve complete with boardwalk.

Continue along the lane as it bends left and go straight ahead at the bench and green, remembering to look back for some fine views. Pass through the **2 metal gate** and along the drystane dyke-edged path, climbing over the steps in the wall at the end and following the waymarkers as they meander up and over the hilltops. The **3 wooden sign** 'Trusty's Hill/Anwoth' offers another short detour contouring up on to **Trusty's Hill**, site of an ancient hillfort and **Pictish rock carvings** (NX589560). Retrace your steps and follow the path in the direction of Anwoth, through a drystane dyke and over gorse- and bracken-covered moorland. The path appears to go away from the hilltop monuments you are heading for, but eventually reaches a wooden sign, 'Rutherford's Monument/Anwoth'. Head left on a gradual that Trusty's Hill could have been a royal site of the Britons who were familiar with Pictish symbols at some time between AD500 and AD900, very possibly the location of Rheged, one of the most mysterious kingdoms of Dark Age Britain.

Anwoth & around

It was the minister of Anwoth who first described the symbols at Trusty's Hill. Here, in a picturesque setting are the remains of the **Old Parish Church**, in the centre of which a sarcophagus monument from around 1635 commemorates the mother and two wives of John Gordon, who by that time had taken ownership of Cardoness Castle (page 169). It's an atmospheric spot that was used as a location in the cult film *The Wicker Man* (see box, page 26).

climb up to **Rutherford's Monument obelisk** (NX587588), dedicated to Anwoth's first parish minister, and enjoy sweeping views of the bay and, on a clear day, to the Isle of Man.

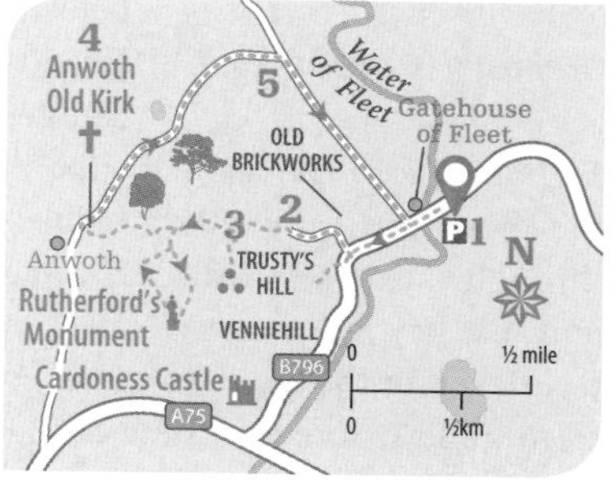

Having rested awhile soaking up the scenery, head to the next hilltop monument, dedicated to the work of the ministers of Anwoth and Girthon, and then on to the trig point (NX586559). Go straight ahead and in the bottom of the dip turn right following a rough path until it rejoins your earlier route. Turn left and then on to the path for Anwoth. Head down the hill and over a soggy field to the track running alongside the **4 Anwoth Old Kirk** (NX582562), turning right at the road. Take time to explore this atmospheric old kirkyard with its fine gravestone carvings and the impressive Maxwell family tomb. For fans of *The Wicker Man*, this will be a familiar location. Follow the quiet road out of the village turning right at the **5 T-junction** (NX592570) and following it back to Gatehouse of Fleet. Go left at the T-junction (NX598562) to return to the start point. This last section is perhaps less interesting but take time to enjoy the smaller pleasures, such as the beauty of the fine oaks and the joy of the hedgerow flowers.

Above Anwoth to the east is the prominent granite obelisk (NX587557) commemorating **Samuel Rutherford**, minister at Anwoth from 1627 to 1638. The monument was installed in 1842, struck down by lightning in 1847 and raised again in 1851. Rutherford was a diligent soul who was eventually banished from Anwoth due to his non-conformity. By then, though, he was regarded so fondly by his parishioners that when it was decided to knock down his manse, which had stood opposite the old church, and use the stones to build the new church, the masons refused to work and went on strike, not for higher wages but out of respect for his memory. A **millennium cairn** opposite the monument lists the names of all of the ministers of Anwoth and nearby Girthon (page 168) up until the year 2000.

South of Gatehouse, the Water of Fleet flows out to Fleet Bay, with its half-mile tides and warm shallow waters. Down the east side of the Fleet is **Sandgreen**, site of a holiday park (page 262) with its own beach, while nearby is one of the region's most visited attractions, the ever-popular **Cream o' Galloway** (see below). To the west of the Water of Fleet is **Cardoness Shore**, with six sandy bays that can be accessed either from the Skyreburn Teapot Café in the layby on the A75 (park here and walk back along the shore, generally only possible when the tide is on the way out), or through **Cardoness Estate Holiday Park** (DG7 2EP) south of the A75 and just beyond the Skyreburn Teapot, where you will need to buy a day ticket for the beach from the estate office. Dinghies can be launched from trailers from the estate car park.

"The masons refused to work and went on strike, not for higher wages but out of respect for Samuel Rutherford's memory."

Cream o' Galloway

Rainton DG7 2DR 01557 814040 creamogalloway.co.uk late Mar–early Sep & early Oct–early Nov 10.00–17.00 daily; early Sep–early Oct 10.00–17.00 w/ends only

The Finlay family have been farming at Rainton since the 1920s and over the years have developed, diversified and reinvented themselves several times in order to survive. The result is impressive – Cream o' Galloway is now not only known for its ice cream and cheese, but also caters for a broad range of interests and offers a number of entertainment options for kids and adults alike (3D maze, adventure playground, electric go-karts and nature trails to name a few). But this is also part of a working farm, which means there's a whole lot more besides: take a farm tour, join an ice-cream tasting session, or even make your own. Sister company, The Ethical Dairy, also based on the farm, offers a cheese-making day or you can join the 'Morning Milking Experience' to view the milking parlour and see the cows. Underpinning it all is the Finlay family's commitment to ethical farming and 'cow contentment'. Their story is an interesting one, especially the new methods that they have been trialling to reach new standards of animal husbandry.

THE COAST ROAD FROM GATEHOUSE TO CREETOWN

Kirkdale Estate (page 262), **GG's Yard** (page 262)

There is a story that Thomas Carlyle (page 53), when asked by Queen Victoria which was the finest road in the kingdom, replied 'the coast road from Creetown to Gatehouse'. And when he was asked whether there was not another one as good, he replied 'Yes, the coast road from Gatehouse to Creetown'. Carlyle's attachment to the scenic delights of this route was not unjustified. Pinched between the hills on one side and the dramatic sweep of Wigtown Bay on the other, it offers some fine views, especially on a sunny day when the sea is sparkling blue. This is the fastest route west, along the A75, and passes **Mossyard Bay**, where the perfectly formed small sandy bay affords good views of the islands at the mouth of Fleet Bay.

Cairn Holy (NX518538 year-round; free; Historic Environment Scotland) is an easy jaunt off the A75, around half a mile up a single-track road. Here lie two chambered cairns, Cairn Holy I and Cairn Holy II, the former the more elaborate of the two but the latter of which has been named as the tomb of the legendary Galdus, the great warrior king of the Scots. Up this same road is Kirkdale Estate (holiday cottages offered, page 262), which has been in the Hannay family since 1532.

13 CARSLUITH CASTLE

NX494541 Apr–Sep 09.30–17.30 daily, last entry 17.00; Oct–Mar 10.00–16.00 daily, last entry 15.30; closed 25–26 Dec & 1–2 Jan; free; Historic Environment Scotland

Carsluith Castle sits just off the A75 towards Creetown, overlooking Wigtown Bay. Built in the 1560s, it was a typical tower house, the home of one Richard Brown, whose family remained here until emigrating to India in 1748, after which it lay empty. Gilbert Brown, the last abbot of

Sweetheart Abbey (page 130) was born here. Visitors can climb right to the top for superb views out over the bay.

Next to the castle is the **Marrbury Smokehouse** café (see below), a convenient stopping place, and one of two smokehouses along this route. The second is the **Galloway Smokehouse** (page 176), just a little further west.

FOOD & DRINK

Gather Laggan DG7 2ES ✆ 01557 840217 no website available at the time this guide went to print. On a hill above the A75, a smart, glass-fronted café-restaurant offering superb views out over Mossyard Bay and the Solway.

Marrbury Smokehouse Just off the A75 at Carsluith Castle, DG8 7DY ✆ 01671 820476. The smokehouse itself is at the home of owners Ruby and Vincent Marr, up at Bargrennan near Glen Trool, but the *fruits de mer* of their labours can be enjoyed here and/or bought to take home. Marrbury is the house smoker for the famous Gleneagles Hotel in Perthshire.

THE HIGH ROADS FROM GATEHOUSE TO CREETOWN

The high roads to Creetown offer slower, single-track alternatives to the coast road. Our suggestion would be to take the coast road in one direction and one of the high roads in the other. And if you have time, we'd recommend exploring both of the high roads, partly for the jaw-dropping views but also for the chance to visit the **Big Water of Fleet Viaduct** (see opposite) on the old railway line.

Cairnsmore of Fleet National Nature Reserve (NNR)

Cairnsmore NNR covers 4,650 acres in the hills above Gatehouse of Fleet and Creetown, and makes up around half of the area of the Cairnsmore of Fleet SSSI. One of the wildest and most remote areas of southwest Scotland, it is dominated by the imposing granite hill of Cairnsmore (2,333ft). The privately owned Cairnsmore Estate was at one time the home of the wildlife photographer F W Champion.

Dromore Visitor Centre (NX555637 year-round) is reached on the B796 north of Gatehouse, up the western side of the Water of Fleet, and then by taking the turning to the right where indicated. The area is a walker's paradise and there are three suggested routes detailed in a leaflet available at Dromore. There is also a path to the summit of Cairnsmore from Palnure, about three miles east of Newton Stewart. Summit heath, heather moorland and blanket bog make up the terrain, supporting a range of iconic birdlife, including both red and black grouse, peregrine falcon and (if you're lucky) golden eagle. Also to be spotted are red deer, mountain hare and adders.

A short walk from the visitor centre stands the **Big Water of Fleet Viaduct**, an impressive 900ft span of 20 arches built in the late 1850s as part of the Portpatrick and Wigtownshire Joint Railway (the 'Port Road') linking Stranraer to Castle Douglas. Alas the line didn't survive the Beeching cuts and closed in 1965. The viaduct is not as graceful as it would have been originally as its piers have been strengthened by brick encasings; however, it has fared better than its smaller sister, the Little Water of Fleet Viaduct, which was blown up some years ago by the military as part of a training exercise.

"Summit heath, heather moorland and blanket bog make up the terrain, supporting a range of iconic birdlife."

The 18th-century Pibble Mine is found in the hills between here and Creetown. Beyond Pibble the road drops down into Creetown, following the course of the teasingly named Moneypool Burn.

Corse of Slakes Road

NX535587

In 1808, in the First Report from the Committee of the Highways of the Kingdom to the House of Commons, it was recorded that the Marquis of Downshire, despite 'having labourers with tools attending his coach, which was then a necessary part of the retinue' while travelling through Galloway, was forced to spend a night in his coach on the Corse of Slakes (corse is old Scots for 'crossing' while slake is from an old Galloway word meaning an opening in the hill). This unfortunate incident prompted consultation between the Marquis and the Duke of Queensberry (of Drumlanrig; page 91), which resulted a couple of years later in a workforce of soldiers being sent to construct a road through the hills, a task that kept them busy for almost 30 years. The result was the Corse of Slakes, also known as the **Old Military Road** (marked as such on OS maps) which, unlike other such roads, notably General Wade's in the Highlands of Scotland, was not built to repel the Jacobite threat but to allow easier passage of troops to Ireland.

Today the Corse of Slakes takes off up into the hills via a track from Anwoth (page 171). Alternatively, it can be accessed by car through the lovely countryside north of Skyreburn (take the signposted Skyreburn turning off the A75 west of Gatehouse). It is a route of exquisite hill and moorland vistas which, towards the western end, opens up into a glorious panorama taking in points west and south to the Rhins and right down to the Mull of Galloway as you come around Stronach Hill. This is countryside to be savoured, take it slowly (it would be difficult not to on this single-track lane) and keep an eye open for birds. We spotted a hen harrier up here. **Walking** it is also an option, from Gatehouse via Trusty's Hill and Anwoth, and then taking the gated track at the Old Church.

As you head down into Creetown, you will pass **Garrocher Market Garden** (page 179), where, believe it or not, tea is being grown in the Galloway Hills. I wonder what the Marquis of Downshire would have had to say about that?

THE GALLOWAY SMOKEHOUSE

For an insider's perspective on how to smoke food, head for the Galloway Smokehouse (page 179) at Carsluith, just east of Creetown, where you can see first-hand how the smoking process works, sample the end product in the restaurant and buy anything from bacon and black pudding to mussels, mackerel, salmon and squid (not to mention crab and lobster), much of it caught locally, in the shop. There's not much that proprietor Allan Watson doesn't know about the smoking process and he has kindly supplied the following text to give a flavour of what's on offer. (Allan's more in-depth account of smoking salmon is available on the SlowBritain website: slowbritain.co.uk).

Where we are Situated on the banks of Wigtown Bay overlooking the Kirkbride salmon nets.

What we do In our traditional smokehouse we hand fillet and hand slice all our salmon. Oak is the fuel and many different products are smoked. We also source our own venison, catch fish from the bay, and buy fish and shellfish from local boats.

The smoking process is one of the oldest food preservation methods. Food cooked on a wood fire lasts longer than the raw material due to the drying and natural antibacterial properties of smoke. Hardwoods are the preferred fuel, for the naturally occurring resins in softwoods give an unpleasant paraffin-like smell when they burn. However, the heat generated while burning can be a problem as it warms up the food, increasing bacterial activity. To slow this down salt is used as a preservative, which not only removes moisture but adds salt, both of which have antibacterial properties.

14 CREETOWN

Barholm (page 261)

Towards the far western fringe of the Stewartry lies Creetown, feeling as if it is more of the Machars than points east, not least in its outlook to Wigtown Bay and its proximity to Newton Stewart. However, Creetown is definitely within the boundaries of the Stewartry as any local will tell you. In early days it was called Ferrytown of Cree, providing a crossing point across the Cree for pilgrims on their way to Whithorn (page 211). In the 19th century it became one of the wealthiest towns in Scotland thanks to its famous local quarries, granite from which was used to build the town itself and was shipped far and wide for use in, among other places, the Liverpool Docks, Thames Embankment and London Bridge. Creetown is therefore noticeably different from most other local towns in its physical appearance; the grey granite is cold and austere on a dull day but in the sun it sparkles.

There is, however, a downside to the use of salt, as too much is unpleasant. Therefore, sugar is added to counteract the harshness (hence honey-glazed ham etc). The addition of the smoke and salt, and the removal of water, all reduce bacterial activity but also reduce palatability. A balance therefore has to be found: we can eat smoked goods with a three-week shelf life (held at 4°C) but if the shelf life is longer the food needs to be treated before it is edible. This usually means soaking in water overnight to rehydrate and remove some of the salt. Some long-life foods are still edible (for example, Parma ham, beef jerky, candied salmon) but the quantities eaten are usually fairly small.

The process of smoking salmon is complex and subject to variations in temperature. To produce a gentle, lightly flavoured product white sugar and beech can be used, for a stronger flavour brown sugar and oak, and for a very heavy flavour molasses and heather or peat. Each smokehouse has its own recipe. We use golden syrup with added dark rum and oak. Sourced from America because of its straight grain, the oak has been turned into sherry casks in Spain and Portugal, filled, sent to the UK and emptied, then taken apart, the joints planed and the casks reassembled to be filled with whisky. The remaining sawdust is a waste product, which when burned produces a wonderful aroma of oak infused with the sweetness and flavour of the sherry.

Other foods can also be smoked: duck, venison, beef, chicken, cheese, haddock, cod, bass, bream, sausage, haggis, black pudding, bacon, eggs, seaweed, tea... and we have even smoked juniper berries for the gin trade.

Appropriately for somewhere that has relied so heavily on rock, Creetown is the location of the excellent **Gem Rock Museum** (Chain Rd, DG8 7HJ ✆ 01671 820357 🖱 gemrock.net ⏲ Apr–Sep 10.00–17.00 daily; Oct 10.00–16.00 daily; Nov–20 Dec & Feb–Mar 10.00–16.00 Wed–Sun), which was started by the father of Tim Stephenson, who now runs it, and which houses a very impressive and wide-ranging collection. This is a lovingly curated showpiece with an impressive and fascinating range of items, presented in a smart exhibition space complete with mini film theatre, café and shop. Tim is often on hand himself to talk about how the museum got going and what it offers today, and how he was inspired by his father to become not just a gemmologist but also a lapidary (stone polishing takes place here, too). Crystals, minerals, fossils, meteorites and even a dinosaur egg are on display, as well as the complete skeleton of a 50,000-year-old fossilised Russian female cave bear. The range of stones and rocks is extraordinary and displays the most fantastic spectrum of colours.

"This is a lovingly curated showpiece with an impressive range of items, presented in a smart exhibition space."

For a closer look at the area's local and natural history, **Creetown Heritage Museum** (91 St John St, DG8 7JE ✆ 01671 820267/78 🖱 creetown-heritage-museum.com ⏲ Apr–May & Sep–mid-Oct 11.00–16.00 daily except Wed & Sat; Jun–Aug 11.00–16.00 daily except Sat, otherwise by appointment) offers a mix of insights, including images from *The Wicker Man* (see box, page 26), some of which was filmed in this area (notably in the Ellangowan Hotel just along the street).

Right next door to the museum is the **Barholm Enterprise Centre** (St John's St, DG8 7JE ✆ 01671 820810 🖱 barholm-centre.co.uk), where a range of community-operated services is offered, from accommodation and a shop to an electric car-charging point. The Arts and Crafts Cooperative within the centre stocks a wide range of locally made items, including pottery, jewellery, paintings and knitwear.

The main street is dominated by two notable features. The granite **clock tower** with its drinking troughs and bowl was built in 1897 from a public subscription to commemorate Queen Victoria's Diamond Jubilee and is reminiscent of the clock tower in Gatehouse. Next to it is **Adamson Square**, which was remodelled in 2007 and is itself dominated by a stark granite sphere. The square was designed and created by renowned Japanese sculptor Hideo Furuta, a remarkable man who lived in the area for many years before his death. A film of his work can be seen in the Creetown Museum, outside which one of his sculptures, depicting quarry workers, is built into the wall.

In the hills above Creetown, tea is grown in the Galloway hills at **Garrocher Market Garden** (garrochermarketgarden@gmail.com), a horticultural oasis tucked into an old sand quarry. It's not generally open to the public, but the owner, Angela Hurrell, is happy to be contacted via email or Facebook.

FOOD & DRINK

Galloway Smokehouse Carsluith DG8 7DN 01671 820354 gallowaysmokehouse.co.uk 09.00–17.30 Mon–Sat, 10.00–16.00 Sun. Husband and wife team Allan and Kim Watson have established a popular eatery next to their much-visited smokehouse just off the A75, with gorgeous views straight across the bay to Wigtown (spot the town hall on the skyline). Open for most of the year, including evenings during summer, everything from bacon butties to lobster is offered. For starters try the venison pâté, baked camembert or a smokehouse sharing platter, while for mains there's an emphasis on fish, from Kim's signature seafood pancake to dover sole, kedgeree and specials of trout fillet, monkfish bites or king prawn linguine. The adjoining shop offers all manner of tasty goodies, many direct from the smokehouse below, which is also open to visitors (see box, page 176).

KIRKCUDBRIGHT & THE SOUTHERN COAST

The southernmost part of the Stewartry is considered by many to be the jewel in Dumfries and Galloway's highly ornamented crown, and there are many who return here year after year for their annual holiday. What makes it so special is its mix of attractions: the historic harbourside town of Kirkcudbright and the strikingly beautiful and unspoiled coastline abutting the pastureland of gently undulating lush green hills, with the higher ranges of the Galloway Hills in the background. Combined with a pleasant climate for much of the year, this area and the neighbouring Colvend Coast (page 162) have been referenced as the 'Scottish Riviera' and, much as the description smacks of a brashness that is far from the reality, we can understand why the soubriquet might stick (though we hope it doesn't). Genteel, cosy, even couthy (a good Scottish word), are adjectives that more accurately fit the bill.

'A CAR BUILT BY LADIES, FOR THOSE OF THEIR OWN SEX'

The Galloway car plant at Tongland owed its existence to Dorothée Pullinger (1894–1986), who persuaded her father, a manager at Arrol-Johnston, to make use of the disused World War I factory to provide employment. At the age of just 20, Dorothée had been in charge of 7,000 women in an aircraft and ammunition factory during the war. Once her father opened the Tongland plant, she managed production in a workplace that famously included a tennis court on the roof, a swimming pool, a hockey team and a piano room for relaxation. Many of the employees were women and Dorothée ran a ladies engineering college, which offered apprenticeships in three years rather than the five undertaken by men, since women were believed to be faster learners.

The car that they produced was the Galloway 10/20HP, a lightweight vehicle designed specifically for women and described as 'a car built by ladies, for those of their own sex' (*The Light Car and Cyclecar* magazine, 1921). It was the first car with a standard mounted retro-visor and it was designed without protruding handles or pedals that could snag a woman's skirt. As women were on average shorter than men, measurements and fittings were adjusted so that the driver could look over rather than through the steering wheel.

Dorothée was not only a founding member of the Women's Engineering Society, but was also accepted as the first female member of the Institution of Automobile Engineers (albeit having to apply twice, since the first application was turned down on the grounds that 'the word person means a man and not a woman'). In 1920 she was awarded an MBE for her work during World War I and in 1924 she won the Scottish Six Day Car Trial driving the Galloway. After the war she came in for flack, like so many women did, for taking jobs that were perceived to be men's. She subsequently moved south with her husband, to Croydon, where she opened a large, technically innovative steam laundry, commenting that 'washing should not be doing men out of a job'. During World War II she set up the women's industrial war work programme and later she was the only woman on a post-war government committee formed to recruit women into factories.

NORTH OF KIRKCUDBRIGHT

The village of **Twynholm**, just off the A75, is the birthplace of Formula 1 racing driver David Coulthard and the location of **The Cocoabean Factory** (Ashland DG6 4NP ✆ 01557 860608 thecocoabeancompany.com ⏲ 09.00–17.00 daily), a family-run business started by Claire Beck in 2005 on her kitchen AGA, which has since grown and moved to these purpose-built premises. In addition to producing handmade chocolates and confectionary, the Cocoabean Factory runs popular children's chocolate-making workshops and has a kids' play area, a factory-viewing area and a café. Adult workshops (make your own truffles) are run from time to time, too. Combine it with Cream o' Galloway (page 172) for a truly calorie-tastic day.

The other place of note north of Kirkcudbright is **Tongland**, where the main thing you will notice is the striking power station, the most southerly in the Galloway Hydroelectric Scheme, in a Modernist building of 1935 on the banks of the Dee. Tongland was also the location in the 1920s for the **Galloway automobile plant**, a subsidiary of Arrol-Johnston in Dumfries (page 114). The plant was housed in an old World War I factory and was started up by the engineer T C Pullinger, who was a manager at Arrol-Johnston. His daughter, Dorothée (see box, opposite), was instrumental in persuading her father to keep the factory going to provide employment.

"Much involved in organising entertainments, he was also an alchemist and directed the building of chemical furnaces."

In medieval times, Tongland was the site of a **Premonstratensian monastery** founded by Fergus, Lord of Galloway. Its remains can still be seen. The monastery's most famous resident was John Damian, an Italian (real name Giovanni Damiano de Falcucci) who attended the court of James IV of Scotland and who was abbot at Tongland in the early 16th century. He was, by all accounts, quite a character. Much involved in organising entertainments, he was also an alchemist and directed the building of chemical furnaces at Stirling Castle and Holyrood. His most infamous venture was his attempt to fly when he launched himself from the battlements of Stirling Castle. The birds' feathers he was wearing failed to do the trick and he was lucky only to break his thigh.

From Tongland it's a short hop down into Kirkcudbright, crossing **Thomas Telford's bridge** of 1808 over the River Dee.

FOOD & DRINK

The Schoolhouse Café Ringford DG7 2AL ✆ 01557 820250 closed Wed & all of Jan. Handy location for travellers on the A75 (page 165).

15 KIRKCUDBRIGHT

The Selkirk Arms Hotel (page 261) **Orroland Holiday Cottages** (page 262)

Kirkcudbright ranks highly for having one of the most confounding names in Scotland. Pronounced 'kir-coo-bree', the popular belief is that it is derived from the church/kirk of St Cuthbert, but it is also possible that this in itself was a derivation of an earlier name, Caer Cuabrit, meaning 'fort on the bend in the river'. Whatever the truth, there is no doubting that the first Christian church here was dedicated to Cuthbert, the 7th-century saint whose uncorrupted body was carried around the country in the late 9th century by monks from Northumbria fleeing attacks from the Danes. The church was most probably situated on the hill to the east of town, where St Cuthbert's graveyard can now be found.

Kirkcudbright's – and Galloway's – history is both long and abundant, with more twists, turns and anecdotes than can be told in full here. From Celtic tribes to the Roman general Agricola, Galloway Picts and St Cuthbert and one of the earliest Christian churches in Scotland, so the town developed. By 1140, on land at Lochfergus east of today's town, Fergus, Lord of Galloway lived in his castle, the first of five hereditary

KIRKCUDBRIGHT – ARTISTS' TOWN

Anne Ramsbottom is Museums Curator of Dumfries and Galloway West and looks after a range of museums and galleries from Castle Douglas to Stranraer, including The Stewartry Museum, Kirkcudbright Galleries and Tolbooth Museum in Kirkcudbright. She has kindly written this piece on Kirkcudbright's rich artistic heritage.

Kirkcudbright has a unique place in the history of Scottish Art as the only town where an artists' community or 'colony' flourished for a long period.

By the early 1880s, inspired by the success of the Faed family of artists from nearby Gatehouse of Fleet, a group of local artists were regularly exhibiting in the town alongside several of the 'Glasgow Boy' artists who found inspiration for their painting in the Kirkcudbright area. The town's reputation was established by 1900 with the Kirkcudbright-born 'Glasgow Boy' E A Hornel, the pre-eminent resident artist.

A younger generation of artists was drawn to visit the town, some of whom eventually settled here. Of these residents perhaps the most famous, both within the town and throughout Scotland, were Jessie M King and E A Taylor. This husband and wife team were multi-talented, with Jessie M King designing jewellery and fabrics for Liberty of London, illustrating books and decorating ceramics while E A Taylor, a prolific artist, also designed musical instruments. In the 1920s and 1930s they set up artists' studios behind their home in Kirkcudbright's historic High Street, and through their teaching they encouraged and nurtured a further generation of younger Scottish artists until 1940.

Post war, the town was noted for its summer art school involving artists and resident craft lords who ruled Galloway for a century. Edward Bruce, younger brother of Robert, was granted the Lordship of Galloway in 1308 following his efforts to rid the area of the English in the Wars of Independence. Douglas rule and disharmony followed until on 26 October 1455 Kirkcudbright became a royal burgh. The 16th century was a time of prosperity but despite the Union of the Crowns in 1603 more trouble was to follow, for nowhere was religious persecution felt more harshly by the Covenanters (page 24) than in Galloway. During the 17th and 18th centuries the town fell into decline, so much so that Daniel Defoe commented:

> Here is a pleasant situation yet nothing pleasant to be seen. Here is a harbour without ships, a port without trade, a fishery without nets, a people without business; and that, which is worse than all, they do not seem to desire business, much less do they understand it.

workers such as Tim Jeffs and the potter Tommy Lochhead. The Stewartry area still has a high number of practising artists and craft workers. With a thriving Wasps facility in the town (Wasps is an arts-based charity that provides studio spaces across Scotland), a nationally acclaimed summer exhibition programme, a range of art galleries and well-established branding, the Artists' Town has come into its own.

Kirkcudbright's artists have been a part of the town's social history for the last 150 years, and they have engaged with the local community in many different ways – from serving on the town council to arranging pageants and operating local craft businesses. Kirkcudbright's artist community inspired Dorothy L Sayers to write her Lord Peter Wimsey crime novel *Five Red Herrings*, and the daughters of the artists Bill Johnston and Dorothy Nesbitt were the models for Ronald Searle's 'St Trinian's Girls'.

The town's artistic heritage can be explored at various places, including Broughton House, the home of E A Hornel, now a National Trust for Scotland site. The newly established Kirkcudbright Galleries displays the region's Nationally Significant Collection of these artists' paintings and crafts, including jewellery, ceramics, woodwork and sculpture. The Stewartry Museum collection boasts a significant archival, documentary and photographic record of the artists' lives and careers. The Kirkcudbright Tolbooth displays a collection relating to the Tolbooth and its history, an interactive display on the story of this 17th-century building, and a 10-minute video on the History of Kirkcudbright and Surrounds.

The 19th century saw the beginning of the revival of Kirkcudbright's fortunes, not least thanks to the influx of artists who made this their base (see box, page 183), drawn by the quality of the light and the availability of affordable housing. The cachet that had always been attached to the town was enhanced further and its profile as the county town and capital of Kirkcudbrightshire was raised, although economically it was given a run for its money and ultimately overtaken by Castle Douglas.

Kirkcudbright today is still known as 'The Artists' Town' and is as enticing a place as you can imagine. Compact but with wide airy streets, the old town with its brightly painted houses clusters around the remains of the 16th-century **MacLellan's Castle**, which stands prominently overlooking the fishing boats moored at the harbour. Such a mix of attractions has a timeless appeal that gives this small town a perpetual charm. It is a place to explore, to linger, and to get to know. Standing at the harbour, reflect on the fact that Kirkcudbright can claim over 800 years as a commercial port, from warfare, piracy and smuggling to passenger services and international trade. And what's more, it's still in use today.

"The old town with its brightly painted houses clusters around the remains of the 16th-century MacLellan's Castle."

The town's most iconic attraction is **Kirkcudbright Galleries** (St Mary St, DG6 4AA ✆ 01557 331276 ⌂ kirkcudbrightgalleries.org.uk ◷ 10.00–16.00 Tue–Sat, noon–16.00 Sun; see box, page 182) a four-storey display space housing 600 works in what was formerly the Town Hall, including some of the very best items of the nation's holding of art and antiquities. Paintings, jewellery and correspondence from names such as the Faed family, Peploe and Jessie M King are all here, and there is an on-going series of talks, in addition to workshops, family activities and events, and a delightful café.

Just along the road from the gallery is **The Stewartry Museum** (St Mary St, DG6 4AG ✆ 01557 331643 ⌂ dgculture.co.uk ◷ Oct–mid-Apr 11.00–16.00 Mon–Sat, mid-Apr–Sep 11.00–17.00 Mon–Sat & 14.00–17.00 Sun). The museum was purpose-built in 1892–93 and stepping inside is a like stepping back in time. Glass-fronted wooden cabinets are positioned around the ground floor while the upstairs balcony is fitted with glass-topped display cases of the type that are only found in museums of this vintage. The collection is crammed with items of historical interest, from artworks and book covers to old rifles and pistols, a model railway and newspaper clippings telling the gruesome story of the 'Lighthouse Murder' in 1960 on Little Ross Island at the mouth of Kirkcudbright Bay. Upstairs is dedicated to natural history, with stuffed animals, birds and fish, as well as pinned butterflies and birds' eggs.

The old high street, just round the corner from the museum, is lined with period cottages and houses. The **Selkirk Arms** (High St, DG6 4JG; page 261) dates from 1777 and takes its name from the Earl of Selkirk, whose family had acquired lands in Wigtownshire and the Stewartry through marriage and who were the original owners of the inn. Thomas Douglas, fifth Earl of Selkirk, was born in 1771 at St Mary's Isle to the south of Kirkcudbright and became one of the town's most famous sons. The Selkirk Arms' most famous guest was Robert Burns, who came to stay here in 1793, during which visit it is believed he may have written his famous *Selkirk Grace*.

Further down the high street stands the 17th-century **Tolbooth Art Centre** (High St, DG6 4GL 01557 331556 dgculture.co.uk mid-Apr–Sep 10.00–16.00 Mon–Sat, 13.00–16.00 Sun; Oct–mid-Apr 11.00–16.00 Mon–Sat) which, along with some of the narrow closes (passageways) that run off the high street will be recognisable to fans of the film *The Wicker Man* (page 26). On top of the outside stone staircase is the **Market Cross** of 1610, below which is **St Cuthbert's Well**. Look for the town **jougs** or iron collar on the wall of the Tolbooth, in which ne'er-do-wells of days past were chained. In 1698, Elspeth McKewan was held here before being burned alive, the last witch to be executed in Scotland. She was accused of making 'a compact and correspondence with the Devil', of drawing off milk from her neighbour's cows with a magical wooden pin and of interfering with the hens' egg laying.

> *"Upstairs is dedicated to natural history, with stuffed animals, birds and fish, as well as pinned butterflies and eggs."*

The following century the Tolbooth was prison to a number of Covenanters, and it was from here on 16 December 1684 that there was a mass break-out, assisted by Robert Stewart and John Grierson (page 141), both of whom ultimately paid for their sympathies with their lives. In the 18th century **John Paul Jones** (page 132) was held in the Tolbooth. Today it houses a display about the building's history and a short film about Kirkcudbright and the surrounding area.

Continuing down the high street from the Tolbooth, on the left-hand side at number 46 is **Greengate** (now a B&B), the home of the artist, illustrator and designer Jessie M King and her artist husband E A Taylor (see box, page 182) for much of the first half of the 20th century. Students would come and stay with them here and Jessie gathered around her a group of Glasgow-trained female artists who became known as the Greengate Close Coterie, which was still in existence when she died in 1949.

The town also has a range of shops and is particularly noted for its commercial galleries, full details of which (and more besides) can be found on the local website 🖱 kirkcudbright.co.uk.

Broughton House & Garden

12 High St, DG6 4JX ⏲ late Mar–Nov 10.00–17.00 daily; National Trust for Scotland; free entry for members

Broughton House was acquired in 1901 by E A Hornel, whose ancestors had lived in Kirkcudbright since the late 1500s and who had by then achieved fame as one of the Glasgow Boys. To the back of his home Hornel added a large studio, which along with the rest of this fine Georgian building is now open to the public. In addition to around 40 Hornel paintings on display, visitors can also see Hornel's **library**, which by the time of his death contained a staggering 15,000 items. His Burns collection is one of the largest in private hands and contains many early and valuable editions, including the first 'Kilmarnock' edition of Burns's *Poems, Chiefly in the Scottish Dialect* from 1786. Behind the house is Hornel's garden, a serene and beautiful retreat looking out over Kirkcudbright harbour.

MacLellan's Castle

DG6 4JD ⏲ Apr–Sep 09.30–17.30 daily, may close 13.00–14.00, last entry 17.00; Historic Environment Scotland

The northern end of the high street bends round to the right on to Castle Bank, site of the remains of MacLellan's Castle, a fine example of late 16th-century domestic architecture as it evolved from more heavily defended tower houses.

A much earlier castle, first mentioned in 1288, had stood on a site to the west on the banks of the Dee near what is now Castledykes Road. The town also had a Franciscan convent, founded in the mid 15th century, the site of which was granted to Thomas MacLellan of Bombie, provost of Kirkcudbright, in 1569, and it was here that he built his own mansion partly from stones from the convent and early castle.

Today, the castle is remarkably complete inside apart from the roof. Of particular note is the **Great Hall**, over 42ft long and almost half that in width, where the enormous fireplace boasts a lintel over 10ft long made out of a single stone. Hidden at the back of the fireplace is a **peephole**, a 'lairds lug' (literally 'lord's ear'), from where the castle owner could keep an eye on, and listen to, his guests.

Thomas MacLellan himself is commemorated in the **Episcopalian church**, which stands across from the castle on Moat Brae (not to be confused with the Dumfries literature centre of the same name, page 116). The current building dates from 1919 but incorporates various parts of older churches. One of the 19th-century buildings was used as a school and it is said that the children used to sharpen their slate-pencil on Thomas's nose!

On the outskirts of Kirkcudbright

On a hill to the east of the town lies **St Cuthbert's Graveyard**, burial place of Billy Marshall, of Romany stock, who was regarded as the king of the gypsies in southwest Scotland in the 18th century. A little further up the hill, overlooking the town, are **Barrhill Woods**, where a trail runs through beech, spruce and larch woodland. A well-positioned hide makes a good place for spotting birds and red squirrels.

North of the town centre, on the road in from Tongland, is the **Elizabeth MacGregor Nursery** (Ellenbank, Tongland Rd, DG6 4UU ✆ 01557 330620 elizabethmacgregornursery.co.uk ⏲ end Apr–mid-Oct Mon–Wed, Fri & Sat) where for over 20 years owners Elizabeth and Alasdair MacGregor have been cultivating their half-acre walled garden to take advantage of Galloway's mild climate and specialise in choice perennials.

One of the best views of Kirkcudbright is from the Stell on the west side of the Dee, from where the town presents itself clustered around the harbour with the mixed deciduous woodland of Barrhill behind. From here there's a glimpse of Broughton House and, next door to it, the imposing white Blair House, of the fishing boats and yachts in the marina, and of the castle. It is a scene so inviting that it makes quite clear, if it weren't already, just why so many artists have been attracted to the town.

FOOD & DRINK

Kirkcudbright Galleries Café St Mary St, DG6 4AA ✆ 01557 331276 🖱 kirkcudbrightgalleries.org.uk. Lovely light, bright café on the first floor of the gallery, serving soups, snacks, sandwiches, baguettes and jacket potatoes, and, of course, tray bakes, cakes and scones.

Polarbites Fish and Chips Harbour Sq, DG6 4HY ✆ 01557 339050 🖱 polarbites.co.uk ⏲ Jul–Sep Tue–Sun; Oct–Jun Tue–Sat. This place is legendary! Alas, at the time of writing it was also up for sale, but don't let that deter you from seeking it out. Sit in or out, or take away – this is not your average chippy. Scallops, lobster and crab might be found on the menu or, if not, can be sourced from the sister shop, Polarpak, next door. Cod and haddock are on the menu too, along with lemon sole, monkfish, mussels, and so the list goes on. This is one serious fish and chip shop.

The Selkirk Arms High St, DG6 4JG ✆ 01557 330402 🖱 selkirkarmshotel.co.uk; see ad, 4th colour section. Owners Chris and Sue Walker are old hands at running a successful hotel and restaurant and The Selkirk Arms is thriving under their tenure, with a reputation for good food so strong that people drive from miles around to come for a meal. Needless to say, booking is advised. Homemade dishes and local ingredients feature strongly, all prepared and served according to head chef Ryan's exacting specifications. Smoked salmon with samphire, quail's egg and buttermilk scones might be a starter, bacon and black garlic burger a main, and a crumble or passion fruit crème brûlée to round off. Vegetarian sous chef Melissa has helped devise a 'Green Menu' of vegetarian and vegan options: vegetarian haggis, bang bang halloumi salad and raspberry and white chocolate vegan cake all feature.

The Station House Café St Mary St, DG6 4DN ✆ 07484 915709 🖱 stationhousecookeryschool.co.uk. What could be better than a café attached to a cookery school in an old train station? Breakfasts, brunches, lunches and afternoon tea are all offered. On Sunday evenings pizzas are made – and delivered – to order. Book in advance.

Thai Kitchen Kirkcudbright Golf Club, Stirling Cresc, DG6 4EZ ✆ 07465 812331 🖱 kirkcudbrightgolf.co.uk. It seems an unlikely combo, golf and Thai food off the beaten track in southwest Scotland, but in Kirkcudbright it's working a treat. Opened in February 2019, the Thai Kitchen has been named by *The* [Glasgow] *Herald* newspaper as one of the top 15 Thai restaurants in Scotland. Take-away only.

THE KIRKCUDBRIGHT COAST

Balcary Bay Country House Hotel (page 261)

The coastline in the area around Kirkcudbright is one of the finest in the UK. There are enough rocky bays, sandy beaches and tales of smugglers to make you feel as if you've stepped into a Famous Five story. There's also a **Ministry of Defence (MOD) Exercise Area** to the southeast that was used during World War II for training for the D-Day invasion. Take note though: it's still in use today (see below).

East to Auchencairn

The A711 south of Kirkcudbright hugs the shoreline for a short distance with views out to **St Mary's Isle** (a peninsula, not an island), once the seat of the Earl of Selkirk. It was to the earl's house in 1778 that John Paul Jones (page 132) came, landing his ship the *Ranger* on St Mary's Isle and intending to capture the fourth earl. On reaching his house, however, Jones's men discovered that the earl was away from home. Jones did nothing more than authorise his men to loot the house of its silver, which he later purchased back from them and returned to Lady Selkirk along with a lengthy note of apology.

Heading east you very quickly hit **MOD land** (see the entry for Kirkcudbright Training Centre at 🔗 gov.uk/public-access-to-military-areas#scotland) which reaches as far as Dundrennan. No restrictions apply to the main A711 road itself, nor to the land north of the road but if you want to explore the area to the south of the road you will need to be clued up on where you can go and at what times it is safe to do so. Access to the area is possible at four different points, at each of which you must leave your car and walk. The MOD publishes a leaflet that is available from Kirkcudbright tourist information centre (see box, page 136), which shows the extent of the area and walking routes within the range. It also emails out times of live firing exercises usually two weeks ahead of time to the tourist information centre and library – if you want to walk in the relevant area make sure to check in advance if it is safe to do so. Firing times can also be found online at 🔗 gov.uk/government/publications/scotland-firing-times. If in doubt, the MOD flies a flag during the day and has red lights at night to indicate that no access is allowed. You can also telephone the Guard Room at the Kirkcudbright Training Centre, which is manned 24 hours a day (☎ 0141 224 8502). The number has a Glasgow code but goes through the exchange automatically to reach Kirkcudbright.

"Jones did nothing more than authorise his men to loot the house of its silver, which he later purchased back from them."

Of the 13 Cistercian monasteries in Scotland, the most impressive that still remains is **Dundrennan Abbey** (📍 NX749475 🕘 Apr–Sep 09.30–

17.30 daily (last entry 17.00); Historic Environment Scotland). It was founded by Fergus, Lord of Galloway in 1142 and the monks who came here went on to found the abbeys at Glenluce (page 231) and New Abbey (page 130). The graceful ruins that can be seen today are known for their bucolic setting, for the well-preserved transepts from the late 12th century, and for the fact that it was here that Mary, Queen of Scots spent her last night on Scottish soil. Linger a while soaking up the atmosphere then pop into the tea room just along the road (opposite).

From Dundrennan it's a short hop over the hills to Auchencairn, passing a large straw effigy of a wicker man en route, recollecting use of the area as a location for the cult film. Wickerwork is also on display in **Auchencairn** itself, for this pleasant, unpretentious village is the home of Trevor Leat (trevorleat.co.uk), one of the UK's foremost creators of willow sculptures, whose work can usually be spotted on the main street. It's also the home of Esther Stevenson, whose holistic retreats offer an ideal way to slow down and rejuvenate (9–11 Main St, DG7 1QU 01556 640574 gallowayholisticretreats.co.uk); she also runs the Dragonfly Restaurant from the same address (see opposite). A little further down the main street, towards the bottom, is the village shop (see opposite), where Vicky Pitts keeps a good range of essentials as well as offering a cuppa, bite to eat and a chat.

Auchencairn, and more specifically Auchencairn Bay, was smugglers' country, with the most ostentatious sign of those times being **Balcary House** (now a hotel, page 261) at Balcary Point. Depending on which account you read, the house, which dates from 1625, was built either by a shipping firm or on the proceeds of smuggling. The road out to Balcary Point is a dead end but worth the trip. It runs for two miles up the side of Auchencairn Bay with fine views out over the sands and, from the end, to the diminutive **Hestan Island** (hestan.co.uk), which in the 12th century was used by the monks from Dundrennan for fishing and which in slightly more recent times became the Isle of Rathan in *The Raiders* by S R Crockett (page 147). A **circular walk** of around 3½ miles can be done around Balcary Point along the coast to Rascarrel Bay, then looping back inland, with spectacular clifftop views (not recommended for vertigo sufferers). It's possible to walk over to Hestan Island, too, but

"From Dundrennan it's a short hop over the hills to Auchencairn, passing a large straw effigy of a wicker man en route."

only at certain low tides. Misjudge it and you risk getting into trouble, so caution is advised and any attempt is at your own risk. Check tide times and ask locally for the best advice before setting out.

FOOD & DRINK

Auchencairn Store 7 Main St, Auchencairn DG7 1QU ✆ 01556 640385. Vicky Pitts and her partner James have created a warm and welcoming hub; a great place to drop in, catch up on the news and meet the locals. In addition to teas, coffees and home baking, Vicky also cooks main meals to either eat in or take out. Being greeted by the smell of her beef stew, lentil soup and cake is blissful!

The Crown and Anchor Tea Room Dundrennan DG6 4QH ✆ 01557 500579. Jacqui and John Pendleton's cosy tea room is a perfect stop-off point if touring the area or if you just fancy a change of scene. Jacket potatoes, burgers, soups and sandwiches, vegetarian options, cakes and scones… and a wood-burning stove for cooler days.

The Dragonfly 11 Main St, Auchencairn DG7 1QU ✆ 01556 640088. From edible flowers during the summer to healthy, hearty meals in winter, not to mention take-away pizza, curry, chilli, chocolate cheesecake and Eton mess, Esther's menu is wide-ranging. There are also good vegetarian and vegan options: tofu 'fish', falafel, hummus and salad platters, roasted vine tomato, sweet potato and pepper soup. Everything is made from scratch and as many ingredients as possible are sourced locally.

West to Carrick

To get the most out of the west side of the Dee head out of Kirkcudbright across the stark concrete-arched bridge of 1926 and take the B727 south, signposted for Brighouse Bay. The road follows the shoreline of the Dee, offering ever-changing views of the estuary and passing a convenient stopping point at **Dhoon Bay**, a pleasant spot for a picnic. Keep heading south on the road as it turns inland and take the first turning on the left for both Brighouse and Ross bays.

This stretch of coast is a succession of slow-shelving bays and inlets, with the sandy horseshoe of **Brighouse Bay** a particular favourite. The surrounding parish of **Borgue** has long enjoyed a reputation as 'the land of milk and honey', with fine pastureland for grazing and farms famed for producing honey. It also makes a comfortable habitat for the alpacas at Senwick Farm (✆ 01557 870199 senwickalpacas.co.uk), who you can join for a trekking experience on the Solway coast. The area was the home in the 18th century of one Hugh Blair whose condition, it is believed, may have been the first recorded case of autism.

THE GALLOVIDIAN ENCYCLOPAEDIA

A short walk across the fields from the road to Ross Bay lie the remains of **Senwick Church** (NX655460) on the west side of Kirkcudbright Bay. Here in the kirkyard is buried **John Mactaggart**, author of *The Gallovidian Encyclopaedia* ('Gallovidian' being 'of Galloway'), published in 1824. The full title of his work, as it appeared on the title page, was more than just a mouthful: 'The Scottish Gallovidia, or the original, antiquated, and natural curiosities of the South of Scotland, containing sketches of eccentric characters and curious places, with explanations of singular words, terms, and phrases, interspersed with poems, tales, anecdotes, &c., and various other strange matters; the whole illustrative of the ways of the peasantry and manners of Caledonia, drawn out and alphabetically arranged, by John Mactaggart'.

Mactaggart was in his lifetime a poet, teacher, author, and engineer, forging his various careers in Scotland, London and Canada. It is his notorious *Encyclopaedia* for which he is remembered, though not necessarily for the right reasons. Into this book he poured his heart and soul. No character and no custom of his native land did he leave unexplained, all told in his own inimitable, perplexing style. In a display of uncharacteristic *sangfroid* he then declared: 'It will be a book that will never create much noise, yet still it will not be in a hurry forgotten'. He was almost right, for not long after publication his book was withdrawn due to the threat of libel from the father of a local Kirkcudbright girl and the tale of both the man and his work has endured ever since. In fact, so persistent has the story been that in recent years the Wigtown Book Festival (page 205) commissioned a sequel or modern-day version, *McMillan's Galllovidian Encyclopaedia*.

The coast from **Borgue to Knockbrex** and then on to Carrick is gorgeous. It takes in a few curiosities, all of them dating from the late 19th and early 20th centuries and attributable to James Brown, part owner of Affleck and Brown, Manchester's 'Harrods of the north' in what is now the city's iconic Smithfield Buildings. **Kirkandrews Kirk, Corseyard Farm and Model Dairy** and the estate house at **Knockbrex** all display a unique style, combining influences from the Arts and Crafts movement, Celtic motifs and Brown's fondness for outlandish castellated finishings. So extravagant is the model dairy (visible from the road at Corseyard) that it has for years been known as the 'coo [cow] palace'! Today it has been restored to its former glory by a holiday

"So extravagant is the model dairy (visible from the road at Corseyard) that it has for years been known as the 'coo [cow] palace'!"

DARK SKIES

Dumfries and Galloway is one of the best places in the country for stargazing. Galloway Forest Park was the UK's first Dark Sky Park, and Moffat was the first Dark Sky Town in Europe.

SIMON ROBERTSON/I

EDDIE J. RODRIQUEZ/S

HOLY PLACES

The region is home to a wide range of religious architecture, reflecting the many and varied influences that have found their way to this corner of Scotland and been brought to bear over the centuries. From simple handmade crosses to extravagant marble monuments, the variety is striking.

RICHARD P LONG/S

WALTER BAXTER/W

DG/DF (SLOW BRITAIN)

DG/DF (SLOW BRITAIN)

OTTER/W

DG/DF (SLOW BRITAIN)

1 Romantic Sweetheart Abbey. 2 The Durisdeer marbles. 3 Peace and beauty are found in the ruins of Dundrennan Abbey. 4 Striking Dalswinton Barony Church was built in 1881. 5 Kagyu Samye Ling Tibetan Monastery in the hills of Upper Eskdale. 6 St Ninian's Cave. 7 Hallmuir Prisoner of War Chapel. 8 The grave of Covenanters John Stewart and Robert Grierson at the parish church in St John's Town of Dalry.

DG/DF (SLOW BRITAIN)

GRAEME ROBERTSON

THE ARTS

The arts are thriving in Dumfries and Galloway and the region has a growing national and international reputation for the quality and breadth of its artistic offering. Music, literature, art, drama, sculpture, photography and much more besides are on offer all year round.

1 Moat Brae, 'home' of *Peter Pan*. 2 Henry Moore's *Glenkiln Cross* stands on a hill overlooking Glenkiln Reservoir. 3 Robert Burns's statue at the top of Dumfries High Street and, behind him, Greyfriars Kirk. 4 The face of German artist Kurt Schwitters adorns a caravan at the Merz art space in Sanquhar.

STOCKSOLUTIONS/S

DG/DF (SLOW BRITAIN)

MERZ

property bond company. Look out for the castellated **bathing hut** on the beach at Knockbrex.

Beyond Knockbrex the sandy bays give way to a wonderful rocky shore. Keep going to **Carrick**, though, down a rough track, and you'll reach another small sandy bay among the little chalets dotting the shoreline.

Lying just offshore between Knockbrex and Carrick is **Ardwall Isle** (NX572493), the largest of the Islands of Fleet. This is a magical place for kayaking and makes for a popular walk, too. Beware, though, for the island can only be reached at low water and the tides can be treacherous. Check tide times before setting out and keep an eye on them on the way. The island itself is believed to have been an early Christian site possibly dating from the 5th century. In the 13th century a hall house stood here, and towards the end of the 18th century a tavern, catering – one likes to think – to the many smugglers who made this their haunt.

FOOD & DRINK

Borgue Hotel Main St, Borgue DG6 4SH 01557 870636 borguehotel.co.uk. Bar meals and snacks, popular with both locals and visitors.

SEND US YOUR SNAPS!

We'd love to follow your adventures using our *Dumfries & Galloway* guide – why not tag us in your photos and stories on Twitter (@BradtGuides) and Instagram (@bradtguides)?

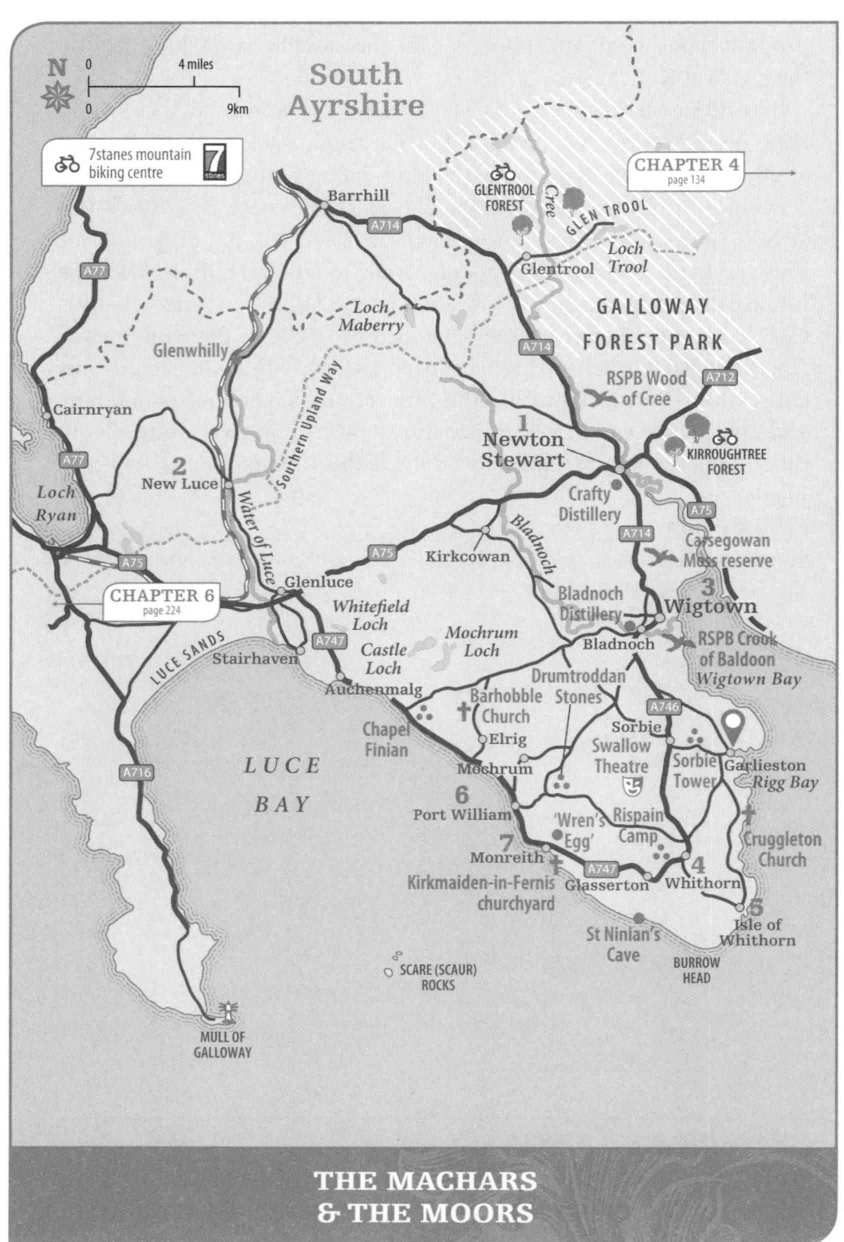
N
0
4 miles
0
9km
South Ayrshire
7stanes mountain biking centre
CHAPTER 4
page 134
Barrhill
A714
GLENTROOL FOREST
Cree
GLEN TROOL
Loch Trool
Glentrool
GALLOWAY FOREST PARK
A77
Loch Maberry
Glenwhilly
Southern Upland Way
A714
RSPB Wood of Cree
A712
Cairnryan
1
Newton Stewart
KIRROUGHTREE FOREST
A77
2
New Luce
Water of Luce
Crafty Distillery
Loch Ryan
Bladnoch
A75
A714
Carsegowan Moss reserve
A75
A75
Kirkcowan
Glenluce
3
Wigtown
CHAPTER 6
page 224
Whitefield Loch
Bladnoch Distillery
Mochrum Loch
Bladnoch
RSPB Crook of Baldoon
Wigtown Bay
LUCE SANDS
Stairhaven
A747
Castle Loch
Drumtroddan Stones
Auchenmalg
Barhobble Church
A746
Sorbie
Chapel Finian
Elrig
Swallow Theatre
Sorbie Tower
Garlieston
Rigg Bay
A716
LUCE BAY
Mochrum
6
Port William
'Wren's Egg'
Rispain Camp
Cruggleton Church
7
Monreith
A747
4
Kirkmaiden-in-Fernis churchyard
Glasserton
Whithorn
5
Isle of Whithorn
St Ninian's Cave
BURROW HEAD
SCARE (SCAUR) ROCKS
MULL OF GALLOWAY
THE MACHARS & THE MOORS

5
THE MACHARS & THE MOORS

Occupying the tract of land between the high hills and ragged coastline of the Stewartry to the east and the gentler landscapes of the Rhins to the west, the Machars and moors offer a compelling mix of upland wilderness, undulating interior and idyllic coast for discerning travellers in search of somewhere just a wee bit off the beaten track.

North of Newton Stewart stretches empty moorland, while to the south, the peninsula of the Machars – from the old Scots word meaning low-lying coastal plain – is perfect for pootling around quiet lanes by car or bike or venturing into the countryside on foot. Exploring is a real treat with a wealth of attractions and features that are as notable for their diversity as they are for their compact geography: it takes less than an hour to drive the 28 miles from Newton Stewart down to the Isle of Whithorn (though the going is slower if you head north to the moors).

Culture and history abound, notably in **Wigtown**, Scotland's National Book Town, and at **Whithorn**, the cradle of Christianity in Scotland. There is also a plethora of prehistoric sites: stone circles, cup and ring marks, Iron Age settlements, crannogs, chambered cairns… historical evidence of life down through the centuries in such abundance that separate books have been written on them alone. We have selected some of the best to include here, but there are lots of leaflets and information points around the region, so if you have a specific interest, keep an eye open for relevant literature. As ever, OS maps provide an indispensable reference source, too.

Strictly speaking, the Machars start at Newton Stewart on the west side of the River Cree, which means that Minnigaff, on the east side, falls into the Stewartry. However, it makes no sense to separate the two and so both are dealt with in this chapter.

GETTING AROUND

The Machars and Moors are bisected east–west by the A75 and north–south by the A714 from Whithorn up into Ayrshire and beyond. The A75 is sometimes busy, particularly shortly after a ferry docks at Cairnryan, and masks the tranquil areas and quiet roads that lie just a short distance either side. Cautious drivers may want to note that some of the roads across the interior are distinctly rough with potholes.

Ferries operate between Northern Ireland and Cairnryan, on the eastern side of Loch Ryan, which is 26 miles from Newton Stewart. P&O Ferries operates services to Larne, and Stena Line sails to Belfast.

PUBLIC TRANSPORT

The Scotrail **train service** has two railway stations within 25 miles of Newton Stewart at Barrhill (18 miles) to the north, and Stranraer (25 miles) to the west, which connect to Glasgow. Dumfries station is 48 miles away, with services also operated by Scotrail, which has more frequent services along its Newcastle and Carlisle to Glasgow route.

There are regular **bus services** between Dumfries and Stranraer, which stop at Newton Stewart, Kirkcowan and Glenluce. Between Stagecoach Western services 500 and X75 there are 11 departures a day (Mon–Sat) from Dumfries railway station and Whitesands to Stranraer. The journey can take up to 2½ hours depending on the time of day. McCulloch Coaches also offers one service a day. On Sundays there are four departures of service 500. Return journeys run as frequently.

Once at the Machars, daily buses run from Newton Stewart through many of the key villages and towns to Port William (Service 415; DGC Buses/Stagecoach West Scotland). Stagecoach West Scotland also runs the infrequent 416 service from Stranraer down to Whithorn and back up to Newton Stewart.

Local public transport information is provided by South West of Scotland Transport Partnership (🖱 swestrans.org.uk), or alternatively Traveline (☎ 0871 200 22 33 🖱 traveline.info).

CYCLING

The quiet, triangular-shaped peninsula of the Machars is fertile low-lying ground, making for flatter cycling when compared to the rest of the county. **National Cycle Network Route 7** passes Newton Stewart on its way north to Inverness.

TOURIST INFORMATION

There is no VisitScotland information centre on the Machars. *Our Wigtownshire* is a local magazine published every two months with lots of information about local people, businesses and events; it's available from high street shops across the region.

The Belted Galloway Visitor Centre and Café Riverside Rd, Newton Stewart DG8 6NQ ✆ 01671 403458. Craig and the team do a grand job of providing visitors with information.
The Whithorn Trust 45–47 George St, Whithorn DG8 8NS ✆ 01988 50050 whithorn.com Apr/Easter–Oct 10.30–17.00. Carries lots of information in its shop in the centre of Whithorn and has a good website.

There are four signed and colour-coded Machars Cycle Routes as designated by Dumfries and Galloway Council (info.dumgal.gov.uk/mapviewers/pathsmap). The Yellow Route (25 miles) heads west from Wigtown; the Red Route (17 miles) starts from Whithorn taking in Sorbie and the Isle of Whithorn; the Orange Route (22 miles) loops from Wigtown, down to Garlieston and back via Sorbie; and the green route (20 miles) passes through Mochrum, Port William, Monreith and Whithorn.

CYCLE HIRE

Kirkcowan Cycles The Old Red Cross Hall, Victoria Ln, Newton Stewart DG8 6DA ✆ 01671 401529 kirkcowancycles.co.uk

WALKING

The quiet peninsula of the Machars and the wild and remote moors to the north provide a fine range of scenery for walkers to explore. The rugged moors and hills offer a wonderful sense of isolation. **The Merrick Trail** from Loch Trool takes you to the highest point in Dumfries and Galloway, rising to 2,766ft. Along the way, look out for some of the rarest plants in Scotland such as dwarf willow, mossy saxifrage, thrift and juniper, all montane species and extremely tough, surviving harsh mountaintop conditions.

The long-distance **Southern Upland Way** wiggles its way across this northern area, while part of the **Whithorn Way** (whithorn.com/walk-the-whithorn-way) works its way down the west coast of the Machars

MACHARS MOVIES

Fancy catching a film while you're in the area? In addition to the cinema in Newton Stewart (see opposite), Machars Movies (Scotland's most southerly community cinema; macharsmovies.weebly.com) screens films at venues across the area, from its base at St Ninian's Hall in the Isle of Whithorn (page 216) to various village halls and the Swallow Theatre (page 215).

before cutting across to Whithorn. Although 149 miles long in total, it's divided into manageable sections.

On the coast, green pastures roll to the water's edge and merse (saltmarsh), providing contrast with stretches of dramatic cliffs carpeted in coastal flowers. Inland, pockets of native broadleaved woodlands, particularly along the River Cree, are important sites for birds and wildlife. Available in many local shops is our *Galloway 40 Coast and Country Walks* book, published by Pocket Mountains (pocketmountains.com).

Walkers may want to note that Newton Stewart offers a good outdoor shop, Cunninghams (14–18 Victoria St, DG8 6BT 01671 401115 srcunningham.co.uk).

3 NEWTON STEWART & AROUND

Flowerbank Guest House (page 262) **Cairnharrow** (page 263)

Pleasantly positioned on the banks of the 'silv'ry winding Cree', Newton Stewart (newtonstewart.org) is a likeable and functional town, servicing all of the outlying areas (the next town of any size is Stranraer, 25 miles to the west; page 234) with its mix of restaurants, shops, cafés and supermarkets. 'Gateway to the Galloway Hills' is a description that's used to describe it today, while the novelist S R Crockett, who came from neighbouring Kirkcudbrightshire, said it was the 'natural gateway and distributing point for much enchanted ground'. No surprise then that it's the hub for southern Scotland's largest **walking festival**, held each year in May. It's also the home of the unusual sport of **tambourelli**, a version of badminton invented in Galloway in the 1970s in which a shuttlecock is hit back and forth using a bat similar to a tambour. The annual World Championships are held here every three years, rotating between Newton Stewart, Devon and Dresden.

In times past this was a river crossing point on the cattle droving route from the west along to Dumfries and beyond to the markets in England. Cattle (and sheep) continue to play a role in the life of the modern town thanks to Wigtownshire's last remaining **livestock market**, which can be found in a listed octagonal building at the junction of Queen Street and Station Road at the southern end of town (see box, page 200). Sales are held weekly, and at the end of the trading year in October there is a world-famous Blackface ram sale.

Newton Stewart developed when William Stewart, second Earl of Galloway, secured the royal burgh charter from Charles II in 1677. However, its name was changed to Newton Douglas 200 years later when aspiring merchant William Douglas, of Castle Douglas fame (page 154), bought the estate. Douglas's ego surpassed his business acumen, for the £20,000 cotton mill that he built here failed and he was compelled to retreat from the Shire, leaving locals to revert their town name without fuss to Newton Stewart.

For an introduction to the town, take a short circular walk from the riverside car park at the southern end of Victoria Street. Cross the bridge over the river and turn left along the east bank and then return via the handsome granite **Cree Bridge** of 1813. Here on the west bank stands a **monument** to Randolph Stewart, ninth Earl of Galloway, by all accounts a credit to his title having held the position of Lord Lieutenant of both Wigtownshire and Kirkcudbrightshire.

"Here on the west bank stands a monument to Randolph Stewart, ninth Earl of Galloway, a credit to his title."

From the monument continue along Victoria Street, noting the community-run **Art Deco cinema**, which has been going for over 85 years. Beyond the cinema, walk up the hill and turn left to drop back down to the riverside car park.

Newton Stewart's **museum** (York Rd, DG8 6HH newtonstewart.org Easter–Jun & 3rd week Sep–1st week Oct 14.00–17.00 Mon–Sat; Jul–2nd week Sep 10.30–17.00; last admission 16.30), housed in the former St John's Church in a residential area above Victoria Street, is perhaps the town's greatest unsung attraction. Nothing really prepares you for the sight that hits you on stepping inside. Thousands of exhibits are crammed into every nook, niche and cranny. It's a fantastic collection of accumulated paraphernalia – a joy in its range of interest, local

A DAY AT THE MARKET: FROM LIVESTOCK TO CHRISTMAS TREES

Craig Wilson Ltd Queen St, DG8 6LH ☏ 01671 402051 ⌂ craigwilsonltd.co.uk

Selling Livestock by Auction as a method has defied improvement so far in practice or theory. It is the most efficient method of distributing and directing, to where each is wanted, the infinite varieties and qualities which present production methods turn out.

Such was the belief in the late 19th century of one James Craig of Ayr, which lead him to successfully establish a livestock auction house in his home area. This quickly went on to expand, acquiring the auction mart in Newton Stewart.

Unlike many marts that have moved out of town, Newton Stewart's still operates from town-centre premises, with its distinctive, B-listed, six-sided building that houses the auction ring.

Anyone can wander in to take a look – the door is always unlocked if there is someone around – and anyone can go along to the livestock auctions (every Wednesday and one Friday a month). The Machars area relies heavily on agriculture and the auction offers an honest perspective of an industry at the heart of a rural economy.

James Craig would be proud of how his business has fared. Still in the hands of his family, it has also diversified – of necessity, to weather the storm of the 2001–02 foot and mouth outbreak – and now also owns two Christmas tree farms, one in Ayrshire and the other in the hills north of Creetown. In December the auction ring doubles as a display space for Christmas trees. It has been so successful that it now supplies trees to 10 Downing Street and the Ritz Hotel in London.

personality, anomaly and the downright bizarre. The collection was started in the 1970s and pursued with vigour by a number of local people, not least Miss Helen Drew, a name that according to the local *Galloway Gazette* is 'synonymous not just with the museum but with Newton Stewart as a whole'. Miss Drew, who passed away in 2010, purchased the church and gifted it to be used as a museum. She also spent her life collecting for it and donated around 50% of the items that are on display. The collection here is one of the most eclectic and wide-ranging that we have ever come across in a local museum, rivalled perhaps only by the collection at Dalbeattie's museum (page 159). Make time for it if you can, it is quite something to behold.

On the edge of Newton Stewart is the new **Crafty Distillery** (see opposite), while just a few miles south of the town, down a lane off the main road to Wigtown, lies the Scottish Wildlife Trust's **Carsegowan Moss reserve**, one of the best examples of a lowland raised peat bog in Galloway. Cranberry and bog rosemary grow in the sphagnum moss carpet and, depending on when you're here, you might spot large heath butterflies, adders, hen harriers and short-eared owls.

CRAFTY DISTILLERY

Wigtown Rd, Newton Stewart DG8 6AS 01671 404040 craftydistillery.com check website for opening hours & tour times

Occupying smart and stylish purpose-built premises with enviable views out to Cairnsmore of Fleet and the Cree Estuary, this bold and – dare we say it – slightly funky new business, producer of the increasingly popular Hills & Harbour gin that you're likely to come across while in the area, has taken the gin world by storm.

"Keeping it all as local as possible, Crafty forage their own botanicals, favouring the citrus hints of the noble fir."

With a lightning bolt logo, punchy lines like 'Distilled by the nation that invented almost bloody everything', a grain-to-glass approach, and extensive research and testing (they tried over 100 recipes before deciding on the one to go for, and then tested it on 400 people to refine the flavour), Crafty's efforts paid off in 2018 when they won Scottish Gin Destination of the Year at the Scottish Gin Awards.

Keeping it all as local as possible, Crafty also forage their own botanicals, favouring the citrus hints of the noble fir – fresh sprigs of which, incidentally, are foraged on land managed by Craig Wilson's Garrocher tree farm (see box, opposite) – and the saltiness of Solway seaweed.

There's a lot more to the Crafty story that is worth telling. Check out their website and go along and see for yourself. Two different tours are offered (both involving tastings, of course) and you can also book to go on a foraging experience, at the end of which you can make your own cocktail. Bottoms up!

FOOD & DRINK

The Belted Galloway Visitor Centre Riverside View, DG8 6NQ 01671 403458. Café, shop and information in a convenient location by the riverside car park. Serves tea, coffee, sandwiches, snacks, fish and chips and more.

The Riverbank Restaurant Goods Ln, DG8 6EH ✆ 01671 403330. On the riverside next to the supermarket, this popular café serves sandwiches, soups, fish and chips and more.

GALLOWAY FOREST PARK

🏠 **House o' Hill Hotel** (page 262)

Newton Stewart offers easy access to **Galloway Forest Park**; this western side of the park also offers the only vehicular access to **Glentrool Visitor Centre** (NX371787; page 151). Immediately east of Newton Stewart is **Kirroughtree Visitor Centre** (page 151). For more information on Galloway Forest Park see page 148.

FOOD & DRINK

House o' Hill Hotel Bargrennan DG8 6RN ✆ 01671 840243 houseohill.co.uk. The only hotel within Galloway Forest Park has a strong reputation for its food. The menu, which ranges from afternoon tea to venison, fish and shellfish, changes with the season. It's a 20-minute drive from Newton Stewart but worth the trip. Alternatively, plan your day's touring to include it for lunch or dinner.

RSPB WOOD OF CREE RESERVE

Running up the east side of the Cree north of Minnigaff is the **RSPB Wood of Cree** reserve, the largest ancient woodland in southern Scotland. It's a good place to spot pied flycatchers, tree pipits and numerous warblers, along with scotch argus and small pearl-bordered fritillary butterflies and otters at the Otter Pool on the River Cree. There are various stopping points and parking areas along the wood edge, from where different trails head off. The main habitat is oak woodland.

THE MOORS

Miles upon miles of empty moorland lie north of the A75 where it runs between Newton Stewart and Glenluce. If you feel like getting away from everyone and everything, this is the place to come and, depending on how you like your countryside, you will either love it or loathe it. There is a stark beauty in the endless moorland vista, but there is also a loneliness and isolation that can shake even the most positive spirits.

One way to experience this area is to take the train from Stranraer (page 234) up to **Barrhill** in South Ayrshire, get off there and then catch the next train back, but train times don't tie in very neatly and you're likely to find yourself killing time for several hours. Barrhill is a small village with limited amenities and the station is a 15-minute walk outside the village itself. Alternatively, driving – or cycling for the very fit – offers greatest flexibility. Whether you start at Glenluce or Newton Stewart, it's just less than 20 miles by road to Barrhill.

If going from **Glenluce**, once north of New Luce, stick to the road on the east side of the Main Water of Luce and you'll find isolated hilltop farms and views that make you feel as if you're on top of the world. There really is nothing here. It is bleak, desolate, wonderful, superlative moorland where Blackface sheep roam the road and the old disused station at **Glenwhilly** (⚲ NX173715) sits forlorn and empty since closing in 1965. The road follows much the same route as the train line and you may be forgiven for wondering if you have reached the emptiest place in Scotland. From Newton Stewart the A714 travels through large stretches of Forestry and Land Scotland plantation, as does the smaller B7027, the latter having the added interest of a series of lochs roughly halfway. The **River Bladnoch** rises at pretty **Loch Maberry** (⚲ NX285755), which marks the regional boundary and which is gemmed with a number of small islands, on one of which stand the remains of a fortified castle. **Canoe trips** are run here by the Adventure Centre for Education (✆ 01465 710077 during office hours; ✆ 07920 406982 at other times 🖱 adventurecarrick.com), catering to both adults and (accompanied) children.

2 NEW LUCE

The pretty village of New Luce sits at the junction of five roads and the confluence of the Main Water of Luce and Cross Water of Luce. At one time it was a bustling small community of tradesmen and labourers serving the surrounding farms, but today it's a quieter place of whitewashed cottages, neat gardens and hanging baskets, and a combined post office and shop. At the southern entrance to the village, right by the river, stands the Kenmuir Arms Hotel, which, at the time this guide went to print, was in the process of being refurbished by its new owners, the New Luce Community Trust (🖱 newlucect.org), to offer a pub, tea room and guest rooms. Located just a mile or so north of the **Southern Upland Way**, it's a good spot for walkers in search of retreat.

During the 17th century, from 1659 until his ejection in 1662, New Luce came under the care of the renowned **Prophet Peden** –Alexander

Peden, Covenanter preacher and minister. He was one of the 300 or so ministers who were forced to leave their churches after the restoration of Charles II. During the 11 years he spent on the run, he gained notoriety preaching in fields all over southern and central Scotland. Eventually government troops caught up with him; he was arrested in 1673 and spent four years imprisoned on Bass Rock in the Firth of Forth. In 1678 he was put on a slave ship bound for the US but he was set free by the captain and spent most of the rest of his life in Ireland. It is said that when he left New Luce, after preaching his farewell sermon, he closed the door of the pulpit and, knocking on it three times with his Bible, declared 'I arrest thee in my Master's name, that none ever enter thee but such as come in by the door as I have done.' His prophecy was correct for the pulpit at New Luce wasn't used again until after the Revolution.

Various places of archaeological interest are found in the surrounding area, all of them detailed on a sign at the top end of the main street, from Neolithic cairns to Bronze and Iron age remains.

North of New Luce the road follows the line of the railway over rolling hills and farmland for 13 miles up to Barrhill.

3 WIGTOWN

Craigmount Guest House (page 262), **Hillcrest House** (page 263) **Beltie Flat** (page 263), **Cairnharrow** (page 263) **Drumroamin Farm Camping and Caravan Site** (page 263)

With its plethora of bookshops, quiet streets, views over Wig Bay, abundant birdlife and a colourful history, **Scotland's National Book Town** is an overgrown village where you can wrap yourself in the comfort of a slower way of life. There is something unreservedly appealing about a town that has a bowling green at its very heart, set out neatly in the town square in front of the disproportionately large and imposing County Building, a sign of past prosperity. Looking at today's peaceable town with its gaily coloured houses and its delightful dedication to matters bookish, it is difficult to believe that this was once a major centre with a trade built upon the fortunes of a port that is now silted up, where cattle were corralled in the railed enclosure in the town centre and the green was the common dunghill, and where the savage murder of innocent victims occurred during Covenanting times.

Settled for at least 1,000 years, Wigtown was once the main town of Galloway west of the Cree. It also lent its name to the old county of Wigtownshire, an administrative region that was lost in the reorganisation of county boundaries in 1975, but which still exists as a lieutenancy area for the Queen's representative, the Lord Lieutenant of Wigtownshire. A castle was built here by the 13th century, but little is known about it other than the fact that, contrary to the siting of most defensive buildings, it was located on the flat plains of the River Bladnoch, where it could command control of the port, while the town and church were above it on the hill. A Royal Charter was granted in 1457 and during the 15th and 16th centuries the port of Wigtown thrived, competing first with Kirkcudbright (page 181) and then, later,

THE WIGTOWN BOOK FESTIVAL – AND MORE

Founded in 1999, the Wigtown Book Festival is now in its third decade and the town itself now boasts almost 20 independent shops that sell books, from full blown bookshops to a café and gallery with book sections, covering vintage and antiquarian tomes as well as modern and recently released editions (all detailed on wigtown-booktown.co.uk and on a leaflet available from all of the bookshops and the Wigtown Festival office). There's even one – appropriately named The Open Book – where you can book (no pun intended) a working holiday to see what it's like running a bookshop (details on the website above), an initiative that has proved so popular that it is often fully booked for up to two years in advance. And mention should also be made of The Bookshop, Scotland's largest secondhand bookshop, whose owner Shaun Bythell is also the author of the hugely successful and entertaining book (and sequel), *The Diary of a Bookseller*.

The Book Festival itself is run by the Wigtown Festival Company and is held every year in late September/early October. It's a fun affair with a wide range of talks on all manner of topics given by everyone from international celebrities to local authors. The *Telegraph* newspaper said it is 'one of the best autumn festivals in the world'. As attendees and speakers ourselves, we would have to agree!

Not content with running just one annual extravaganza, the Festival Company has in recent years established a range of events, programmes and charitable projects and schemes in Wigtown and across the region throughout the year, from the Big Dog – 'A Children's Book Festival for Dumfries' (named after Nana, the big dog who looks after the children in *Peter Pan*) – to the Big Bang Mini Science Festival, an annual arts award, a local writer's magazine and much more besides.

Full details about the festival, the company and its work can be found at wigtownbookfestival.com.

with nearby Whithorn (page 211). It was in the 17th century, during the Killing Times (page 24), that Wigtown gained notoriety for the execution of the **Wigtown Martyrs**, including a 63-year-old woman and a girl of 18 who stood accused of attending 20 field Conventicles. Margaret McLachlan and Margaret Wilson were sentenced to death by drowning and, on 11 May 1685, both were tied to the stake in the channel of the Bladnoch near the entrance to Wig Bay, where they were left to the incoming tide. They were laid to rest in **Wigtown Parish Church** at the bottom of Bank Street, where their graves can still be seen along with those of other martyrs, and they are also commemorated in the **Martyrs' Memorial**, an obelisk built on Windy Hill in 1858, from where there is a good view over the town down to the bay (and which is a good place to come bat spotting of an evening). To reach the memorial head up High Vennel from the main square, turn left at the garage and take the last turning on the left at the top.

"It is awful to contemplate the horror that befell those who lost their lives for remaining true to themselves."

Down on the bay stands the most poignant of all the memorials, the **Martyrs' Stake**, which can be reached via a path past the Parish Church and then on to a boardwalk across the merse. Standing here in this lonely spot, it is awful to contemplate the horror that befell those who lost their lives for remaining true to themselves.

By the end of the 20th century, Wigtown was beginning to lose its life and lustre. That all changed when it won a competition to become the National Book Town, since when its fortunes have been significantly revived.

Wigtown Bay, a huge expanse of saltmarsh and mudflat, is the largest Local Nature Reserve in the UK, brimming with food that attracts waders throughout the year, notably Svalbard geese in winter. Ospreys have also nested here for the past few years and are observed via osprey cams at the **wildlife centre** on the top floor of the County Buildings, from where there's a great view over the bay.

FOOD & DRINK

Beltie Books & Café 6 Bank St, DG8 9HP ✆ 01988 402730 www.beltiebooks.co.uk. Proprietor Andrew Wilson offers a warm welcome and lots of information about the area. He bakes a scrumptious range of cakes, scones and bread.

Cobwebs 31 South Main St, DG8 9HG ✆ 01988 402097 [f]. All the old favourites – soup, baked potatoes, lasagne, macaroni cheese – plus a literary-themed burger menu packed with puns so groan-worthy you have to read it the whole way through, including 'Lord of the [onion] Rings' and 'Mush-ROOM with a View'...

Craft 30 South Main St, DG8 9HG ✆ 01988 403236 🖱 crafthotelwigtown.co.uk. Bar and restaurant in the heart of Wigtown with an olde-world bar and tartan-carpeted dining room with log stove. Live music every weekend.

The Green Room 19 Bank St, DG8 9DS ✆ 07511 469321 🖱 greenroomwigtown.co.uk. Bistro and bar; classic seasonal cooking and enticing twists on traditional dishes (for instance, Egyptian eggs: toasted sourdough topped with hummus and eggs).

ReadingLasses Bookshop and Café 17 South Main St, DG8 9EH ✆ 01988 403266 [f]. Cosy and comfortable, and serves irresistible cakes; the sort of place you could sit for hours.

Shoots & Leaves 20 South Main St, DG8 9EH ✆ 01988 402249. Dumfries and Galloway's first 100% vegetarian and vegan café; replete with rave reviews and plenty of gluten-free options, too.

AROUND WIGTOWN

The area around Wigtown encompasses gentle scenery, ancient standing stones, small villages and all the attractions of the coast. Northwest from Wigtown on the B733 in a field just next to the road is the impressive **Torhouse Stone Circle** (⚲ NX383565; Historic Environment Scotland). Known as a recumbent stone circle due to one of the stones being laid flat, it is one of the best examples of its type in Britain and something of a rarity in Scotland.

Bladnoch, just south of Wigtown, grew up as a crossing point for pilgrims on their way to Whithorn. Today it's the location of a popular pub (page 210) and home to a community of artisans and musicians. Its main claim to fame, though, is the recently reopened and extremely impressive **Bladnoch Distillery** (DG8 9AB ⚲ NX420543 ✆ 01988 403605 🖱 bladnoch.com), a stunning, modern refurbishment that combines the best of the old and new on the banks of the Bladnoch River. Bladnoch is one of the oldest distilleries in Scotland, dating from 1817, and is also the oldest privately owned Scotch distillery. The new still room is breathtaking, a triumph of brilliantly polished copper and finely tuned alchemy.

"The extremely impressive Bladnoch Distillery, a stunning, modern refurbishment on the banks of the Bladnoch River."

Advance booking is recommended for the regular tours; there's also a café with an enticing range of local produce, cakes and treats.

Bargain hunters head for **Beyond the Bridge Emporium** (Unit 3, Bladnoch Bridge Estate ✆ 07470 457175 f) which offers vintage furniture and collectables in old industrial units on the banks of the river. To reach it, cross the river heading south from Bladnoch, take the road immediately on the left and you'll find it in the brick-built units on the right.

Continue down the same road to reach the **RSPB Crook of Baldoon** reserve (⚲ NX445531), accessed across an old World War II airfield. From the reserve a short footpath runs to Wigtown harbour, and a noticeboard and audio installation offer further information on the restored wet grassland, an ideal breeding habitat for lapwing and redshank.

Garlieston to Cruggleton Castle

OS Landranger map 83, Explorer map 311; start: Village Hall, Garlieston, ⚲ NX478463 (accessible by bus 415/416); 6.5 miles; easy to moderate (some inclines). Note that refreshments are available at the Harbour Inn in Garlieston.

Starting from the **1 Village Hall** on Garlieston waterfront, head towards the caravan parks and on to the old harbour. Take the track at the end of the harbour wall as it passes along the water's edge through old gnarled oaks, past fine estuary views and in front of the stately **Galloway House**. Look out for grey seals, the silhouette of open winged cormorants and a motley crew of wading birds. Follow the path around the headland and in to the lovely Rigg Bay. The track becomes less distinct **2** but follow your nose along the small paths through the woods, enjoying the estate gardens as you go and keeping the bay to your left.

Once at the **3 picnic area** (⚲ NX476447) the path becomes clearer along the back of the bay and on in to the woods. At the cottage ruins, veer off to the left and enjoy the gentle climb up through beautiful mixed woodland and over numerous bridged small streams. When the path meets the stone dyke (wall) and turns right, pause a second and head over to an old **4 wooden bench** and enjoy the view.

Exit the wood to find yourself by a solitary cottage standing atop towering cliffs complete with stunning views – if you feel like staying a while longer the cottage can be rented out (gallowayhouseestate.co.uk). Continue along the clifftop following the drystane dyke; go

On a separate note, if you head down to Crook of Baldoon, keep an eye open for the remains of **Baldoon Castle** 👇 (private) at Baldoon Mains. Around three miles south of Bladnoch is **Kilsture Forest**, the largest patch of woodland on the Machars and a good place to spot roe deer, red squirrels and great spotted woodpeckers. It's particularly pretty in spring when the bluebells are out and also has short waymarked walks of one and three miles.

Continue south for another couple of miles to reach **Sorbie**, a small village once known for its damask weaving, which has an exceptionally solid-looking church, immediately east of which is the half ruined 16th-century **Sorbie Tower** 👇 (⚲ NX451471), seat of the Clan Hannay, who have carried out a number of remedial works. Last occupied in the 18th century, the tower's setting is pleasant and peaceful, with a small colourful garden with picnic tables.

through the gate, turn left and along the edge of the fields to **5 Cruggleton Castle** (⚲ NX485428). All that remains of this 13th-century castle is a reconstructed arch, but what it lacks in walls it certainly makes up for in atmosphere and views.

Retrace your steps back to the picnic area at Rigg Bay. Once at the benches and information board take the hard surface track to the left, through the gate and on past the cottages and walled garden. Turn right and follow the signs through the gardens to the car park and out along the access road, with its fine views of Galloway House. At the **6 crossroads** go straight ahead over the cattle grid, and just before the farmyard turn left; continue for approximately 30yds then turn right on to the track back to Garlieston.

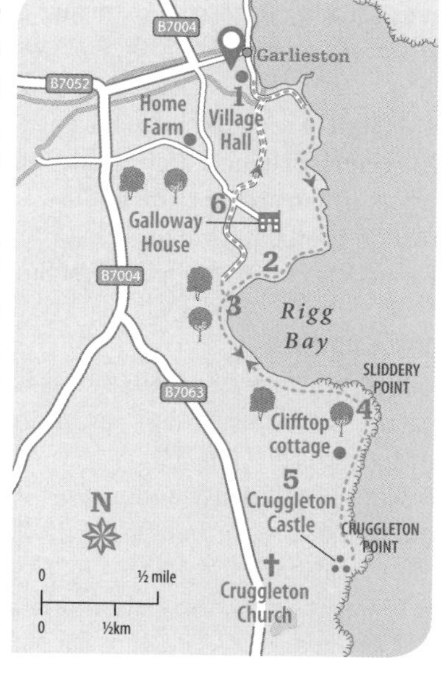

The pristinely maintained waterfront cottages of **Garlieston** on the Machars' east coast look out to Garlieston Bay, an endearing setting that draws in the visitors to the local caravan park. This was once the richest village in Galloway thanks to boat building, fishing and cargo, while in more recent times nearby Rigg Bay was a testing site for the Mulberry Harbour used in the Normandy Landings. In the 18th century the sixth Earl of Galloway redesigned the village to incorporate the neat terraces, and it's from his eldest son, Lord Garlies, that it takes its name. The Earl also built neighbouring **Galloway House** (gallowayhousegardens.co.uk), an enormous pile that was sold off by the 11th Earl in 1909. (At the time of writing it was on the market once again.) Its grounds are open seasonally to the public and are well worth a visit and there are also holiday cottages for rent (gallowayhouseestate.co.uk). Delightful walks run from the small parking area (honesty box for payment) through what were once fine woodland gardens that are today maintained by a stalwart team of volunteers. A short stroll brings you to the sands of **Rigg Bay**.

"The pristinely maintained waterfront cottages on the Machars' east coast look out to Wig Bay, an endearing setting."

South of Garlieston on the B7063 stands **Cruggleton Church** (NX478428), the former chapel of nearby **Cruggleton Castle** (NX485428), only a fraction of which can still be seen on a rocky peninsula about one mile south of Rigg Bay (see box, page 208). Its chief point of interest is the 12th-century chancel arch inside, one of the few surviving examples of early Norman architecture in the area. Access is via Scotland's Churches Trust (scotlandschurchestrust.org.uk) or by attending the one service held here each year – on the first Sunday in September at 15.00.

FOOD & DRINK

Bladnoch Inn Bladnoch DG8 9AB 01988 402200 the-bladnoch-inn.com. Always popular for both lunch and dinner, and especially on a sunny evening when you can sit outside on the banks of the river.

Harbour Inn 18 South Cresc, Garlieston DG8 8BQ 01988 600685 the-harbour-inn.co.uk. Popular shorefront pub offering a friendly welcome and sea views from the cosy bar. Traditional pub fare.

The Pheasant 2 Wigtown Rd, Sorbie DG8 8EL 01988 850270 thepheasantsorbie.com. Chef Andrea and his wife Morag offer authentic, mouth-watering Italian food in this friendly, award-winning country inn-turned-restaurant. Booking recommended.

4 WHITHORN

The Pend (page 263).

This section has been written in conjunction with Julia Muir Watt, Development Manager for the Whithorn Trust. We are extremely grateful to Julia for her input, and especially for the box on page 212.

With a population of less than a thousand people, Whithorn at first glance appears to be little more than a quiet country town, isolated from the rest of the world towards the southern tip of the Machars. But Whithorn's appearance today belies its past, for it was once a major trading centre located conveniently close to major shipping routes. What's more, its place in history is assured thanks to its reputation as the first place where Christianity made landfall in what is now Scotland, as is attested by the modest yet crucially important 5th-century stone in the Whithorn Museum that begins with the overtly Christian message, written in Latin, 'We Praise you Lord'.

Significantly, the evidence at Whithorn, which includes a huge collection of imported pottery and glass, would indicate Christian activity on-site a century before Columba, Scotland's best-known early saint, reached the island of Iona in the west of Scotland. Scholars now working with the Whithorn Trust are retelling the story of early Christianity in Scotland, studying the massive archaeological collection unearthed here; their conclusions are that Scotland's first Christians were not monks, as at Iona, but powerful lords, bilingual elites, who had learned late Roman ways and were quick to adopt Christianity and access international sea routes for trade and luxury goods.

"It did become a monastery, at least by the 7th century, and made its fortune thanks to the thriving cult of its saint."

Undoubtedly, Whithorn did become a monastery, at least by the 7th century, and made its fortune thanks to the thriving cult of its saint, known as Ninian. By the Middle Ages, **St Ninian** became the most venerated in Scotland's canon, right up to the Reformation, with a reputation for cures that attracted thousands, including Scotland's Royal House of Stuart, and pilgrims from England (Richard III was a devotee), Ireland and beyond. Those roads traced by pilgrims are now under development as long-distance walking routes (page 14); recognised again, in a different age, for their benefits to health, both mental and physical.

WHITHORN, CRADLE OF CHRISTIANITY IN SCOTLAND

Julia Muir Watt, Development Manager, Whithorn Trust (whithorn.com)

The international importance of Whithorn as an archaeological site, and its seminal role in Scottish history, is not immediately apparent from this small royal burgh's attractive and well-preserved Georgian streetscape. Yet the observant eye will already detect from the narrow ports closing either end of George Street that a medieval town underlies its later frontages; glimpses of the 'burghage plots' – the narrow strip gardens running down from the houses to the back – further confirm Whithorn's early credentials.

Its real claim to national importance, however, lies after you leave behind the secular world at the mouth of The Pend, the arched gateway into the former Priory precincts, adorned with the Stuart Coat of Arms (c1500), and walk up historic Bruce Street to the crown of the small hill. In so doing, you walk in the footsteps of countless pilgrims, who came to seek forgiveness, healing and even absolution from crimes at the shrine of St Ninian, Scotland's earliest saint, whose cult reached a peak in the high medieval period. At the top of the hill, the roofless ruins of the medieval cathedral, once a tall structure dominating the surrounding countryside, are what remain of the latest of a series of churches built on the site; it is here that the earliest evidence for Christian practice, belief and settlement has been found in the country.

Much scholarly controversy surrounds the exact date and identity of St Ninian, a debate begun by the Venerable Bede in the early 8th century, when he wrote that the saint's evangelising mission had pre-dated the much better-known Columba's by a great many years. A series of archaeological excavations from the late 19th century onwards have sought the grail of the original white-plastered Ninianic church, *Candida Casa*, or the 'white shining house', and in so doing have uncovered, if not the church itself, a remarkable body of evidence that proves that Whithorn, probably by the 5th century AD, was a thriving, sophisticated and literate community with Christian beliefs, importing luxury goods, in touch with the outside world of ideas and trade, with a Latin-speaking local elite acquainted with late Roman feasting culture. Much of the evidence for this was excavated during the 1980s and 1990s by archaeologist Peter Hill, and the finds from the dig are on display in the Whithorn Trust's visitor centre. The inscribed 'Latinus'

To get to grips with the ins and outs of this crucial part of Scottish history, head straight for the well-planned **Whithorn Story Visitor Centre** (45–47 George St, DG8 8NS whithorn.com Apr/Easter–31 Oct 10.30–17.00 daily; see ad, 4th colour section) run by the Whithorn Trust, where an introductory film sets the scene followed by a wander through the chronologically arranged exhibition that stone, the iconic stone that testifies to the very early origins of the Whithorn site, dates from its earliest Christian period and can be seen at the adjacent Priory Museum.

The continuing reverence in which the early church and its saint were held is attested by the way in which Whithorn was constantly resettled and reinvented in the following centuries and by successively invading or colonising peoples. In Bede's day, the Anglo-Saxons dominated Whithorn and claimed St Ninian as their own; an 8th-century poem speaks of the volume of pilgrims seeking miraculous cures at his shrine. Just after, Whithorn (which has kept its Anglo-Saxon name, 'Hwitan-Aerne', the White House) acquired its own school of sculpture and the distinctive disc-headed crosses, seen in the museum, were carved here and have been found at critical points in the countryside, as preaching crosses, at places of judgement or at the sites of other medieval churches within Whithorn's sphere of influence. The later carved stones of the 10th and 11th centuries display perhaps less skill, but belong to a period of Hiberno-Norse settlement, from Viking Dublin, whose culture and symbols blended with Anglo Saxon design and Christian imagery; incidentally, they gave their name to Galloway (the 'Gall-Ghàidheil', or the foreign Gaels).

Wealth and power accumulated from the pilgrimage trade (the pilgrims' detritus fortunately survived for archaeologists to analyse) and allowed Whithorn to become a broker in the murky world of Scottish medieval power politics. Whithorn's Prior had the power of life and death within his extensive lands, a trading fleet sailing from the Isle of Whithorn, and was in the confidences of princes. At the peak of its influence James IV of Scotland visited this remote, and not always obedient, part of his kingdom yearly on pilgrimage, dispensing largesse and begging forgiveness for his sins at the shrine of Scotland's most powerful saint. His treasurer's accounts paint a lively picture of his visits, occasionally accompanied by Italian minstrels, dancers and a baggage train, arriving from across Scotland. The wide open space in front of The Pend still has a ceremonial grandeur, and the town's older civic buildings cluster round the entrance to the Priory.

With the banning of pilgrimage after the Reformation, Whithorn settled into a more modest role as a small centre for trade and a service centre for the surrounding, rich countryside, and that is what it remains today.

lays out clearly the town's development. The importance of this small community to the evolution of a nation can't be overstated and the insights offered here make all the difference in appreciating just how special a place this is. Over the centuries many Scottish kings and queens have visited, including – so tradition has it – Robert the Bruce who came to the shrine of St Ninian in 1329, just three months before his death, to pray for a cure for leprosy. Pick up copies of a couple of leaflets while here: *Whithorn Story* and *Whithorn Town Trail*.

The entry ticket to the Whithorn Story also includes access to Historic Environment Scotland's **Whithorn Priory & Museum** (DG8 8PY ⏲ Apr–Oct 10.30–17.00, last entry 16.30), just around the corner, which forms an integral part of the tale. Enter through the arched gateway of **The Pend**, noting James IV's sculpted coat of arms above. He was known for his devotion to the veneration of the relics of the saints, and visited Whithorn frequently. Of the original large compound only the roofless nave and crypts survive, the latter gloomy but impressive in their scale. The neighbouring museum houses an effectively displayed collection of carved Christian stones from the 5th to 11th centuries. Even if this sounds like a dry subject, we recommend a visit as there is much to be learned and discovered especially if Debbie, the museum curator, is on hand. Her father looked after the museum before her and there is little that she doesn't know on this subject, helping to bring it alive in ways that are truly enlightening. Crosses such as these would have been spread across the landscape in centuries past and the collection here is particularly fine, including the so-called Whithorn School crosses and the earliest Christian monument in Scotland, the 'Latinus' Stone.

"The sheer scale of the building (32ft at the apex) gives an insight into the skill of the Celtic peoples of the time."

Also included in your ticket (which lasts a year) is access to the Whithorn Trust's full-scale **Iron Age roundhouse**, based on recent excavations on a nearby wetland site, which had preserved unprecedented details of Iron Age carpentry. The sheer scale of the building (32ft at the apex) gives an insight into the skill of the Celtic peoples of the time – named the *Novantae* by the Romans. The reconstruction roundhouse adds weight to the Trust's new research, which shows that Christianity was grafted on to local traditions and adopted by local peoples, rather than being imposed by a foreign elite. Such round constructions were built anywhere between the 5th Century BC and as late as the 7th Century AD; two were found by excavators in the Early Christian layers at Whithorn.

There is still an **annual pilgrimage** at Whithorn on the last Sunday in August, when between 500 and 600 people gather and make their way to **St Ninian's Cave** (⚲ NX422361), four miles southwest of Whithorn at Physgill. Tradition has it that here on this pebbly shore St Ninian would retreat to the cave at the end of the beach for personal prayer. The cave can be visited at any time by parking in the car park around one mile from the beach and wandering down through the woods. A small enclave with a good view back along the beach and coast, it's an ideal spot for quiet contemplation. Over the centuries many pilgrims have come to give thanks for a safe journey and in among the offerings from present-day visitors are 8th-century crosses carved into the walls. Depending on when you come, look out for the house martins nesting above the entrance to the cave and the dainty purple thrift flower dotted along the edge of the beach. We've also spotted seals just off shore.

Whithorn's **main street** hasn't changed much since 1760 and still retains much of its medieval shape. Scattered along it is a goodly range of local shops, including the appropriately named **Priory Antiques** (29 George St) with a small but interesting collection in an outhouse at the back and the **Central Café** just a few doors along offering tasty homemade ice cream. There's also the **Wee Garden Gallery** (104 George St), where husband and wife team Robert and Teresa design and make leaded clocks, vases and mirrors.

If you're here in summer, look out for family events, especially some with ancient crafts as their theme. And, on a more prosaic note, you're very likely to come across the name of Tyler Jolly while here, for Whithorn is the youth boxing champion's home town.

FOOD & DRINK

The Whithorn Trust 45–47 George St DG8 8NS ✆ 01988 500508. Light lunches, local ingredients, fresh coffee and home-baked cakes in the heart of historic Whithorn.

AROUND WHITHORN

Just over three miles northwest of Whithorn is the **Swallow Theatre** (Moss Pk, Ravenstone DG8 8DR ✆ 01988 850368 swallowtheatre.co.uk), Scotland's smallest professional theatre, set in a permaculture garden next to the owners' home and run on environmental grounds in the rolling countryside of the central Machars. Seating a maximum audience of just over 50 in eight tiered rows and occupying a converted cow byre (heated, but rugs also provided), this delightful performance space offers audience and players alike pretty much everything that could be wished for, but in miniature. Around 40 to 50 performances are staged a year, ranging from topical drama to opera, classical music to jazz, in a curated programme of shows hand-picked by the owners and, in many cases, adapted by the players to work in this intimate setting. Founded in 1996 and born of a love of theatre, this was a 'BYO' place in the early days – bring your own chair, that is. These days it's a fully fledged, professionally lit theatre – pleasingly quirky and altogether charming. As for pre-theatre drinks… well, they're served in the converted stable, of course.

Around one mile west of Whithorn, behind Rispain Farm off the A746, lies **Rispain Camp** settlement. A source of much debate over the years, Historic Environment Scotland now asserts, thanks to archaeological excavations between 1978 and 1981, that this is not a Roman fortlet nor a medieval manor-place, but was probably the home of a tribal chief, inhabited between 100BC and AD200. The defences are among the most impressive surviving from Iron Age Scotland. Rispain can be reached on foot from Whithorn, on a newly installed off-road path, the last segment of the 149-mile Whithorn Way (page 14), which leaves from the rear of Whithorn Priory.

Continue a little further down the A746 to reach the hamlet of **Glasserton**, once an estate village with its prettily set 18th-century church down a lane off the main road (if approaching from Whithorn go straight over at the war memorial crossroads). It is home to **Woodfall Gardens** (Glasserton DG8 8LY ✆ 01988 500692 woodfall-gardens.co.uk), part of Scotland's Gardens Scheme (scotlandsgardens.org), covering roughly 3 acres and known as 'Galloway's Secret Garden'.

5 ISLE OF WHITHORN

The Steam Packet Inn (page 262) **7 Ninian's Landing** (page 263)

Down at the southern tip of the Machars sits one of the most enticing fishing villages in Dumfries and Galloway, the **Isle of Whithorn** (isleofwhithorn.com). A cluster of cottages with their backs to the sea nestles around the small harbour, creating a cosy enclave and the perfect retreat. Needless to say it can be busy, but its charm is undeniable. Despite its name, this is no island but more of a peninsula, just about as far south in Scotland as you will find a village, rivalled only by Drummore on the Rhins (page 253).

The remains of an early tower house are here, and so too are the remains of **St Ninian's Chapel**, from around 1300, where pilgrims landing on the shore en route to Whithorn gave thanks for safe passage. Later, this was a place of trade, from where goods from the medieval

Prior of Whithorn's estates were exported. Just south of the chapel stands a simple granite-hewn memorial to the seven local men who lost their lives when their boat, the *Solway Harvester*, sank in a storm off the Isle of Man in January 2000.

Burrow Head, the most southerly point of the Machars, is just a couple of miles south of the Isle of Whithorn. Today it is a holiday village, but film buffs may know it as the location for the final scene in the cult film *The Wicker Man* in which a young Edward Woodward is (spoiler alert) sacrificially burned alive inside the wicker man effigy. Despite a cast of big names (Britt Ekland and Christopher Lee), the film never took off, although it has endured as a cult classic.

The Isle of Whithorn today is home to around 300 people and its harbour remains in use with regular landings from the Irish Sea shell fishing boats. The local fleet brings in lobster, which is served up at the **Steam Packet Inn**.

FOOD & DRINK

St Ninian's Hall Cafe and Shop Main St DG8 8LH 01988 501197. Smart glass-fronted tea room and shop overlooking the harbour serving breakfast and lunch, teas, coffees and home baking. The Hall is also the home base of Machars Movies (page 198).

The Steam Packet Inn Harbour Row, DG8 8LL 01988 500334 thesteampacketinn.biz. Popular CAMRA inn, cosy and welcoming with a wood-burning stove, idyllically situated right on the waterside and serving quality, wholesome food in the bar. The Scoular family have owned the Steam Packet for many years and also have a micro-brewery on the other side of the harbour, where they brew the six beers that make up the Five Kingdoms brand (fivekingdomsbrewery.com). The name stems from the fact that five 'kingdoms' (a loose definition!) can be seen from the back of the inn: England, Ireland, Scotland, Wales and the Isle of Man. There are plans to open the brewery to visitors.

STAIRHAVEN TO PORT WILLIAM

Hills that drop to exquisite sandy beaches and superb views over Luce Bay to the Rhins distinguish the west coast of the Machars. At **Stairhaven**, the Milton Burn marks the boundary between the Machars and the Rhins, according to Tom Stevenson, a native of these parts (see box, page 229). Inland, numerous **lochs** dot the interior: **Whitefield** is popular for fishing (permits from Keystore, Glenluce 07766 572266, and The Sports Shop, Stranraer 01776 702705), while the remains

A GALLOWAY LEGACY

Polly Pullar is a field naturalist, wildlife rehabilitator and photo-journalist. She was the wildlife writer for *The Scottish Field* for ten years and contributes to a wide range of publications, including *The Scots Magazine, People's Friend, Tractor & Farming Heritage, BBC Wildlife* and *Scottish Wildlife*. She is the author of eight books, including *Dancing with Ospreys* and *Rural Portraits: Scottish Native Farm Animals, Characters and Landscapes*. We met her at the Wigtown Book Festival when she was talking about her lovely book, *Fauna Scotica: People and Animals in Scotland*. We are indebted to her for providing the text below about Galloway's native farm livestock. For more details about Polly and her work, see 🖱 pollypullar.com.

The Belted Galloway is formally recognised as a sub-species of the Galloway. It has its own separate breed society and a herd book that began registering animals in 1922. Though the Beltie has essentially the same origins as the Galloway, an infusion of Dutch blood from sheeted cattle in Holland during the 17th century is thought to be the reason for the distinctive white band. The black Beltie is the most common but there are also red and dun Belties as well as pure white animals attractively marked with clearly defined black etched around eyes, black hairy ears and a black nose. The riggit with a dark or red ground colour, and a white line and greyish markings down its back, was thought to be extinct. They had indeed almost died out, when years ago a white cow and bull produced a beautifully marked riggit bull. Soon after this the late Miss Flora Stuart of the Old Place of Mochrum (1941–2005), discovered that several other cows had produced riggits too. They remain unusual and seldom seen.

The Stuart family have been famed for their Belties for generations, and theirs is one of the few herds left in the country that formed the foundation of the breed for the Belted Galloway Herd Book.

I had the fortune to meet the late Miss Flora Stuart on several occasions; she was without doubt one of the most dedicated and unusual people I have ever been lucky enough to spend time with. She left her gentle mark on all who met her and she was a world authority on the breed, revered as such. Her father, Lord David Stuart, a son of the fourth Marquis of Bute, spent 15 years researching his book, *An Illustrated History of Belted Cattle*.

Hidden in a wood of lichen-covered trees, the Old Place of Mochrum has parts that date back to 1400. Mochrum is a hidden gem. The dense hedgerows are filled with berries and wildflowers and, as few agricultural pesticides

of several crannogs are in **Castle Loch** (📍 NX285536). **Mochrum Loch** forms part of the Mochrum Estate and may be open for pike fishing (contact the estate for details 🖱 mochrumestate.com). This is a particularly pretty part of the Machars, full of classic views of rolling are used, wildflowers and butterflies are abundant. Drive or bike along the narrow lanes on balmy spring and summer days and you may spy peacocks settling on bramble leaves or small tortoiseshells on purple spear thistle, while thistledown and rose-bay willow-herb fluff float along the ditches, back-lit by low rays of sun. The Galloway landscape is patterned with drystane dykes and, as you travel nearer to the sea, the trees become shaped by the salt-laden winds driven in off the western seaboard. Knobbly hawthorns are laced with soft green lichens, and ivy grows in abundance, often forming a thick curled stem almost as dense as a small tree trunk. This part of Galloway has a timelessness, the pace of life appears slower. Though the fields are mostly small in size, the moorland around Mochrum stretches for miles, edged with scrub woodland, and fringed with bog cotton and flag iris. Kestrels hover by the grey dykes, and hen harriers are frequently seen quartering the heather-clad ground. A sparrowhawk may dash low over the road, while otters frequent the abundant watercourses. This is the childhood haunt of the well-known author Gavin Maxwell, and Elrig, his old family home close to the sea, is surrounded by wild landscapes that clearly inspired his beautiful writing. Flora Stuart knew him well.

Close to the farm, the Mochrum Lochs provide rich habitat for goosanders, mergansers and golden-eye ducks. Greylag geese, snipe and curlews nest on the moorland's raised blanket bogs; this is one of few inland-nesting sites for cormorants. Nicknamed the Mochrum Elders, owing to their habit of perching with wings outstretched to dry themselves, they were amusingly thought to resemble the somewhat forbidding Presbyterian kirk elders that once presided over the area.

Flora Stuart bred Belties of all varieties. She knew every animal, its calving record, bloodlines and history, and explained their background to me as she took me round. She had a bovine family tree as an integral part of her psyche, and she was a highly skilled stockwoman. There was an unspoken rapport between her and her animals.

Having spent precious time in her company, and briefly shared a part of the Old Place of Mochrum, I know that the survival of the gorgeous Belted Galloway is largely down to Miss Flora Stuart and her family, for no-one could have been more truly dedicated to their survival. Today, the cattle are still farmed by a new manager and Flora's nephew.

For more information about Belted Galloways, contact The Belted Galloway Society (beltedgalloways.co.uk).

hills and **Belted Galloway** cattle, for which the Mochrum Estate is world famous. We recommend exploring at will the network of roads that criss-cross the landscape from Bladnoch or Garlieston in the east over to the west coast.

Back on the coast, walkers can make the popular loop of five miles or so from Stairhaven to Auchenmalg, taking the quiet back road in one direction and the coastal path in the other. Beyond **Auchenmalg**, a long stretch of pristine **beach** is a perfect place for a picnic and a paddle, while a little further on still are the remains of Historic Environment Scotland's **Chapel Finian**, humbling in its simplicity and another place where pilgrims on their way to Whithorn would have stopped. It was the Irish St Finnian [sic] who taught St Columba, and today there is debate among some scholars as to whether he could actually be the historical figure who has come to be known as St Ninian (page 211).

Continuing south, a mile or so inland lies the charming village of **Mochrum**, part of the eponymous parish that extends over the western side of the Machars and also incorporates the picturesque hamlet of Elrig to the north and the village of Port William to the south. **Barhobble Church** (NX311494; park at the barn on the entrance road to Elrig House and walk up to the church site following the signs) is an intriguing example of modern detective work unearthing a historic site. The discovery in the northern part of Mochrum parish of fragments of a 10th-century building led to a search for the source and excavations in 1984–94 revealed a previously unknown religious site thought to be from AD700 to 1300. Some of the finds are on display in Whithorn (page 211).

PORT WILLIAM & MONREITH

Beaches, wildlife spotting, ancient monuments, and a glimpse into the early life of author Gavin Maxwell are all to be found here.

6 PORT WILLIAM

Port William huddles around the village square with a row of fisherman's cottages running out on each side and a small harbour tucked into the hill. Fishing boats still head out from here and a range of tourist boats operate in the summer. In the 17th century Port William was something of a smuggler's village, with all manner of contraband being landed from the Isle of Man, where duty on imported goods had been slashed to encourage settlement by wealthy merchants.

A **bronze statue** of a man gazing out to sea, leaning on a post, stands at the waterfront. It's an evocative work and you can't help but go and stand next to him, lean on the post, and pause for a moment. On a clear day the Mountains of Mourne in Ireland can just be made out through the dip in the land at West and East Tarbet (page 254) at the southern end of the Rhins.

An inscription on a plaque in front of the statue reads 'What is this life if, full of care, We have no time to stand and stare', from W H Davies's poem 'Leisure'. We defy you not to slow down here! Otters are sometimes seen in the surrounding waters, so too are seals, basking sharks and dolphins. There's a large and varied bird population and adders can be found locally, so watch where you walk on warm sunny days. Picnic tables on the green are a good place to linger if you've brought your own food. Alternatively, there's a good café, **The View**, next to the green (see below), on top of the shed housing Port William's independently run lifeboat. It's a relaxing space from which tea drinkers can gaze out to sea over the lobster pots and harbour.

If you fancy **fresh fish, lobster or crab** in Port William, seek out Paul Maguire (✆ 07766 700671), whose family boasts five generations of local fishermen. Paul still sails on his boat, *The Galilee*, and has a shed on the harbour with tanks for keeping his catch fresh. He's happy for visitors to pop in to take a look and to buy lobster or crab for dinner straight from the tank.

Good **beaches** can be found both north and south of the village where the road hugs the shoreline. A couple of miles to the south is **Barsalloch Fort**, or at least the footprint of it, a fortified farming settlement accessed by a flight of steps up the hillside. The fort is believed to date from around 1000BC, but on the land below it, at **Barsalloch Point**, evidence of human settlement has been found dating from 6000BC, making it the oldest dated settlement in Galloway. All along here there is easy access to the rocky beach.

FOOD & DRINK

The View Harbour Rd, Port William DG8 9QF 🖱 pirsac.org. Port William's glass-fronted café is an enticing place in which to linger and sea watch, whatever the season. Teas, coffees, sandwiches and cakes on offer.

7 MONREITH & AROUND

Monreith village was originally an estate and mill village serving nearby **Monreith House** 👆 (⚲ NX356430; private, but grounds can be accessed), home to the **Maxwell family** since the late 18th century, and the local grain mill. The grounds of Monreith House are described as a 'best-kept local secret' by those in the know and can be accessed (within reason) via either the north or south gates. A designated parking area for visitors is most easily reached from the South Gate. There are some fine trees, including old wych (or Scots) elm, English elm and some Japanese rarities, and wildlife is also abundant, including red squirrels. Fishing is offered but all equipment must be scrupulously cleaned to avoid contamination from signal crayfish. Permits can be bought on the bank or from ghillie-cum-handyman-cum-mechanical designer David Williams, who lives at the South Lodge.

Also in this area, three miles to the south, is the **Galloway Astronomy Centre** (Craiglemine Cottage, Glasserton DG8 8NE ✆ 01988 500594 🖰 gallowayastro.com), where Mike and Helen Alexander have for the past 25 years been enjoying the lack of light pollution and offering courses on the night sky.

The area around Monreith House is known in part for the several groups of standing stones and cup and ring markings that can be found here. Near the north gate entrance to the Monreith Estate are the **Drumtroddan Stones** 👆 (⚲ NX363447), three large stones in alignment, though only one remains standing, believed to have been erected at some time between 3000BC and 2000BC. Around 400yds to the northwest, and most easily accessed via Drumtroddan Farm off the road to Whauphill (drive up the farm track and park where indicated), are associated **cup and ring markings**. Two sites, both fenced off in the middle of a field, consist of a series of markings on the bedrock. Their function and date remain a mystery, but they are definitely prehistoric.

Also in this area is the **'Wren's Egg'** (⚲ NX36104199), a large glacial erratic boulder in the vicinity of two pairs of aligned standing stones dating from the Bronze Age. Stand on top of the Wren's Egg on the shortest day and the sun will set directly behind Big Scaur rock, several miles offshore in Luce Bay in the direction of the Mull of Galloway.

Just south of Monreith, take the road to the right down to the golf club, at the end of which is easy parking and access to **sandy beaches** and bays in both directions. Halfway down this road a path goes off to the right, leading to Penny Wheatley's delightful **otter sculpture**, set atop a rock and gazing out at the mesmerising view, placed here to commemorate **Gavin Maxwell**, author of *Ring of Bright Water*, which told the story of his life with otters in the West Highlands of Scotland. Although Maxwell's life as an adult was based in northwest Scotland, when he returned to Monreith he could often be seen exercising his otter on the beach below. From here you also catch a glimpse below of **Kirkmaiden-in-Fernis** churchyard (NX366399), associated with St Medan (page 252) and which can be accessed via a path opposite the parking area a little further down the road. Here stands the family mausoleum of the Maxwell family, with something of an enchanted, magic garden feel about it. This is also the resting place of the McCullochs of Myrton Castle, which was acquired by the Maxwell family and now stands ruined on their Monreith estate. Legend tells of how the pulpit and bell from the church here were lost in Luce Bay while being transported to Kirkmaiden Church on the Rhins (page 252) following the joining of the parishes of Kirkmaiden and Glasserton here on the Machars. Ever since then, it is said that every time a McCulloch's death approaches, a bell rings from the depths of Luce Bay.

Also buried in the graveyard is **François Thurot**, whose death in action off the Isle of Man on 28 February 1760 ended four years of terror against the British Navy and marked a pivotal moment in the Seven Years War between France and England (and many others besides, between 1756 and 1763). Defeated by one Captain Elliot, in the chaotic aftermath of battle, Thurot's body was thrown by mistake off his ship and washed ashore here at Monreith. A memorial to him was erected by the ancient Order of Coldin, a secret society of mariners, which Thurot had introduced to Sweden.

Beyond the first parking area, carry on down the track and round the hill at the bottom to another, from where you can walk along the shore to the south to **Johnnie Logie's Cave**, where the raised beach meets the cliff. Originally a miner from Ayrshire, Johnnie Logie retreated from life to his cave here after being injured in an accident which left him half blind and deaf. Cultivating his own crops, he became almost self-sufficient and in 1960 was the only troglodyte recorded living in Scotland.

FOOD & DRINK

St Medan Golf Course Clubhouse Monreith DG8 8NJ 01988 700358 stmedangolfclub.com Apr–Oct. Offers a small selection of food and refreshments in a course-side setting looking down to the shore.

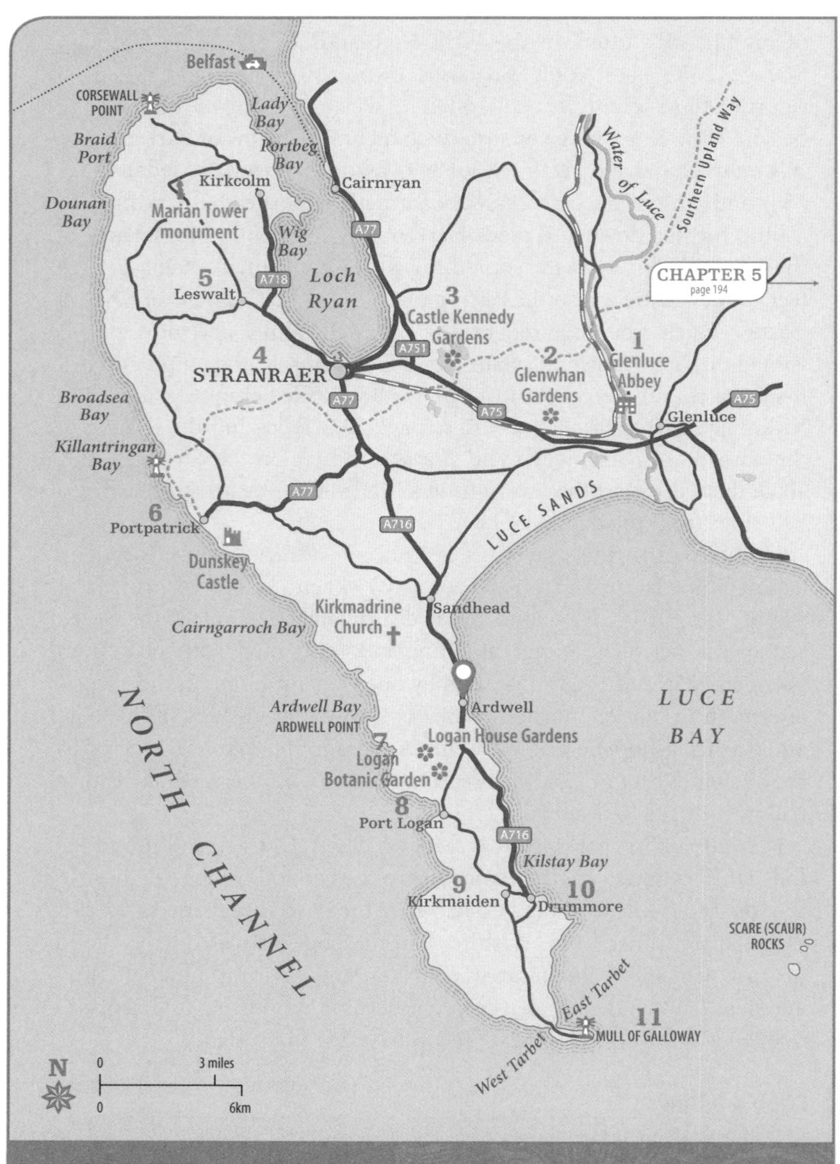
Belfast
CORSEWALL POINT
Lady Bay
Braid Port
Portbeg Bay
Kirkcolm
Cairnryan
Dounan Bay
Marian Tower monument
Wig Bay
A77
Water of Luce
Southern Upland Way
5
Leswalt
A718
Loch Ryan
CHAPTER 5
page 194
3
Castle Kennedy Gardens
1
Glenluce Abbey
A751
2
Glenwhan Gardens
4
STRANRAER
Broadsea Bay
A77
A75
A75
Glenluce
Killantringan Bay
A77
LUCE SANDS
6
Portpatrick
A716
Dunskey Castle
Sandhead
Kirkmadrine Church
Cairngarroch Bay
NORTH CHANNEL
Ardwell Bay
ARDWELL POINT
Ardwell
LUCE BAY
7
Logan Botanic Garden
Logan House Gardens
8
Port Logan
A716
Kilstay Bay
9
Kirkmaiden
10
Drummore
SCARE (SCAUR) ROCKS
East Tarbet
11
MULL OF GALLOWAY
West Tarbet
N
0
3 miles
0
6km

THE RHINS

6
THE RHINS

For anyone who loves peace and isolation, arriving at the Rhins is like reaching the Promised Land. This narrow strip, less than 40 miles long and never more than five miles wide out on the peninsula itself, is almost completely surrounded by water and sparsely populated – a recluse's dream. It would be possible to hole up here in a cottage for a week and hardly see or speak to another soul. On a still day there is an intense calmness about the place that penetrates the consciousness and makes you wonder if you've been teleported to a lost land. On a blustery day, it is invigorating and life-affirming. We find the Rhins beguiling.

The beech hedgerows and copse woodlands of east and central Dumfries and Galloway grow ever-more scarce as you approach the Rhins, giving way to a landscape of undulating hills of lush green fields sprinkled with patches of scrub gorse and sedge. It is an open and stark place wrapped in a vast, uncompromising sky. The only wood to be seen is in the mile upon mile of fence posts and leaning telegraph poles linking isolated cottages and farmsteads. In the sun the Rhins is a place of vivid colours: lime green fields, shocking blue skies, dark blue seas, the sharp tangy yellow gorse of spring, startlingly white cottages, red-painted barns, and not forgetting the mixed black and white of both Friesian and Belted Galloway cattle.

The peninsula stretches from Corsewall Lighthouse, the most northerly point you can reach by road, down to the Mull of Galloway, Scotland's most southerly point (on land, that is; strictly speaking, Gallie Craig rock just off the Mull is Scotland's most southerly point). The name Rhins is derived from the Gaelic 'roinn' for 'nose' or 'promontory'. The west coast is etched by a line of cliffs, the east is gentler. No matter which direction you travel, you soon hit a coastal road and you don't have to be here long before an island mentality sets in. The pace is just that little bit slower, pleasantly soporific in parts. The mobile library still does the rounds of the villages, country lanes wind through the middle of farmyards, and people you don't know wave as you pass in the car. And like any good 'island', the Rhins also boasts not just a super choice of **beaches**, most of which are covered throughout this chapter, but also a number of **lighthouses** ☛.

Tourism and farming (dairy and beef) are the main industries on the Rhins, the latter in particular having long been important. Galloway cattle are renowned for their hardiness and quality of beef: in addition to local stocks, by the late 18th century 15,000 Irish cattle were passing along the droving route from Portpatrick, on the west coast of the Rhins, where they arrived from Ireland, to Dumfries. Here they were fattened up before being driven south on foot to the Norfolk Cattle Fair. (There are still signs in the centre of Dumfries today that show the droving distances; page 114.)

The mid 18th to mid 19th centuries were also a time of shipbuilding, notably at Stranraer, Portpatrick and Drummore on the Rhins, and also at Port William, the Isle of Whithorn, Garlieston and Bladnoch on the Machars. The largest ships were built at Stranraer, with smaller boats coming out of local yards. The Stranraer crest shows a full-masted sailing ship in a shield, with the Latin motto *Tutissima Statio*

RHINS GARDENS

At Logan Botanic Garden there is a display that describes the Rhins as the Tropic of Scotland, and it fits. Here in this southwest corner of the country is a cornucopia of gardens, the collective likes of which exist nowhere else in Britain, except perhaps in Cornwall and the Isles of Scilly.

Although the Rhins is in the direct line of the prevailing weather coming in from the Atlantic, its climate isn't as bad as you might expect, due to the Gulf Stream – or, as it is known in this particular part of the world, the North Atlantic Current. Suffice to say, don't be surprised to find palm trees in front gardens and herbaceous borders stuffed with a veritable plethora of southern-hemisphere plants and shrubs. It's what many visitors come here for.

Castle Kennedy (page 233), **Glenwhan** (page 231), **Logan Botanic Garden** (page 250) and **Logan House** (page 249) are the Rhins's four key garden sites. Also of note is **Aldouran Wetland Garden** (page 239), while the gardens at Dunskey and Ardwell are no longer open to the public, although both estates are crossed by 'Core Paths' (routes that have access rights under the Land Reform (Scotland) Act 2003 and which are managed by Dumfries and Galloway Council) that offer a glimpse of the grounds.

ONE 'N' OR TWO?

The chances are you will come across both 'Rhins' and 'Rhinns' in your travels around the area. Both are acceptable, but the single 'n' is the more common and is what we have opted for in this guide. To supporters of the double 'n', therefore, we apologise.

or 'Safest Harbour'. As bigger and faster ships were built, though, beef farming became less and less viable since droving was being fast outpaced and cattle could be transported to their destination far quicker than was previously possible. Thus the early 19th century saw the advent of commercial dairy farming with the first large-scale dairy farm going into operation at Kirkcolm in 1802. Farming on the Rhins today remains more dairy than beef, and many farms are tied in to supplying manufacturers in Stranraer and further up the coast at Girvan in South Ayrshire. Stranraer is also the home of the Seriously Strong Cheddar brand that you'll find in supermarkets, as well as the Galloway cheddar: 'the family's favourite', as they say.

The people of the Rhins are custodians of a piece of Scotland that is unique and special, and there is a pride in the area among both established families and incomers, of whom there are a fair few. For some, leaving the Rhins even for a day or two is a wrench, such is the hold that this place can take. Nonetheless, day trips to Belfast are a popular jaunt for locals in need of some retail diversion. Ireland is only two hours away by ferry and 'Galloway Irish' is a term that you will likely come across. There's a distinctive Irish twang to the local accent.

GETTING AROUND

The best way to experience the 'real' Rhins is to get off the main A roads. **Driving** here is a pleasure but also a challenge. Narrow country lanes make for sedate going, which is the pleasure, but they are also full of sharp corners, blind summits and junctions at which it can be almost impossible to distinguish between a farmhouse track and the public highway. Slow, leisurely, relaxed travel is the way to soak up the spirit of the Rhins and savour the views. No need to rush, just enjoy the experience of being here. It's not uncommon for roads to run through the middle of a farmyard either, with a row of cows stretching their necks

TOURIST INFORMATION

There is no VisitScotland information centre on the Rhins. *Our Wigtownshire* is a local magazine published every two months with lots of information about local people, businesses and events. Available from high street shops across the region.

Kirkmaiden Information Centre 21 Mill St, Drummore DG9 9PS ✆ 01776 840207 visitkirkmaiden ⏲ generally end May–Sep, but check the Facebook page. Volunteer-run centre located by the bus stop on Drummore's main street. Often visited by people researching family history; public internet access available.
Stranraer Development Trust 8 Castle St, Stranraer DG7 7RT ✆ 01776 705849 stranraerdevelopmenttrust.co.uk. Information is available from the trust's office, though they hope to develop the old Harbour Master's Office on Stranraer's waterfront into a tourist information centre, but the plans are still in the pipeline (check the website for updates).

out of the byre to feed on one side and the farmhouse on the other. And don't be surprised if you find livestock roaming the roads: sheep, cattle, deer, hares, pheasants... any of them could make an appearance. Keep your wits about you and take it slowly. Remain conscious of potential oncoming traffic, especially larger vehicles such as tractors, delivery vans, school buses and the mobile library.

Distances are not great but small roads can make timings longer than you may expect: Portpatrick to the Mull is just over 22 miles and takes around an hour to drive, Portpatrick to Corsewall Lighthouse is just under 16 miles and takes around 45 minutes, and Corsewall Lighthouse to the Mull of Galloway comes in at roughly 30 miles and takes around 1½ hours straight up the eastern edge of the Rhins.

One thing to note when driving is that there are very few road signs around the narrow lanes away from the main roads, rendering a good OS map essential.

PUBLIC TRANSPORT

Rail timetable changes in recent years owing to local demand have seen a notable increase in usage of services to and from Stranraer. Although at one time the end of the direct **train service** to Glasgow looked likely, at the time of writing there are still infrequent direct services (Mon–Sat). For-non-direct services a change at Ayr is required.

There are regular **bus services** to Stranraer from Dumfries. Stagecoach West Scotland services 500 and X75 offer 11 daily departures (Mon–Sat) from Dumfries railway station and Whitesands. The journey takes between two hours and ten minutes and 2½ hours depending on the time of day. On Sundays there are four service 500 departures. Return trips run as frequently. Once at the Rhins, buses run with varying degrees of regularity from Stranraer to Stoneykirk, Sandhead, Ardwell, Port Logan and Drummore (service 407 – Stagecoach West Scotland, McCulloch Coaches and Wigtownshire Community Transport) in the South Rhins; to Leswalt, Kirkcolm and Ervie (service 408 – Stagecoach West Scotland and McCulloch Coaches) in the north; and to Knock and Portpatrick (services 367 and 411 run by Stagecoach West Scotland and McCulloch Coaches) in between. Stagecoach West Scotland also run

RHINS PATHS

This is fine walking country with routes to suit all ages and abilities, from gentle strolls to long-distance hikes; an amble along a country lane to a steep cliffside path. The **Southern Upland Way** starts its 214-mile trajectory at Portpatrick and the first two days are entirely within the Rhins, taking you around 20 miles to New Luce (page 203) for an overnight stop.

The **Mull of Galloway Trail** (mullofgallowaytrail.co.uk) runs for 25 miles from the Mull up the east coast to Stranraer and then continues as the 12-mile **Loch Ryan Coastal Path** to Glenapp in South Ayrshire. Both paths were developed and are maintained by the members of the Rotary Club of Stranraer, led by local force Tom Stevenson who has been instrumental in creating and publicising them. Together they are now part of a scheme instigated by Scottish Natural Heritage called 'Scotland's Great Trails' to form the southernmost end of a series of routes by which it is now possible to walk from Scotland's most southerly point at the Mull of Galloway to the most northwestern point of mainland Britain at Cape Wrath. The Rhins paths also form part of the International Appalachian Trail long-distance walking route.

The Mull of Galloway Trail forms one section of the longer, 84-mile **Rhins of Galloway Coast Path** (f), a circular route right around the peninsula with waymarkers and interpretation signage, with its official start and finish in Stranraer. In a clockwise direction, the route picks up the Mull of Galloway Trail heading south to the Mull, then comes up the west coast to Portpatrick before continuing on a section of the Southern Upland Way to Killantringan. From there it carries on up and round the north coast, passing Corsewall Lighthouse before dropping back down to Stranraer via Lady Bay and Wig Bay.

service 416 from Stranraer down to Whithorn and back up to Newton Stewart on the Machars.

Local public transport information is provided by South West of Scotland Transport Partnership (swestrans.org.uk), or alternatively Traveline (0871 200 22 33 www.traveline.info).

FERRIES

The terminus for ferries to Northern Ireland is a few miles up the eastern side of Loch Ryan at Cairnryan. P&O Ferries operates services to Larne, and Stena Line to Belfast.

CYCLING

From the Mull of Galloway in the south to Milleur Point at the north of Loch Ryan, the Rhins offers many miles of quieter lanes to be explored. As a starting point, cyclists may wish to check out routes from and around Stranraer on the MapMyRide website (mapmyride.com/gb/stranraer-sct) and also a small selection of routes featured on Portpatrick's Rickwood House Hotel website (portpatrick.me.uk/cycling-portpatrick-scotland).

WALKING

Mile upon mile of rylock sheep fencing criss-crosses the area and can make roaming the hills a bit laborious as you concentrate on traversing the next barrier rather than taking in the fine views. Don't, however, let this put you off exploring on foot. The rolling fields complete with pockets of woodland and the fact you are almost completely surrounded by miles of fine coastline make walking very rewarding. There are plenty of walking leaflets and books available in local shops, including our own *Galloway 40 Coast and Country Walks*, offering a fine choice of clear and varied routes.

For more on **walking and cycling routes** in the area, visit info.dumgal.gov.uk/mapviewers/pathsmap.aspx and see the box on page 229.

GLENLUCE & THE EAST

This short stretch of Galloway from Glenluce up to Stranraer always seems to us to be a bit of a no-man's land. Although it's regarded as being part of the Rhins, it feels as if it falls between two camps: out of the

Machars but not quite into the Rhins peninsula. Perhaps because of this people tend to pass through and not stop. However, to do so is to miss out on some of the Rhins' most noteworthy sights.

1 GLENLUCE ABBEY

Glenluce DG8 0AF NX185586 Apr–Sep 09.30–17.30 Sun–Tue, last entry 17.00; Historic Environment Scotland

The ruined Cistercian monastery at Glenluce was built over 800 years ago and stands in a peaceful riverside setting by Luce Water. Founded by Roland, Lord of Galloway, it is thought that the monks who established the monastery and lived here would have come from Dundrennan Abbey near Kirkcudbright (page 189). Parts of the chapterhouse survive intact, including a fine entrance doorway, stone-vaulted ceiling and traceried windows. Monastic life continued here for around 400 years until the Protestant Reformation took hold.

There's a small museum and visitor centre with artefacts discovered during preservation work that illustrate the daily lives of the monks.

2 GLENWHAN GARDENS

Glenwhan Gardens Shepherd's Hut (page 263)

Dunragit DG9 8PH NX153586 (follow the signs from the main road at Dunragit up into the hills) 01581 400222 glenwhangardens.co.uk entrance charged Apr–Sep 10.00–17.00; honesty box at entrance & café closed Oct–Mar

Set 300ft above sea level where hill meets moor, this is the only one of Galloway's many gardens to offer such a tremendous view. On a clear day you can see out over Luce Bay and right down the Rhins to the lighthouse at the Mull. The garden itself is a gem and easy to find thanks to the brown tourist signs on the road. Over the years it has been the subject of much praise and inspiration. The story behind it is one of a restless farmer in search of pastures new, moving north from Herefordshire almost on a whim to a patch of land bought hastily in Dumfries and Galloway. In 1971, Bill and Tessa Knott decided they wanted a change of scene from farming and so they put in a very last-minute offer on 105 acres of land above Dunragit, part of an estate that was being split up and sold off by a disinterested landowner. To their delight and consternation, they found themselves the proud owners of a tract of Galloway hillside and moorland covered in bracken and gorse, with a couple of run-down houses thrown in to boot. It was a different time: they got it for a song and their solicitor told them they couldn't go wrong. He was right, too, for today at the heart of Glenwhan is a charming garden of 12 acres surrounding a delightful small country house that the Knotts renovated and extended from one of the original buildings. Make no mistake, though, the garden as it is today has come only with years of dedication and hard work. Take a look at the photographs in the tea room of how it was when the Knotts first arrived and you'll soon appreciate how much has gone in to making Glenwhan what it is today.

What is so appealing about this garden (apart from the red squirrels) is that it feels so homely, albeit on a slightly grander scale than most of us are used to. It is with a slight sense of embarrassment at intruding into a private space that you realise you are actually walking in the Knott's back garden, where the lawn behind the house runs seamlessly into an array of shrubs, borders and trees arranged around a couple of lochans, laboriously dug out then filled with water piped down from the moor. Domestic details of family life punctuate the gardens: a diving board and bathing hut at the edge of the lochan, which the family use for swimming; a statue of Buddha and prayer flags in the trees positioned carefully by Tessa and Bill's son, Richard. A series of 'rooms' work their way up the hillside to a striking **slate sculpture** by local craftsman Joe Smith, before leading you out into the 17 acres of moor where there are over 120 species of wildflower and a **circular walk** among the gorse and bracken for something a little wilder to finish off. There is also a tree trail taking in 150 trees. Each section of the garden has a name. 'Choice Valley' is so called because it is full of choice plants. We particularly liked 'Thinking Rock' – 'a good place to come and think', says Tessa Knott.

"What makes the whole thing even more impressive is that Tessa, the driving force, never considered herself a gardener."

What makes the whole thing even more impressive is that Tessa, who has been the driving force behind Glenwhan, never considered herself a gardener. 'I was a cordon bleu cook first and a bit of a gardener', she says. Everything she has learned has been on the job, resulting in a VisitScotland four-star rating plus partner garden status with the Royal Horticultural Society.

It would be so easy to overlook Glenwhan on a visit to this area. Don't. It's quite special. Dogs are allowed on leads, and there's a cosy tea room. And, for those in search of peaceful escape, there's also a quirky accommodation option in a beautifully appointed shepherd's hut (page 263). Marriage ceremonies and cultural courses are also offered, the latter ranging from watercolour painting to vegetable propagation.

3 CASTLE KENNEDY GARDENS

Castle Kennedy DG9 8SL NX111608 castlekennedygardens.com Easter/Apr–Oct 10.00–17.00 daily

The original Castle Kennedy was the home of the Kennedy family but it then passed to the current owners, the Dalrymples and Earls of Stair. It is known to have been standing in the 14th century but was destroyed by fire in 1716, though the ruins can still be seen in the grounds today. The story goes that on hearing of the imminent return of the second Earl of Stair, the staff aired his bedding in front of an open fire, with disastrous results.

Nowadays the castle is known as **Lochinch Castle**. 'Inch' means spit (as in a spit of land) and the castle gardens are situated on a peninsula between two lochs: Loch Crindle, which is known as the Black Loch because of its peaty water, and Loch Inch, which is known as the White Loch. The castle itself isn't open to the public, but the gardens are, 75 acres that have been nurtured and curated by successive generations. Today they are under the watchful eye of John Arthur, who is not only head gardener but also chief of the clan Arthur. He's also a regular bagpipe player with the Cairnsmore Pipers, who you might catch playing at one of the local festivals

It was the second Earl of Stair who was so inspired by the gardens at Versailles that he resolved to develop his own. He was a military man, having attained the rank of Field Marshal, and this is reflected in areas of the gardens that are named after battles in which he took part, thus Mount Marlborough and Dettingen Avenue. He also enlisted the help of the Royal Scots Greys and Inniskilling Fusiliers in developing the gardens, and it is said that the distinctive embankments were created by his own private army. By the 19th century the gardens had become neglected and overgrown, but a bundle of plans was found in a gardener's cottage showing how they had once been and, on his succession in 1814, the eighth earl took it upon himself to restore them to their former glory.

As with most gardens in the Rhins, one of the chief attractions is the **rhododendrons**, which come in every size and colour and attract enthusiasts from all over the world. Between March and July the rhododendrons are in flower, from the early large-leafed variety to the later, wild *Rhododendron ponticum* (the one that gets all the bad press for being so invasive). The 12th earl was a great rhododendron fan and would compete in shows in London. To get there he would book two sleeper compartments: one for the gardener and one for the exhibits!

There are plenty of other plants and wildlife, too, including a splendid 1,000-foot avenue of monkey puzzle trees, a perfectly circular mirror pond with stunning reflections on a still day, giant redwoods and several Scottish champion trees, and an impressive walled garden, originally the kitchen garden. But while the gardens offer one of the finest collections of plants in the area, the main delight is their architecture – the long vistas along the terraces, the avenues of trees radiating from the old castle, and the gentle stretch of the old canal linking the two lochs and spanned by a lovely formal bridge.

4 STRANRAER

Stranraer has all the ingredients of a good old-fashioned seaside town: a superlative setting at the head of Loch Ryan, some fine old buildings, enticing narrow lanes and alleys, a quirky old harbour master's office on the seafront and brightly painted houses. There's even a castle in the middle of the main street. Despite suffering from loss of industry and

STRANRAER OYSTER FESTIVAL

If you're planning on coming this way, then one date to bear in mind is Stranraer's hugely successful Oyster Festival (🖰 stranraeroysterfestival.com) in September. First held in 2017, this three-day extravaganza celebrates the fact that the oyster beds that lie 1½ miles up Loch Ryan are the last remaining wild and natural oyster beds in the UK. The beds date back to 1701, when William III granted a Royal Charter to fish them to the Wallace family, whose descendants have retained the rights ever since and still live on Loch Ryan's shore.

During the festival, marquees are erected, boats bring in the oysters, which are piped ashore, and an *Ode to Oysters* is recited. Food, drink, fireworks, live music and stalls of everything from whisky to cupcakes are the order of the day, including a mouth-watering marine paella in the chef's tent. Gin fans will be pleased to find some of the various local gin producers here, too. The festival also hosts Scotland's first-ever shucking championship, an oyster dash on the ice rink and kite-flying workshops.

investment, notably the relocation of the ferry terminal to Cairnryan, thanks to the sterling efforts of the Stranraer Development Trust (stranraerdevelopmenttrust.co.uk) and a wide range of other groups and individuals Stranraer is starting to reassert itself. Events, awards and initiatives are now generating significant amounts of money for the local economy and pulling in a lot of people who might otherwise never have come here.

One such event is the Oyster Festival (see box, opposite), which has quickly shot to prominence and been a triumph, while the Stranraer Jazz Festival (October) draws performers and punters from all over the UK. Looking ahead, it is hoped that the town might develop further as a leading watersports centre, especially following the enormous success of the Skiffieworlds World Championship, which was held here in 2019. The potential is terrific.

The best way to discover Stranraer is through the **town trail**, starting off at **Stranraer Museum** (The Old Town Hall, 55 George St, DG9 7JP 01776 705088 dgculture.co.uk 10.00–17.00 Mon–Fri, 10.00–13.00 & 13.30–16.30 Sat), from where leaflets about the trail are available. The museum explains the history of the region, from the first settlers in 7000–4000BC, nomads who travelled inland to the Galloway Hills in the summer, through to the present. It also houses the unique **Chilcarroch plough**, which is the only remaining example in the country of the old Scotch plough. This particular one was first used in the area in 1793 but lay in a barn for many years from around 1870 before being discovered in the 1950s. It's a fearsome looking thing, heavy and cumbersome, and it would have taken a strong animal to pull it and stamina to walk behind it.

From the museum, follow the trail, which makes for an easy and interesting walk of a couple of hours. Plaques around the town provide information about specific points of interest. Along the way the story of Stranraer from the 16th century onwards will emerge, from the Castle of St John, built around 1510 for the Adairs, a powerful local family, through to the prosperity of the late 18th century and an economy based on tanning, fishing, boat building and weaving. The **Castle of St John** (Charlottte St, DG9 7EJ 01776 705088 dgculture.co.uk Jun–Sep 10.00–16.30 Tue–Sat) is worth a visit for its displays about its origin as a tower house and subsequent use as a prison, not to mention the great view from the top.

Extant from the 19th century around Stranraer is a range of buildings, including **North West Castle**, which was built in 1820 as the home of Arctic explorer Admiral Sir John Ross, who was born in nearby Kirkcolm in 1777. It's now a hotel with the curious distinction of being the first hotel in the world to have its own indoor curling rink. The trail also passes the **Princess Victoria Monument**, which commemorates one of the three transport disasters for which Dumfries and Galloway is known, the sinking in the North Channel (the strait that separates northeast Ireland from southwest Scotland) of the Stranraer to Larne car ferry MV *Princess Victoria* in 1953 with the loss of 135 lives. (The other two disasters are the Lockerbie bombing and the Quintinshill rail disaster, see page 48 and the box on page 58.)

"This was once the town house of the Maxwell family, whose coat of arms can still be seen above the front door."

One building that isn't mentioned as part of the town trail is **32 Charlotte Street** in the centre of Stranraer. This was once the town house of the Maxwell family, whose coat of arms can still be seen above the front door. The most famous member of the family was **Gavin Maxwell**, who grew up at the family home near Monreith on the Machars (page 221) and whose tales of rearing and living with otters made him a household name.

FOOD & DRINK

Bunker Snack Bar On the A77 just east of Stranraer. Small café right on the beach on the road to Cairnryan. Much praised for its breakfasts, friendly staff and views up the loch.

D'nisi Café 62–64 Charlotte St, DG9 7DB 01776 702123. Popular with visitors and locals with a memorable location slap bang in front of the castle. Sit outside on a sunny day and take in the view. A tasty selection of cakes and tray bakes, and enormous cheese scones (ask for a doggy bag to take half away). Wi-Fi available.

Driftwood Café Agnew Pk, DG9 7JZ 01776 706361. Licensed café in the pleasant surroundings of Agnew Park on Stranraer's waterfront, light and airy with garden and sea views, serving everything from cooked breakfasts to crispy fried halloumi, lentil and mixed bean chilli, whitebait, fishcakes, paninis and sandwiches, cakes and tray bakes. Popular with families (the playground is right next door). Wi-Fi available.

Fig and Olive 99 George St, DG9 7JP 01776 700099 figandolivecafe.co.uk. In our opinion, this is one of the best cafés in Dumfries and Galloway. Australian Maria Salzmann didn't expect to land up in Stranraer but we're rather pleased she did. Bright and bubbly, she and her team have hit on a winning formula with her relaxed, café/bistro in the centre of town that offers an original menu. Instead of the usual panini and toasties there are breakfasts of sourdough bread with smashed avocado, rocket, feta, red chilli, beetroot, hummus and lime, or eggs Benedict with ham and hollandaise. For lunch, try homemade savoury tart or a truly tasty chicken and bacon club sandwich. Then there's a host of diet-breaking cakes and tray bakes, including Maria's own baked cheesecakes, plus its own range of teas, and books and artisan chocolate for sale. It won Best Café in the Dumfries and Galloway Life awards in 2017 and the standard has been maintained ever since. Wi-Fi available.

The Grapes 4–6 Bridge St, DG9 7HY ✆ 01776 703386. The Grapes has been pulling the punters – and the pints – for many years. One of the oldest pubs in Stranraer, if not Scotland, its mix of real ales and music hits the spot for visitors and locals alike. Low ceilings and wood-panelled walls redolent with the spirit of revellers past set the scene.

Henry's Bay House Restaurant Cairnryan Rd, DG9 8AT ✆ 01776 707388 henrysbayhouse.co.uk. John Henry and his wife Jane offer diners a prime setting, with views and an outdoor terrace looking straight up Loch Ryan. Prices are reasonable, ingredients sourced locally and the menu changes regularly. Starters might include black pudding and bacon salad or smoked mackerel pâté, and mains like seafood pancake or strips of fillet. Grills, sides and indulgent desserts are also offered.

Landos Restaurant 41 Hanover St, DG9 7RX ✆ 01776 702020 landos-restaurant.business.site. Popular and award-winning Italian restaurant.

THE NORTH RHINS: EAST OF LOCH RYAN

Other than the views across the loch, which are good, the main reason people come this way is for the ferry terminals. **Cairnryan** itself consists of not much more than a village shop and a row of waterfront cottages, its low-key presence giving little away of its maritime history. It was here during World War II, when Cairnryan was designated 'No.2 Military Port' and operated as a secret base for troopships, that parts of the floating Mulberry Harbour were built for testing.

For a detour completely off the beaten track and a taste of the moors described on page 202, head northwards on the small road just north of where the A751 meets the A77. From here you can loop around and back down to New Luce (page 203) to the east on a route that is mostly single-track road with passing places and cattle grids, where sheep roam the hills, buzzards perch on top of telegraph poles and in August the landscape turns purple with heather. It's a glorious area of desolate moorland, where the landscape is rife with signs of ancient history. The remains of farms and fields, burial places and ritual monuments have survived relatively well because the uplands have not been altered by modern agriculture, and there's a small patch of mixed woodland still standing shortly before the road runs beneath the railway viaduct into New Luce.

THE NORTH RHINS: WEST OF LOCH RYAN

Corsewall Lighthouse Hotel (page 263)

Travel north from Stranraer up the west side of Loch Ryan and you find yourself in a sparsely populated landscape of undulating hills with views to water on three sides, especially at the northernmost reaches of the peninsula. This is a good area for enticing bays and beaches – if you know where to go (see box, below). Birdwatchers are in their element here, with plenty of seabirds and waders to look out for, not to mention porpoises, dolphins, seals and otters.

Loch Ryan played a significant role during World War II when its sheltered waters were used by the RAF as the location of one of the

NORTH RHINS BAYS & BEACHES

Wig Bay About half way up the eastern side of Loch Ryan NX036678. Lots of World War II history, information boards and a nice short walk out to the old lookout at Kirkcolm Point, where there are a couple of viewfinders for enjoying the outlook. You can also walk up the shore northwards from the point for around a mile. Easy access straight off the main road.

Lady Bay Northeast coast NX026717. This is a lovely sandy beach, a good spot for a picnic, with views across the bay to the boundary between Dumfries and Galloway and South Ayrshire. We've spotted eider, cormorants and goosander here, as well as roe deer. In spring the lower slopes of the surrounding hill are covered in daffodils. Access by car other than 4x4 is not recommended. Park at the top and walk down, or walk along from Portbeg.

Portbeg Bay Northeast coast NW960630. A peaceful, sandy beach and delightful stretch of coast. Access by car is possible but getting back up the track can be tricky if it's muddy. The small beach has parking space for no more than two medium-sized cars and turning round is tight, but it's worth the effort.

largest flying boat bases in Britain. The concrete bases on which the planes sat can still be seen at Wig Bay and a lookout tower still stands at Kirkcolm Point.

5 LESWALT

Just a few miles outside Stranraer is Leswalt, where there are the remains of a medieval church, the burial place of some of the Agnew family, whose hereditary ancestral home was in nearby Lochnaw Castle. The Agnews no longer occupy Lochnaw, but their descendants can still be found in Dumfries and Galloway and the **Agnew Monument** (NX008646) stands just north of the village at the top of Tor of Craigoch, from where there are good views in all directions taking in Loch Ryan and the Irish Sea.

Aldouran Wetland Garden (DG9 0LJ NX015637; look for roadside signs on entering Leswalt village aldouran.org year-round) is a community-based, volunteer-run garden consisting of a mix of raised flowerbeds with native and non-native plants and trees, and a wetland area with one large pond, several smaller ones and a large reedbed, all linked by paths and a boardwalk. There's also a bird hide and a

Genoch Rocks At Braid Port, northwest coast NW968708. A secluded spot where there's a good chance of seeing seals. It's a tricky one to reach as you'll need to walk from either Corsewall Point further north or Dounan Bay to the south.
Dounan Bay Northwest coast, a little further south from Genoch Rocks (see above) NW966688. Come for the sandy bay, the beach and the walks along to Dally Bay and up to Genoch Rocks.
Broadsea Bay Roughly two-thirds of the way down the west coast between Corsewall Point and Portpatrick NW974595. It's best to access this lovely beach with a wander from Killantringan Bay, near Portpatrick. Seek out the remains of an Iron Age fort above the bay.
Killantringan Bay around 2½ miles north of Portpatrick as the crow flies, accessed from the B738, following signs to Killantringan Lighthouse NW983566. The lighthouse here has been decommissioned and is now privately owned. Next to it, though, is the wonderful bay, easiest to get down to at low tide, offering dramatic views northwards up the coast, and a great spot to come whatever the weather, either to enjoy the beach in the sunshine or to blow away the cobwebs in a blustery breeze.

woodland walk and sculpture trail (spot the fairy doors at the base of the tree trunks). As well as many species of birds, red squirrels can be seen at the feeding station by the hide and roe deer frequent the wood, while the pond has a huge diversity of invertebrate life and also provides a home for mallard ducks and greylag geese.

THE NORTHERN TIP OF THE PENINSULA

In the 18th century Balsarroch House (now ruined), north of Leswalt, was the home of **Sir John Ross** (1777–1856), who was known for his expeditions to the Arctic and for his explorations to try to establish the route of the Northwest Passage. His nephew, Sir James Clark Ross (1800–62), accompanied him on several expeditions, one of which saw them become the first Europeans to reach the North Magnetic Pole. If you come up this way, keep an eye open on the right-hand side for the white-painted **Marian Tower monument** on the top of Craigengerroch Hill above Drumdow Farmhouse, from where there are views out to the distinct volcanic rock of Ailsa Craig in the Firth of Clyde. A plaque on the monument states simply 'Marian Hill 1818', giving rise to two different tales about its origins. One is that it was built as a memorial to one of the ladies of the Ross family, while the other is that it commemorates a local girl killed by a bull.

"At Kirkcolm, roughly halfway down the North Rhins on the east coast, stands a curious 10th-century stone cross."

At **Corsewall Point** (⚲ NW981727), the most northerly spot on the Rhins that can be reached by car (if you dare drive it; at our last visit the track was severely pot-holed), stands one of the three lighthouses on the peninsula and, like its southern counterpart at the Mull, this one is still in operation (although it has been automated since 1994), its light helping to guide boats to the mouth of Loch Ryan. The surrounding buildings now form the Corsewall Lighthouse Hotel (open to non-residents; page 263). On a clear day the views from here take in Ireland, Ailsa Craig, the island of Arran, the Kintyre Peninsula and the Firth of Clyde. Sit here a while and you might spot gannets, seals, porpoise, dolphins and otters, as well as roe deer in the surrounding fields. It's also particularly atmospheric in the fog.

In the churchyard at **Kirkcolm**, roughly halfway down the North Rhins on the east coast, stands a curious 10th-century stone cross, the

Kilmorie Stone. Kirkcolm has long had Christian associations, the name itself means church of St Columba, and one interpretation of the cross is that it illustrates the triumph of Christianity over Paganism, with Christ on the cross appearing above a figure who is believed to be a hero from Viking mythology. The carvings on each side appear to be by different hands revealing both Celtic and Scandinavian influences.

FOOD & DRINK

The Blue Peter Hotel 23 Main St, Kirkcolm DG9 0NL ✆ 01776 853221 ◷ restricted hours: food served only on Fri & Sat eve & 1st Sun of the month. Serves up hearty, wholesome and tasty home-cooked food in the cosy bar (log fire in winter) and also outside in the summer. The spacious rear garden is a good place for spotting red squirrels.

Soleburn Garden Centre Mill Croft, Leswalt, Kirkcolm DG9 0PW ✆ 01776 870664. Locally owned and run garden centre with a pleasant conservatory-style café serving filling hot dishes, sandwiches, cakes and tray bakes.

6 PORTPATRICK

Knockinaam Lodge (page 263), **Rickwood House Hotel** (page 263)

Portpatrick's luck has waxed and waned over the years as much as the Atlantic tides that batter its harbour, and it's those very tides that have been at the root of the town's fluctuating fortunes. From the 17th to 19th centuries came a succession of entrepreneurs and statesmen who were convinced that Portpatrick should and could be the official port for all boats coming from Ireland. With just 21 miles separating its harbour from that at Donaghadee, it was an obvious but ill-advised choice. Sir Hugh Montgomery from neighbouring Ayrshire – one of the founding fathers of the Ulster Scots – was to blame. He acquired both harbours and capitalised on a Royal Warrant of 1616 that restricted travel between the Irish Ards Peninsula and the Rhins of Galloway to Donaghadee and Portpatrick. Thus started 150 years of engineering folly in which successive attempts to build, strengthen and enlarge the harbour at Portpatrick were destined to end in calamity. The 18th-century engineer John Smeaton had a go, followed in the 19th century by John Rennie Senior and, subsequently, his son John Rennie Younger.

"Thus started 150 years of engineering folly – attempts to build and enlarge the harbour were destined to end in calamity."

No-one heeded the warnings of renowned engineer Thomas Telford (see box, page 73), who in 1802 passed judgement that Portpatrick remained 'destitute of the advantages requisite for a perfect harbour'. Finally in 1839, a newly constructed pier was destroyed by storms and the authorities accepted it was time to throw in the towel.

> *Despite such fluctuations, Portpatrick did find favour as the 'Gretna of Ireland' following the Marriage Act in 1754."*

That would have been it had it not been for the mail boats, or at least the promise of the mail boats, and for the perceived need for ease of access for both mail and cattle from Ireland through to Stranraer. The idea of the Portpatrick Railway to link with Stranraer as part of a bigger trunk route between London and Belfast was too tempting to resist, and inherent with it was the need to develop the harbour at Portpatrick. Yet again the scheme was doomed. Just as the advent of faster ships brought an end to the cattle route from Ireland (page 227), so too did it spell the end for the mail route, which the government had transferred south bypassing Dumfries and Galloway – and Portpatrick – altogether. And so when Portpatrick Harbour Railway Station was opened on 11 September 1868 it must have been something of an anticlimax and with a sense of futility, for there was no longer a requirement for it. Alas, it closed two months later.

Despite such fluctuations, Portpatrick did find favour for a period as the 'Gretna of Ireland' following the introduction of the Marriage Act in Ireland (and England) in 1754, the same act that transformed the fortunes of Gretna Green in the east of Dumfries and Galloway (page 56). Eloping couples could cross the sea to wed in Portpatrick, where it is said that the minister was known to relax the requirement for a period of residence so that not much more than hour might pass between an unwed couple disembarking their boat and reboarding for the journey home as a married couple.

Portpatrick Harbour is now in the care of the Portpatrick Harbour Community Benefit Society (portpatrickharbour.org), Scotland's first fully-fledged charitable community benefit society. Formed in 2015 with the aim of raising funds through a community share offer for the benefit of all, it has enjoyed considerable success, with the original share offer selling out within three weeks of opening.

As for Portpatrick itself, reconciled to the fact that it was destined never to become a major port it resolved to make the most of its attractive location and associated leisure opportunities. Step forward C L Orr Ewing, MP, who owned (and whose descendants still own) the Dunskey estates. He saw the potential and in April 1903 opened the Dunskey Golf Club (now the Portpatrick Dunskey Golf Club) on 100 acres of land on the north cliff behind the imposing Portpatrick Hotel (opened 1905). It was a smart move and heralded the start of Portpatrick's success as a popular seaside town.

Portpatrick today is as pretty as a picture, of which there are many to be found, and boasts the highest sunshine record in Dumfries and Galloway. It has all the charm of a quaint fishing village and in summer all the crowds that go with it, too. Come at the end of July/start of August when it's **Lifeboat Week**, and there is a range of activities taking place. Traditional cottages are strung around the harbour and a mix of cafés, gift shops, hotels, restaurants and pubs are dotted along the waterfront and up the adjoining streets. Further up the hill in the residential area, elegant villas enjoy sea views, including a number of guesthouses. If you want to visit by public transport, buses 367 and 411 come here from Stranraer. Fishing trips and coastal tours are offered from the harbour on *Predator II* (✆ 07739 231331) and *Lucky Dip II* (✆ 07841 114489).

"Portpatrick is as pretty as a picture, of which there are many, and boasts the highest sunshine record in the region."

Recent years have also seen the addition of a brewery to the area, producing a range of beers under the banner of Portpatrick Brewery, which are available from many local outlets. All six of their beers are named after aspects of local life, from the Fog Horn IPA (in honour of the restored fog horn at Mull of Galloway, page 256) to Beltie Blonde and Gulf Stream blonde ales.

A WANDER AROUND PORTPATRICK

At the northern end of the harbour it's impossible to resist the urge to walk out on to the rocky islets of **McCook's Craig** and **Dorn Rock**, and feel as if you're on an island. From here, you may see some of the **black guillemots** (or tysties) that return to nest here each year in the nooks and crannies of the harbour walls. Passing the **Lifeboat Station and Museum** you'll find first of all a sign marking the start of the **Southern Upland Way**, which sets off up the cliffside staircase. It's worth the climb for the super view looking back down on the harbour and village.

Further around the seafront northwards, the **Princess Victoria Memorial** on the cliff face commemorates the Portpatrick lifeboat men involved in the attempts to rescue the MV *Princess Victoria* on 31 January 1953 (page 236).

Continuing round the harbour, behind North Crescent and overlooking the putting green is a smart row of black-and-white terraced houses on **Blair Terrace** that look like they've been lifted straight from the English Riviera, an unexpected sight in this very Scottish setting. Carrying on round to the southern side of the waterfront, at low tide there's a small sandy beach, and above it, next to Connor's Restaurant you can see the remains of a 19th-century **lime kiln**, a series of arches dropping down to ground level and now filled in, which was built for use during one of the drives to develop the harbour. **St Andrews Kirk**, built in the 17th century, stands a short way back from the harbour off St Patrick Street. The round tower is thought to be older, possibly medieval, and is believed to have acted as a landmark for sailors. In the cemetery are maritime monuments to sailors, sea captains, customs officers and even shipwrecks.

DUNSKEY CASTLE & ESTATE

A popular walk from Portpatrick is to wander south of the harbour for half a mile or so along the coastal path to **Dunskey Castle** (NX004534), an impressive ruin gazing out to sea from its clifftop vantage point that is only accessible on foot. It's an easy walk but there are steep steps to start with. For a **circular walk**, carry on past the castle and then drop down to the right to the disused railway line, which can be followed back into Portpatrick; in total, it's about 1¼ miles.

In the other direction, between Portpatrick and Killantringan to the north, is the 2,000-acre **Dunskey Estate** (DG9 8TJ dunskey.com), home to the Orr Ewing family. Public access isn't generally permitted as the estate is now a venue for weddings, corporate events and retreats (and as a film location), but it is crossed by one of the region's public access 'Core Paths', which means a walk through the grounds is possible so long as you stick to the designated route. This takes in the bay at Port Kale (also accessible along the coast path from Portpatrick to the south and Killantringan from the north), where the curious double octagonal building was the housing for the telegraph cable, laid from here to Ireland in 1852.

FOOD & DRINK

Connor's Restaurant 1 South Cres, DG9 8JR 01776 810314. Reasonably priced restaurant conveniently located next to the car park on the waterfront and offering a varied menu with a leaning towards fish dishes, from venison shanks to Portpatrick crab and lobster.

Knockinaam Lodge DG9 9AD 01776 810471 knockinaamlodge.com. Definitely one for special occasions, the elegant restaurant at Knockinaam has held a Michelin star for over 20 years and is still wowing diners under the expert direction of head chef Tony Pierce. A range of stylish Scottish-based dishes is on offer, making good use of local produce, especially fish. Even if you don't come for dinner, splash out on a traditional afternoon tea. Reservations recommended for both.

Port Pantry 24 Main St, DG9 8JL 01776 810655 Feb–Dec daily. Breakfast, lunch, speciality teas and coffee, plus homemade cakes and scones are all on offer in this perennially popular and cosy café in the heart of Portpatrick. A selection of vegan and vegetarian dishes is offered, plus a range of local gifts, from Portpatrick beers to throws and scarves.

The Old Colfin Creamery The Colfin, DG9 9BN 01776 820622. Extremely popular and well-established restaurant in a converted creamery with tables made from reclaimed wood and old milk urns. Dishes might include breaded pork belly with chilli jam for a starter, traditional mains such as fish pie or a roast, and scrummy deserts such as fresh berry pavlova or apple and cinnamon crumble. Specials and cocktails also offered. Booking recommended.

The Waterfront Hotel 7 North Cres, DG9 8SX 01776 810800 waterfronthotel.co.uk. Refurbished in recent years; open to non-residents: pop in for light bites or full mains. There's lots of fish on the menu: grilled langoustines in garlic butter, sea bass, seafood crêpe, fresh mussels and a carvery every second Sunday. The restaurant is bright and airy, the dog-friendly bar suitably cosy.

THE SOUTH RHINS

The southern half of the peninsula is a maze of winding lanes and rolling hills edged by cliffs and a rocky shore to the west and (on the whole) a fringe of beaches and gentler drops to the east. Heading down the Rhins there is a choice of either following the more westerly roads, which generally run inland from the coast itself, or the main A716 in the east which pretty much hugs the shoreline all the way to Drummore. Alternatively, a mix of both east and west can work depending on what you want to see and where you're aiming for; it doesn't take long to cross from one side of the peninsula to the other. The further south you go the more remote it feels until you eventually reach the dramatic clifftop lighthouse at the **Mull of Galloway**, Scotland's most southerly point.

SANDHEAD TO LOGAN HOUSE GARDENS

Torrs Warren Country House Hotel (page 263) **New England Bay Caravan Club Site** (page 263)

From Sandhead southwards there are splendid views across Luce Bay to the Machars and easy access to rocky beaches. Neat cottages and a grand house here and there dot the countryside, crow-stepped gables and Scottish baronial flourishes in evidence. You can see how harsh conditions can sometimes be here: the tops of the trees have been flattened by the prevailing winds.

Ardwell coast and country walk

OS Explorer 309; start: Ardwell picnic area (accessible by bus 407) NX109453; 5½ miles; moderate (some boggy and uneven sections).

This figure-of-eight offers a wide variety of scenery from the wild to manmade, and history aplenty, including an old windmill and religious buildings, plus far reaching views over Luce Bay – once a hotbed for smuggling. To access the starting point, follow the A716 coast road to Ardwell; the picnic area and car park are at the southern end of the village.

From **1 Ardwell picnic area** follow the Mull of Galloway Trail (MGT) along the foreshore, heading away from Ardwell towards the large white house of Chapel Rossan, built on the site of an earlier religious building. Cross the A716 road, through the kissing gate and along the hedge, soon crossing back over the road. Follow the path through the woodland, along a burn and the beech hedge running parallel with the road, with good views of 16th-century Auchness tower house.

Go through another kissing gate and here leave the MGT, taking the **2 track straight ahead** through woodland then across more open country – look left for the first views of the old windmill tower. Where the path meets an access road by an intriguing former chapel, turn left for Logan Mills. The late 19th-century St Agnes's Chapel was built by the Laird of Logan and named after his wife, Agnes Buchan Hepburn.

At the **3 Logan Mills shore** follow the access road left, passing the ruined cottage and the remains of Logan windmill, thought to date from the 17th century and which probably continued to turn until the middle of the 19th century. After about 100yds take the path off to the right, along the back of the pebbly beach and then up through the woods, passing a World

The sandy beach at **Sandhead** on the edge of Luce Bay is a popular place to while away a few hours. It stretches for a mile and is seemingly endless when the tide is out. The village is strung along the road and has a good local shop that is supplied each week with fresh baking from the Logan Bakehouse (see box, page 248). They also stock local Clash Farm Bacon, sausages and burgers, all rare breed and free range, perfect for a fry-up.

In the middle of the peninsula stands pretty little **Kirkmadrine Church** (⚲ NX080484 ◷ year-round; free; Historic Environment Scotland) on or near the site of what would have been an important early Christian cemetery in this area. The present church is 19th century, having been rebuilt from the ruins of an earlier medieval one by Lady MacTaggart Stewart of nearby Ardwell (page 248) and

War II lookout. Go up the steep steps and turn left to follow the access road back to the earlier kissing gate and retrace the outbound route back to Chapel Rossan.

Don't cross the road back to the picnic area but instead turn left up the **4 access track**, signed 'Ardwell Church 1¾'. Pass through the Barhill farmyard to the right of the sheds, continuing along the track to soon arrive at the Edwardian Ardwell Church, now a community kirk.

Go through the **5 blue metal gate** to the right of the road junction and then immediately left at the path junction to follow the straight path along the edge of the Ardwell Estate – full of snowdrops, bluebells and daffodils in spring. Follow the waymarker arrows through the grounds, over a track and through another blue gate to join the 'Pond Walk'. Climb the path up to follow a ridge, actually the old shoreline cliffs, leading to Ardwell Motte and an ornamental pond. At the edge of the pond take the downhill path to the **6 stepped water channel** known as a lade, cross the bridge and follow the path left, back to the start.

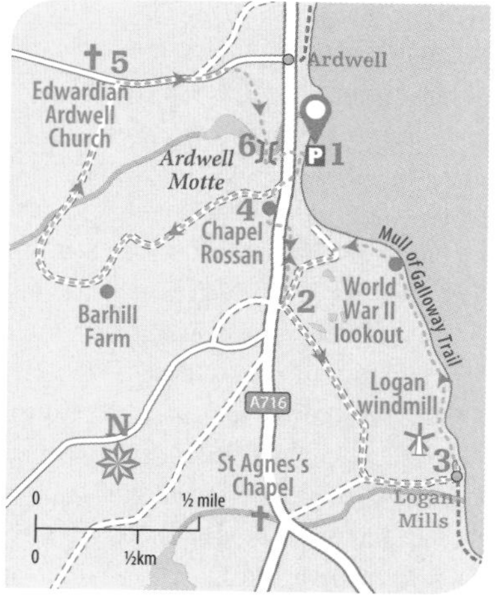

is based on the Romanesque church at Cruggleton (page 210) near Garlieston on the Machars. The main attractions here are the three early Christian stones from the mid to late 6th century, some of the oldest monuments in Scotland outside Whithorn (page 211).

From here it's a short hop down to **Ardwell**, an estate village of whitewashed cottages on the shoreline with a picnic area on now chapel-less Chapel Rossan Bay immediately to the south. Neighbouring **Ardwell Gardens** are no longer open to the public, but a designated path runs through the grounds and can be incorporated into a circular walk from Chapel Rossan Bay.

Not to be confused with Ardwell House, **Ardwell Bay** is a few miles away on the western side of the peninsula. It has a fine beach that is worth the effort of navigating the slightly challenging entrance road. To get there, from Sandhead follow the A716 south and then turn right at the sign for Kirkmadrine Stones. Stay on this road, eventually passing through Low Ardwell and South Ardwell farms and then carry on down a rutted track. Hold your nerve, take it slowly and don't let the potholes deter you. At the bottom of the track is a parking area. The bay is backed by gorse-covered hills and has lovely views of successive headlands up

THE ACCIDENTAL BAKERS

When Logan Bakehouse owners Jo and Lyn moved to the Rhins they hadn't given a thought to becoming bakers. In search of a quieter, more self-sufficient life, they found that their new home offered everything they had hoped for except for the range of bread they had been used to in their former city-based lives. And so they started to make their own. Even then, though, they had no intention of doing so commercially.

In true 'slow' style, they also hoped to grow their own vegetables, but to start with, before their first crops were ready, they opted instead to barter, trading their bread for locally grown produce. And so, by accident, a business was born. Word soon spread, requests started coming in, and before they knew it they found themselves batch baking three times a week. At the same time they were renovating their cottage on the east coast of the Rhins near Logan House. What better opportunity to install a wood-fired oven in their new kitchen?

Today the Logan Bakehouse is a thriving wee business. In keeping with a slower way of life, Jo and Lyn have pulled back from thrice-weekly bakes and now fire up the oven just once a week. They make everything themselves, from scratch. 'This really is a slow business,' says Jo. 'It takes three days to make a batch of croissants!'

There is a definite art to what they do, for the temperature of their oven is uncontrollable.

the western side of the Rhins. You might well have it to yourself, with the cry of gulls and the breaking waves the only sounds to be heard.

Logan House Gardens (DG9 9ND ⏲ Mar–Sep daily; other times by appointment) are just a few miles south of Ardwell. A very long tree-lined drive replete with snowdrops and daffodils in spring gives way to an avenue of rhododendrons that leads to the house. Press the yellow button to pass through the gate, which opens automatically, enticing you in. There is a small charge for entry/parking, and tickets are available from the machine in the parking area. The Queen Anne House (private) is surrounded by sweeping lawns and splendid Victorian woodland gardens. Logan House has seven UK champion and 14 Scottish champion trees, all contributing to the description they use of 'forty shades of green' and between them representing trees from all over the world.

FOOD & DRINK

Tigh Na Mara Main St, Sandhead DG9 9JF ✆ 01776 830210 tighnamarahotel.co.uk. Popular restaurant on the waterfront at Sandhead, serving traditional favourites from local produce.

Once it's been stoked up with wood for five hours, reaching up to 450°C (no electricity required, so even if there's a power cut baking goes ahead), the ashes are raked out and baking can begin. And this is where the expertise really kicks in, for the secret to a successful bake is knowing which breads or pastries to put in at which time as the temperature of the oven cools. Jo and Lyn have penned a few tips and also supplied a recipe for their delicious shortbread (page 21).

And, if you're staying on the Rhins, then keep an eye on their Facebook page. A menu of what's being baked is put up on a Sunday and orders need to be placed by the following Wednesday. Deliveries are made from their little red three-wheeled van between Drummore and Sandhead on a Friday, and even if you're not staying along the route you can arrange a pick-up point.

As to what's on the menu, well it could be anything from rolls, seeded loaves, croissants and pain au chocolat to Portuguese custard tarts, cake or melt-in-the-mouth amaretti biscuits. Keeping it truly local, they also offer a potato, cheese and onion pasty in pastry made with Portpatrick beer.

Orders can be placed via Facebook message, by email to jo@loganbakehouse.co.uk or by phone ✆ 01776 860357. Fresh baking is also supplied to the shop in Sandhead weekly on a Friday.

7 LOGAN BOTANIC GARDEN

DG9 9ND 01776 860231 rbge.org.uk Mar–mid-Nov daily

Right next door to Logan House is Logan Botanic Garden, one of several outposts of the Royal Botanic Garden in Edinburgh. The gardens are officially open from March to mid November, but visitors are welcome to come out of season to have a walk around, for which donations in the box are always appreciated. The gardens have an excellent café, the Potting Shed Bistro, with a strong emphasis on fresh produce from local suppliers, though this is closed out of season. A wide range of walks, talks, music, family and educational events is organised through the year.

SCOTLAND'S MOST EXOTIC GARDEN

Richard Baines, Curator, Logan Botanic Garden

Here on the southwestern tip of the Rhins of Galloway lies Logan Botanic Garden, the holder of Scotland's Most Exotic Garden title – a fitting and well-deserved label as you'll discover yourself when you see the spectacular plants that thrive here, for Logan enjoys the warm climate of the Gulf Stream and basks in Scottish Riviera sunshine. Here you will find plants native to the southern hemisphere, rather than a dreich Scottish coastline.

A stunning entrance awaits in the form of a quarter-mile avenue of 400 cabbage palms (*Cordyline australis*), the first of which were planted at Logan in 1909. This initial approach gives the first hints of exotica to come. As you wander round the garden you will be transported across the world to places like Chile, Tasmania, Madeira and Vietnam.

We are the national collection holders of *Leptospermum, Gunnera, Griselinia, Clianthus and Sutherlandia*. Probably the most famous is *Gunnera manicata*, the giant rhubarb from Brazil that has leaves up to 6.5ft across, a true giant! *Leptospermum* is a very important genus economically as it is the source of the widely used tea-tree oil and the food source for the production of manuka honey.

We specialise in tender maddenia rhododendron and our new Vietnam feature bed is testament to this. We have a vast array of rhododendrons from China, Vietnam, Taiwan and Myanmar. If you look closely you will even find some plants recently discovered in Vietnam that are new to science. Together with evergreen magnolias and schefflera, these are some of the many plants benefitting from Logan's unique climate.

After belonging to the same family for 700 years, Logan was gifted to the nation and became a Regional Garden of the Royal Botanic Garden Edinburgh in 1969. Our exotic Walled Garden dates back to the 18th century when it was a traditional kitchen garden and is now a haven of tropical delights. Alongside camellias and blue poppies are the distinctive bright pink funnel-shaped flowers of

Originally part of the grounds of Logan House owned by the McDouall family, the gardens were initially developed by Agnes McDouall in the 1870s. Today, having recently celebrated being part of Royal Botanic Garden Edinburgh for 50 years, the gardens are in the expert hands of curator Richard Baines with a team of six helpers and a small army of interns. Richard has kindly written a more specialist appraisal of the garden for this guide, which gives a full picture of what you can expect to find here. Suffice to say, within the garden there are 20 different species of palm and 20 of eucalyptus, tree ferns that were originally part of the Great Exhibition at Crystal Palace in 1851, the biggest fuchsia we've ever seen, a strawberry tree native to Portugal, a

Rhododendron kanehirae – until recently one of only two left in the entire world, and now extinct in their native Taiwan. The garden's Cordyline Avenue is one of Logan's most iconic features, calling to mind some distant tropical paradise.

The Woodland Garden is less formal and contains many trees and shrubs, with a particular focus on Australia (including Tasmania) and South America. The giant *Gunnera* is impressive. Children and adults alike love to wander through the *Gunnera* tunnel, while the newly landscaped Woodland Pond is an attractive place to sit and enjoy the peace as well as providing a stimulating place for pond dipping on children's activity days.

Logan has many amazing plants and trees in its collection, with the most famous being our Filo Pastry Tree (*Polylepis australis*) that originates from the Andes in Argentina. Growing at an altitude of up to 16,400ft, it survives by trapping warm air between the layers of exfoliating bark.

Wander a little further round to reach our Tasmanian Creek, surrounded by antipodean forest – 10,000 miles from their native homes of Australia and New Zealand. Nestled within the mass plantings of eucalyptus and tree ferns is Logan's Silent Space, the first of its kind in Dumfries and Galloway, a place to switch off phones, take in the beautiful surroundings and enjoy the endless benefits of spending time in a green space.

In recent years we have been focusing on sustainability, looking at how to balance the need to create a world-class attraction *and* be kind and fair to the planet. In June 2014 we opened the Logan Conservatory, a carbon-neutral, self-sufficient public greenhouse, the first of its kind in the UK. Providing a home to a collection of plants from South Africa rarely seen growing on public display in the UK (such as exotic proteas, spring flowering tree heathers and a large collection of pelargoniums), it's also an exotic haven for visitors in inclement weather. We also have two electric car charging points and places to refill water bottles.

whopper of a giant ornamental rhubarb species from Brazil that grows to 14ft tall, and a Tasmanian creek full of plants from the Anitpodes. Streuth! We particularly like the area known as the 'Bamboosolem', with lots of different types of bamboo to walk through. There's also a Discovery Centre for kids, as well as a children's audio tour.

If you want to visit Logan by public transport, the 407 Stranraer–Drummore bus runs past the bottom of the garden drive from Monday to Saturday and will drop you off or pick you up. There are several services a day in each direction.

8 PORT LOGAN

The McDoualls of Logan House are also to be thanked for the estate village of Port Logan on the west coast. It's a sleepy place with cottages set around a sandy bay with an old lighthouse, and yachts and boats bobbing inside the breakwater. The eye-catching candy-striped trailer parked at the entrance to the village – Cool Licks and Hot Drinks (f) – serves ice cream, cakes and hot and cold drinks on selected days (sometimes just a Sunday) in summer.

On a calm, quiet day, this is the stuff of holiday snaps. But on a stormy day, when the Atlantic pounds the beach, it's said that the sound of the breakers can be heard on the other side of the peninsula, which at this point is less than two miles away.

This little village became known for an aquatic eccentricity, the questionable brainchild of Colonel McDouall who was so keen on a spot of fish for his dinner that he fashioned a living larder out of a naturally occurring blowhole in the rocks where fish caught at sea could be kept until wanted for the table. **Logan Fish Pond** (DG9 9NF ✆ 01776 860606 portloganfishpond.com Mar–Oct 10.00–17.00 daily) is still there today and usually has around 50 fish in it of various species, from cod and turbot to bull huss, conger eels and wrasse.

9 KIRKMAIDEN

Kirkmaiden (the kirk of St Medan) stands proudly atop a hill with a commanding view out to Luce Bay and across to the Machars, both associated with the church's eponymous saint. Medan arrived from Ireland in the 8th century, settling in a cave near East Tarbet (page 254) where she established a church. Her past caught up with her though when her former lover arrived from across the sea. She fled to a rock in

THE LIGHTHOUSE GRAVESTONE

The graveyard at Kirkmaiden has an impressive range of 18th- and 19th-century funerary monuments and memorials, many topped with urns and shrouds. Particularly touching is a gravestone in the form of a lighthouse erected by James B Scott, principal lighthouse keeper at the Mull of Galloway (page 255) in the mid 19th century, in memory of his son James. Maureen Chand of the Mull of Galloway Trust has looked into the history of this and tells us that Scott and his fellow lighthouse keepers were working on a gantry outside the tower at the Mull when his son sneaked up to help but fell off. He was killed immediately. The memorial is based not on the lighthouse at the Mull but on the one at Skerryvore off the south end of the island of Tiree, the most westerly isle of the Inner Hebrides.

After leaving the Mull, Scott went on to Oban where the ships of the Northern Lighthouse Board are based. While there his wife died and so Scott made her gravestone in the shape of one of the lightships.

Luce Bay, but the gods were against her for the rock moved of its own accord, transporting her to Monreith Bay (page 222) on the Machars. Undeterred, her lover followed, proclaiming that it was her eyes that captured him. Desperate for an end to her torment, Medan gouged out her own eyes and her suitor retreated back to Ireland. Medan then bathed her eyes in a nearby well and her sight was restored. (The site of St Medan's Well is believed to lie near Kirkmaiden-in-Fernis on the Machars; page 223.) She spent the rest of her life founding churches all over Scotland.

10 DRUMMORE

The coastal road to Drummore makes for a lovely approach to Scotland's most southerly village, with a lengthy stretch right down by the water. In good weather this is delightful, but in stormy times and at high tides (and particularly when there is a combination of the two) we recommend avoiding it, notably along Kilstay Bay, as the waves can crash in across the road and what in the sunshine looks inviting can become extremely dangerous.

Drummore is as far as you can get by public transport. If you're heading for the Mull, this is frustrating as it leaves you five miles short. From here you have no choice but to walk unless you happen to be staying in one of the cottages at the Mull itself (page 263), in which case a lift can be organised. Alternatively, if you're cycling or if you have a bike with you, there's a good route taking in the Mull and Kirkmaiden (details available from the information centre at Drummore; page 228). Or, for a different view of the Mull, you can take a **boat ride** from Drummore just for the scenery, or to go fishing, seal spotting or birdwatching. Ian Burrett runs trips and can be contacted through his website (onyermarks2.co.uk) or by phone on 01776 840346.

Drummore sits around and above its harbour, with a hotel, coffee shop, post office, tourist office run by volunteers, and general store. Long ago it was said that the sheep of Drummore 'have all their teeth very yellow, aye, and their skin and wool are yellower than any other sheep in the country' because of the presence of gold; however, only thin flakes of the precious metal were ever found.

FOOD & DRINK

Mariner's Coffee Shop 46 Mill St, Drummore DG9 9PS 01776 840550. Way more than your average coffee shop. Sure, they do all the things you would expect (including a mean full Scottish breakfast), but you can also place your orders for fresh cooked or live lobster or crab. And while mains might include sausage, egg and chips, you could equally find scallops, mussels and tiger prawns on offer. The fish platter is something to be seen – and tasted!

DRUMMORE TO THE MULL OF GALLOWAY

Between Drummore and the Mull of Galloway the peninsula narrows to not much more than the width of the road where it's nipped between the two bays of **West** and **East Tarbet**. Here in ancient times boats were rolled on logs between the bays, to avoid having to navigate around the Mull with its dangerous currents. About half a mile north of East Tarbet is **St Medan's Cave**, where Medan came ashore and fashioned her first chapel out of a natural rock formations before fleeing from her pursuing lover (page 252). Nearby are **Chapel Wells**, also referred to as The Well of the Co', of which it was recorded in the mid 19th century: 'To bathe in the well as the sun rose on the first Sunday in May, was considered as an infallible cure for almost any disease'. It was customary to leave a gift at the well, and coins of Charles I and II and William and Mary farthings have been found here.

From the Tarbets the road snakes ahead, crossing the **Double Dykes** that were thought to be the last line of defence of the Picts against the Scots. The road climbs upwards to the top of the 260ft cliffs and the majestic vantage point of the **Mull of Galloway**, Scotland's most southerly point (latitude 54.6351°N) and actually further south than Penrith and Hartlepool. This is an awesome and inspiring place. One guidebook writer in the 1950s described it as: 'grand, high and frightening. A great point of headland thrust down in to the southern seas, a fortress whose stacks of cliffs bristle with knives and spears of rock, buttresses and crenelated and corbelled'. Nothing has changed.

11 THE MULL OF GALLOWAY

Lighthouse Holiday Cottages (page 263)

mull-of-galloway.co.uk. Note: the nearest petrol station is at Stranraer, so make sure you have plenty of fuel before heading down here.

The **Mull of Galloway Experience** (NX155165 late Mar/early Apr–Oct 11.00–17.00 daily) includes the lighthouse and associated buildings run by the Mull of Galloway Trust, adjoining RSPB reserve, and the superbly positioned Gaille Craig Coffee House (page 257), built on the very edge of the cliffs with a grass roof and vertiginous drop from the terrace. At the lighthouse itself is the main tower (small charge) and lighthouse keeper's cottages, which are now run as holiday lets (page 263), plus an exhibition (small charge) in the engine room. Movie buffs will know that the lighthouse was the main setting for the 2018 Gerard Butler film, *The Vanishing*.

There are 93 steps from the bottom of the lighthouse tower up to the first gallery, followed by two ladders, one to reach the outside viewing platform and another from there up to the light itself. The views are worth it: to Ireland and the Mountains of Mourne in County Down, and to the Isle of Man, just 19 miles away (and yet so far if you want to go there; the nearest ferry from the mainland departs from Heysham, just under 200 miles away). On a clear day you can see to Cumbria, too, and of course eastwards across to the Machars and north back up the Rhins. There's no disabled access to the tower, but there is an accessible viewing platform at ground level and access to the exhibition.

"On a clear day you can see to Cumbria, too, and of course eastwards across to the Machars and north back up the Rhins."

'I loved the place... you can see... Scotland, Ireland, Man, and the Kingdom of Heaven' is the famous quote from Bill Frazer, Principal

Keeper 1971–75, and it pretty much sums up the feeling you get when standing on the clifftops or gazing out from the top of the lighthouse.

This is a good place to bring the kids, with lots to see and do. Come on a Sunday if you can to hear the **foghorn** at 13.00. Brought back into working order almost single-handedly by volunteer Stevie Burns, it is the only one working on mainland Scotland and produces the most extraordinary, evocative sound that reverberates off the cliffs and out to sea, conjuring up images of days past when ships relied on it to navigate safely. The sound is unique, as it was for all foghorns, so that ships could identify which one they were hearing. Incidentally, if you choose to get married here, not only can you tie the knot at the top of the lighthouse tower, but the foghorn can be sounded to mark the occasion.

The **exhibition** is fun: huge red tanks that fill with compressed air for the foghorn, an explanation of semaphore and a chance to try out your Morse code, a display on lighthouse keepers past, and the story of James Birnie, the ghost of the lighthouse, who was the only keeper who actually died here.

In front of the lighthouse is a walled garden where produce is being grown in raised beds. In August the heather here and in the surrounding area comes out to provide a vibrant foreground for photographers. Tales of the Mull have long featured heather, or more specifically heather ale, the first ale brewed in the British Isles, for it is said that this is where the recipe for it was lost forever, a story that was immortalised by Robert Louis Stevenson in his poem *Heather Ale: A Galloway Legend*.

Minke whales, porpoise and dolphins, puffins and guillemots are all visitors to the area, and adjoining the Mull lighthouse is the 30-acre **RSPB Mull of Galloway Reserve** (exhibition Easter–Oct daily; reserve year-round). The main display is housed in a cottage that was home to the workers who built the lighthouse. The reserve consists mostly of maritime heath and cliffs, but also includes the **Scare/Scaur Rocks** six miles out to sea, and a wide range of birds can be spotted here. A seasonal ranger runs the reserve and can point out other wildlife, including voles, mice, roe deer, a quite spectacularly iridescent beetle (the rose chafer beetle), and, controversially, weasels, which pose a threat to ground- and low-nesting birds. It's a bit too

"In August the heather here and in the surrounding area comes out to provide a vibrant foreground for photographers."

blustery and exposed for butterflies, but one or two day-flying moths might be spotted, notably the brightly coloured cinnabar moth and similar five-spot burnet. Entertainment for kids is usually on offer, too, including colouring desks, films and webcams, and the chance of an activity tour looking for specific species and items. There are recordings of bird sounds and, for the ghoulish, bird skulls to try and identify. And if you fancy getting a closer look at the wildlife, there's always the option of a boat trip from Drummore (page 254).

FOOD & DRINK

Gaille Craig Coffee House DG9 9HP 01776 840558 galliecraig.co.uk Feb–Mar 11.00–16.00 Sat–Wed; Apr–Oct 10.00–17.00 daily; Nov 11.00–16.00 w/ends only. Angela and Harvey Sloan have been farming at the Mull of Galloway for many years; theirs is the last farm you pass before reaching the lighthouse. Harvey still farms beef and sheep, but some years ago he had a vision for creating an environmentally sensitive visitor facility and so he set about designing and building a café that would fit in with the landscape and provide a refreshment spot at Scotland's most southerly point. The result – a grass-roofed, glass- and stone-encased shed with spectacular views and a cliff-edge terrace that makes the most of its unique location – was so successful that it won the Green Apple Award from the Green Organisation. It's a great place to come for teas or for a fuller lunch (the chicken and bacon pie hits the spot). On a sunny day, the terrace at the end can be a suntrap. And the name? Well that comes from the Gaille Craig rock far below that marks the exact spot of Scotland's most southerly point.

DUMFRIES & GALLOWAY ONLINE

For additional online content, articles, photos and more on Dumfries and Galloway, visit bradtguides.com/d&g and slowbritain.co.uk.

ACCOMMODATION

Below, we offer a selection of accommodation options, all hand-selected places that we have visited ourselves. No business has paid to appear in these listings.

Hotels and B&Bs are indicated in the main body of the book by 🏠 under the heading for the town or village in which they are located. Self-catering options are indicated by 🏠, campsites and caravan parks by ⛺, and glamping by ⛺.

Intrepid travellers wanting to get right off the beaten path might want to check out mountainbothies.org.uk.

Owing to space restrictions, descriptions here are short, but more in-depth entries and additional listings can be found at bradtguides.com/d&gsleeps. For example, compared to the short listing given opposite, the online entry for Summerlea House B&B in Moffat reads:

Summerlea House B&B Eastgate, Moffat DG10 9AB 01683 221471 moffatbedandbreakfast.co.uk Moffat Bed and Breakfast. Ornamental flamingos in the garden, bookcases stuffed with travel guides and maps, Haggis the lusty terrier, and fresh milk in the bedrooms are just a few of the defining features of this B&B in the heart of Moffat's conservation area. It's quietly located, but only a couple of minutes' walk from the shops, bars and restaurants of the high street. Donald and Darren, authors of this guide (and several walking guides) have created a cosy and comfortable haven for couples in search of a country retreat, walkers tramping the hills, tourers stopping off, and cyclists exploring the highways and byways of the Southern Uplands (covered storage for bikes and motorbikes is available). Most guests stay anywhere from two to ten nights, but single-night bookings can sometimes be accommodated.

Just two en-suite rooms are offered, both furnished with a mix of modern, vintage and antique pieces, and with plenty of hanging and drawer space. From the cosy guest sitting room, patio doors lead to the private and spacious courtyard garden where you'll find bird feeders, a sitting area and borders. Full cooked or continental breakfast is served in the country-house-style dining room; muesli, yoghurt and (sometimes) marmalade are all homemade. (Darren's marmalade has won several awards in the annual World Marmalade Festival.) 'Since moving here we've met people from all over the world,' says Donald, 'we know the area inside out and love sharing our top tips with guests. Come and discover Dumfries and Galloway!' 'Best B&B since Lands' End,' according to one long-distance cyclist on a well-known travel website.

1 ANNANDALE & ESKDALE

Hotels

Annandale Arms High St, Moffat DG10 9HF ☎ 01683 220013 ⊕ annandalearmshotel.co.uk f Annandale Arms Hotel. Comfortable and historic coaching inn with 16 en-suite rooms, some pet-friendly, offering great food and a fun (but not raucous) acoustic music night in every Thursday.

Eskdale Hotel Market Pl, Langholm DG13 0JH ☎ 013873 80357 ⊕ eskdalehotel.co.uk f. Ideally located in the town centre, a friendly and welcoming traditional hotel with spacious rooms.

Somerton House Hotel 35 Carlisle Rd, Lockerbie DG11 2DR ☎ 01576 202583 ⊕ somertonhotel.co.uk f. Family-owned, characterful, comfortable and reliable hotel on the edge of Lockerbie, something of a local institution.

B&Bs

Moffat has an extensive range of good B&Bs. In addition to those detailed below, we can also recommend **29 Well St**, **Dell Mar, Ivybeth**, **Limetree House** and **Queensberry House**, all of which have Facebook pages.

Hartfell House Hartfell Cres, Moffat, DG10 9AL ☎ 01683 220153 ⊕ hartfellhouse.co.uk ⊙ Tue–Sun; winter variations f. A handsome Victorian villa with seven en-suite rooms (one on the ground floor) on one of Moffat's smartest streets with grand views.

Hightae Inn High Rd, Hightae, Lockerbie DG11 1JS ☎ 01387 811711 ⊕ hightaeinn.co.uk. Has five tasteful rooms and a cosy restaurant known for its quality food, great for weekends or longer breaks with easy access to Annandale, Eskdale, Dumfries and beyond.

Summerlea House B&B Eastgate, Moffat DG10 9AB ☎ 01683 221471 ⊕ moffatbedandbreakfast.co.uk f; see ad, 4th colour section. Offers two en-suite rooms in the mid-19th century home of the authors of this guide. In the heart of Moffat's conservation area, two minutes' walk from the High Street.

Waterside Rooms Dornock Brow Hse, Dornock, Annan DG12 6SX ☎ 01461 40232 ⊕ thewatersiderooms.co.uk f. Cosy guest suite in a coastal cottage in a memorable location with great views at the eastern end of the Solway.

Self-catering

Cauldholm Bothy Beattock, Moffat DG10 9QA ☎ 01683 300466 f. Cosy, stone-built converted outhouse with all creature comforts on the Annandale Way above Moffat.

Kirkwood Real Farm Holidays Dalton DG11 1DH ☎ 01576 510200 ⊕ kirkwood-lockerbie.co.uk f Real Farm Holidays. Features five cottages around a courtyard (ideal for families and groups) and a separate super-comfortable traditional farmhouse on a working sheep farm.

Nether Boreland Boreland, Lockerbie DG11 2LL ☎ 01576 610248 ⊕ netherboreland.co.uk f. The farmhouse at Chariots of Fire Driving Equestrian Centre offers two en-suite rooms in a rural location near Lockerbie.

Wee Hartfell Cottage Howslack, Annan Water, Moffat DG10 9LS ☎ booking agent 01738 503601 ⊕ cottages-and-castles.co.uk. Set in the beautiful Annan Water Valley, a couple of miles north of Moffat, a three-bedroom, purpose-built log cabin with all mod cons.

Campsites, caravans & glamping

Craigieburn Gardens Bothy Craigieburn Gardens, A708 Selkirk road, DG10 9LF ☎ 07557 928648 f. Charming bothy with wood-burning stove in glorious 6-acre gardens in the hills near Moffat.

Hoddom Castle Caravan Park Hoddom, near Lockerbie DG11 1AS ☎ 01576 300251 ⊕ hoddomcastle.co.uk f. Caravans, 'Chill Pods' and traditional Finnish *kotas* in the grounds of a 16th-century castle.

Moffat Camping and Caravan Site Hammerlands Moffat DG10 9QL ☎ 01683 220436 ⊕ campingandcaravanningclub.co.uk f.

Scenically located 180-pitch site with good facilities, five minutes' walk from the high street.

Moffat Wigwam Holidays Roundstonefoot Farm, Moffat DG10 9LG ✆ 07836 584880 ⊛ wigwamholidays.com/moffat; see ad, 4th colour section. Family-run site with just six very comfortable en-suite wigwams in a glorious setting not far from Moffat.

The Wagon at Arkleton Arkleton Walled Garden, Ewes, Langholm DG13 0HL ✆ 01387 380830 ⊛ the-walled-garden.co.uk. Handcrafted wagon in the beautiful Ewes Valley at the Walled Garden, north of Langholm.

2 NITHSDALE

Hotels

Auldgirth Inn Auldgirth DG2 0XG ✆ 01387 740250 ⊛ auldgirthinn.co.uk. A slightly Gothic-looking inn with striking rooms and a strong reputation for the quality of food.

Blackaddie Country House Hotel Blackaddie Rd, Sanquhar DG4 6JJ ✆ 01659 50270 ⊛ blackaddiehotel.co.uk. Fine dining and luxury accommodation in a country house, plus two self-catering cottages in the grounds.

Buccleuch & Queensberry Arms Hotel 112 Drumlanrig St, Thornhill DG3 5LU ✆ 01848 323101 ⊛ bqahotel.com. Historic and comfortable hotel in the centre of Thornhill with ten mostly spacious en-suite rooms in the main building and three cottage-suites out back.

Friar's Carse Auldgirth DG2 0SA ✆ 01387 740388 ⊛ friarscarse.co.uk. Set in 45 acres of estate land, a historic country house hotel with a splendid wood-panelled hall (perfect for afternoon tea) and contemporary rooms.

Trigony House Hotel Closeburn, Thornhill DG3 5EZ ✆ 01848 331211 ⊛ trigonyhotel.co.uk. Originally a shooting lodge, now a hotel offering ten comfortable en-suite rooms.

B&Bs

Auchencheyne B&B Moniaive DG3 4EW ✆ 01848 200589 ⊛ auchencheyne.co.uk. More than just a B&B: accommodation in an 18th-century farmhouse annexe, eco-conscious hosts and a walled vegetable garden.

Nithbank Country Estate Thornhill DG3 5AP ✆ 07823 773211 ⊛ nithbank.co.uk; see ad, 4th colour section. Three generous rooms, smart bathrooms, beautiful décor, glorious views, handy for Thornhill and the surrounding area, and friendly hosts immersed in local life.

Scaurbridge House Penpont, Thornhill DG3 4LX ✆ 01848 330152 ⊛ scaurbridgehouse.co.uk. Characterful accommodation in a gracious former manse with a charming host who bakes delicious cakes.

Self-catering

Blackaddie Country House Hotel (see left).

Three Glens House Moniaive DG3 4EG ✆ 01848 200589 ⊛ 3glens.com. Luxurious and innovative top-of-the-range eco-lodge with live-in cook.

Campsites, caravans & glamping

Barnsoul Caravan Park Shawhead, Dumfries DG2 9SQ ✆ 01387 730533 ⊛ barnsoulcaravanpark.co.uk. Caravans, camping, pods and mini lodges in a lovely hillside setting west of Dumfries.

Red Squirrel Campsite Glenmidge, Auldgirth DG2 0SW ✆ 01387 740328 ⊛ campingandcaravanningclub.co.uk. Small, popular site in a charming location in the hills, peaceful and well looked after.

The Wanlockhead Inn Gardendyke, Wanlockhead ML12 6UZ ✆ 01659 74535 ⊛ wanlockheadinn.co.uk. A range of affordable glamping pods set in the grounds of Scotland's highest inn.

3 DUMFRIES & THE NITH ESTUARY

B&Bs

20 Castle St 20 Castle St, Dumfries DG1 1DR ✆ 07712 130204 ⊛ sheilacameron1@btinternet.

com. Right in the middle of town, two period rooms – one with kitchenette – on the top floor of an elegant Georgian house. DIY breakfast (food provided) or head out to nearby cafés.

Glenaldor House 5 Victoria Tce, Dumfries DG1 1NL 01387 264248 glenaldorhouse.co.uk. Central location overlooking private gardens in a mid 19th-century terrace with four large en-suite rooms.

Self-catering

Wildfowl and Wetlands Trust Caerlaverock Eastpark Farm, Caerlaverock DG1 4RS 01387 770200 wwt.org.uk/wetland-centres/caerlaverock. The perfect choice for birdwatchers and wildlife lovers, a traditional farmhouse within the grounds of WWT Caerlaverock that sleeps up to 12 in five bedrooms.

4 THE STEWARTRY

Hotels

Balcary Bay Country House Hotel Auchencairn, Castle Douglas DG7 1QZ 01556 640217 balcary-bay-hotel.co.uk. Secluded, romantic and idyllically positioned on the shore of the bay, offering country house comfort with Solway views.

Cally Palace Hotel Gatehouse of Fleet DG7 2DL 01557 814341 mcmillanhotels.co.uk/cally-palace-hotel. A historic country mansion with 56 en-suite rooms and opulent public spaces.

The Selkirk Arms Hotel High St, Kirkcudbright DG6 4JG 01557 330402 selkirkarmshotel.co.uk; ; see ad, 4th colour section. Kirkcudbright's leading hotel has strong historical and literary connections and offers 17 en-suite rooms on the old high street.

The Ship Inn 1 Fleet St, Gatehouse of Fleet DG7 2HU 01557 814217 theshipinngatehouse.com The-Ship-Inn. A welcoming hotel on the main street with ten comfortable en-suite rooms and a popular restaurant.

B&Bs

Chipperkyle Country House B&B Kirkpatrick Durham, Castle Douglas DG7 3EY 01556 650223 chipperkyle-countryhousescotland.co.uk; see ad, 4th colour section. Imposing Georgian house with elegant and beautifully furnished rooms in the rolling hills of Galloway but convenient for nearby towns and attractions. Dinner available by request.

Craigadam Country House Hotel and B&B Near Kirkpatrick Durham, Castle Douglas DG7 3HU 01556 650233 craigadam.com; see ad, 4th colour section. Charming and hospitable country farmhouse offering seven en-suite rooms set around a courtyard and great food. Handily located for all the area's attractions.

Cruachan House Kenbridge Rd, New Galloway DG7 3RP 01644 420865 cruachanhouse.com. Charming Arts and Crafts house with homely bedrooms and relaxing public rooms, loads of character and friendly, welcoming hosts.

Douglas House 63 Queen St, Castle Douglas DG7 1HS 01556 503262 douglas-house.com. Smartly turned-out B&B in a central location offering four rooms and an award-winning breakfast.

Self-catering

Barholm St John's St, DG8 7JE 01671 820810 barholm-centre.co.uk. Friendly, affordable community-run accommodation, sleeping up to 27 in nine rooms, from singles to bunk beds.

Barwhillanty Estate Holiday Cottages Parton, Castle Douglas DG7 3NS 01644 470209 barwhillantyestate.co.uk; see ad, 4th colour section. A stylish five-bedroom farmhouse and four-bedroom country cottage on a working estate in the hills above Loch Ken, perfect for families and groups.

Brockloch Eco-bothy and Treehouse Brockloch Farm, Kirkpatrick Durham DG7 3HU 01556 650249 brockloch.co.uk. Off-grid bothy and tree house on a farm near Castle Douglas, set on a hill with stunning views. Featured on Channel 4's *George Clarke's Amazing Spaces*.

Galloway Activity Centre Loch Ken, Parton DG7 3NQ 01556 502011 lochken.co.uk. Wide range of accommodation, from cabins to the bunkhouse, plus two innovative lochside 'eco bothies', compact but perfectly formed looking out over the water.

Gelston Castle Holidays Gelston, Castle Douglas DG7 1SW 01556 502211 gelstoncastle.com; see ad, 4th colour section. Offering five delightful courtyard cottages sleeping two to eight, plus one other on the estate in a private setting. Grounds to roam, communal tennis court and even an outdoor heated pool.

GG's Yard Gatehouse of Fleet DG7 2ES 01557 840217 ggsyard.co.uk/accommodation . En-suite snugs (18 individual, purpose-built, high-end cabins) with Solway views, plus on-site bistro and Mossyard beach at the bottom of the hill.

Kirkdale Estate Carsluith DG8 7EA 01557 840273 kirkdaleestate.co.uk . Perennially popular and idyllically positioned, three cottages, each sleeping six, on a 2,000-acre coastal estate. Offering woodland walks, a private shore, walled garden and tennis court.

Kirkennan Estate Holiday Cottages Palnackie, Castle Douglas DG7 1PE 01556 600438 kirkennan.co.uk . Sleeping between four and seven in three cottages on a country estate, set within 35 acres of formal lawns, woodland and walled garden.

Nether Ervie Parton, Castle Douglas DG7 3NG 01644 470215 nethererviefarm.co.uk. Well equipped two-bedroom cottage on a hill above Loch Ken, right in the centre of the Stewartry.

New Galloway Cottages High St, New Galloway DG7 3RN 01644 420620 newgallowaycottages.com New Galloway Community Shop and Enterprises. Very smart properties in the centre of the village, owned and run by the community, ideal for couples, families or groups.

Orroland Holiday Cottages Orroland, Dundrennan, Kirkcudbright DG6 4QS 01557 607707 orroland.com . Sleeping between two and 14 in three elegant and cosy cottages on a private coastal estate: whitewashed stone buildings, log fires, comfortable furnishings and immaculate attention to detail.

Campsites & caravans

Loch Ken Holiday Park Parton, Castle Douglas DG7 3NE 01644 470282 lochkenholidaypark.co.uk . Static caravans and 100 camping pitches on a family-owned site on the shores of Loch Ken, plus kayak and pedalo hire.

Lochside Caravan and Camping Lochside Park, Castle Douglas DG7 1EZ 01556 504682 dumgal.gov.uk/tourism (select 'Caravan and camping sites') Castle Douglas Caravan Park. Touring caravan and camping site next to Carlingwark Loch, very handy for the town and good for families.

Sandgreen Caravan Park Sandgreen, Gatehouse of Fleet DG7 2DU 01557 814351 sandgreencaravanpark.co.uk . Long-standing and popular static caravan park (most privately owned) with just two caravans for hire plus one lodge, next to a lovely beach.

5 THE MACHARS & THE MOORS

Hotels

House o' Hill Hotel Bargrennan DG8 6RN 01671 840243 houseohill.co.uk . The only hotel within Galloway Forest Park, with two comfortable and stylish guest rooms.

The Steam Packet Inn Harbour Row, Isle of Whithorn DG8 8LL 01988 500334 thesteampacketinn.biz . Superbly located, very popular inn in a harbourside setting, offering seven rooms.

B&Bs

Craigmount Guest House Fountainblue Tce, High St, Wigtown DG8 9EQ 01988 402178 craigmount.info . A refurbished19th-century manse with four rooms on the edge of Wigtown, handy for the high street.

Flowerbank Guest House Millcroft Rd, Minnigaff, Newton Stewart DG8 6PJ 01671 402629 flowerbankgh.com. Delightfully located on the banks of the Cree, with five rooms, a garden and river views, plus storage for bikes.

Hillcrest House Maidland Pl, Station Rd, Wigtown DG8 9EU 01988 402018 hillcrest-wigtown.co.uk. 'A grand old house', as one guest commented, with six rooms, filling breakfasts and evening meals if wanted.

Self-catering

7 Ninian's Landing Isle of Whithorn DG8 8LL 07824 770968 ninianslanding.co.uk Harbourside Holiday Apartment, Isle of Whithorn; see ad, 4th colour section. Bijou waterside apartment perfect for couples and singles with dreamy views over the harbour from the sitting room. Dogs welcome.

Beltie Flat 6 Bank St, Wigtown DG8 9HP 01988 402730 beltiebooks.co.uk. Quirky and characterful dog-friendly flat, a central location and great views from the top floor.

Cairnharrow Cairnhouse Farm, Newton Stewart DG8 9TH 01988 403217 cottageguide.co.uk/8914. Well-maintained, spacious and homely modern cottage sleeping six in a convenient and scenic location.

The Pend George St, Whithorn DG8 8NS. 01988 500469 pend-house.com; see ad, 4th colour section. Historic and beautifully furnished former monastery gatehouse in the centre of Whithorn sleeping four. Other properties also available. See website.

Camping & caravans

Drumroamin Farm Camping and Caravan Site 1 South Balfern, Kirkinner, Wigtown DG8 9DB 01988 840613 drumroamin.co.uk. A 50-pitch site with a couple of caravans also available. In a rural setting, with views over Wig Bay.

6 THE RHINS

Hotels

Corsewall Lighthouse Hotel Corsewall Point, Kirkcolm DG9 0QG 01776 853220 lighthousehotel.co.uk. Superbly located lighthouse hotel offering six en-suite rooms and three suites. Access road sometimes rough.

Knockinaam Lodge Portpatrick DG9 9AD 01776 810471 knockinaamlodge.com. A special place to stay: luxurious and historic Victorian country house hotel with ten rooms in a secluded location with its own beach.

Torrs Warren Country House Hotel Greyhill Rd, Stoneykirk DG9 9DH 01776 830204 torrswarrenhotel.co.uk. Hugely characterful and comfortable country house accommodation in a former manse offering ten rooms, all refurbished in tartan and oak décor, and with a cosy bar, and resident alpacas.

B&B

Rickwood House Hotel Heugh Rd, Portpatrick DG9 8TD 01776 810270 portpatrick.me.uk. Delightful B&B and charming hosts offering six en-suite rooms in an Edwardian house, plus a hot tub and candy-striped beach hut for changing in the garden.

Self-catering

Lighthouse Holiday Cottages The Mull of Galloway Trust, The Mull of Galloway Lighthouse, Drummore DG9 9HP 01776 980090 lighthouseholidaycottages.co.uk. Comfortable and cosy converted lighthouse keepers' cottages with spectacular views at an iconic location: Scotland's most southerly point .

Campsites, caravans & glamping

Glenwhan Gardens Shepherd's Hut Dunragit DG9 8PH 01581 400222 glenwhangardens.co.uk. Endearing shepherd's hut in the secluded hilltop setting of Glenwhan Gardens, gazing out over Luce Bay.

New England Bay Caravan Club Site Port Logan, Drummore DG9 9NX 01776 860275 caravanclub.co.uk. Coastal caravan site with 150 pitches on the east of the Rhins. Sea views and direct access to the beach.

INDEX

Entries in **bold** refer to major entries; those in *italic* refer to maps.

D

E

F

INDEX OF ADVERTISERS

See 4th colour section.

THE BRADT STORY

In the beginning

It all began in 1974 on an Amazon river barge. During an 18-month trip through South America, two adventurous young backpackers – Hilary Bradt and her then husband, George – decided to write about the hiking trails they had discovered through the Andes. *Backpacking Along Ancient Ways in Peru and Bolivia* included the very first descriptions of the Inca Trail. It was the start of a colourful journey to becoming one of the best-loved travel publishers in the world; you can read the full story on our website (www.bradtguides.com/ourstory).

Getting there first

Hilary quickly gained a reputation for being a true travel pioneer, and in the 1980s she started to focus on guides to places overlooked by other publishers. The Bradt Guides list became a roll call of guidebook 'firsts'. We published the first guide to Madagascar, followed by Mauritius, Czechoslovakia, and Vietnam. The 1990s saw the beginning of our extensive coverage of Africa: Tanzania, Uganda, South Africa, and Eritrea. Later, post-conflict guides became a feature: Rwanda, Mozambique, Angola, Sierra Leone, Bosnia and Kosovo.

Comprehensive – and with a conscience

Today, we are the world's largest independently owned travel publisher, with more than 200 titles, from full-cou and wildlife guides to Slow Travel guide like this one. However, our ethos remai unchanged. Hilary is still keenly involve and we still get there first: two-thirds of Bradt guides have no direct competitio

But we don't just get there first. Our guides are also known for being more comprehensive than any other series. We avoid templates and tick-lists. Each guide is a one-of-a-kind expression of a expert author's interests, knowledge an enthusiasm for telling it how it really is.

And a commitment to wildlife, conservation and respect for local communities has always been at the heart of our books. Bradt Guides was championing sustainable travel before a other guidebook publisher.

Thank you!

We can only do what we do because of the support of readers like you – peopl who value less-obvious experiences, less-visited places and a more thoughtf approach to travel. Those who, like us, t travel seriously.

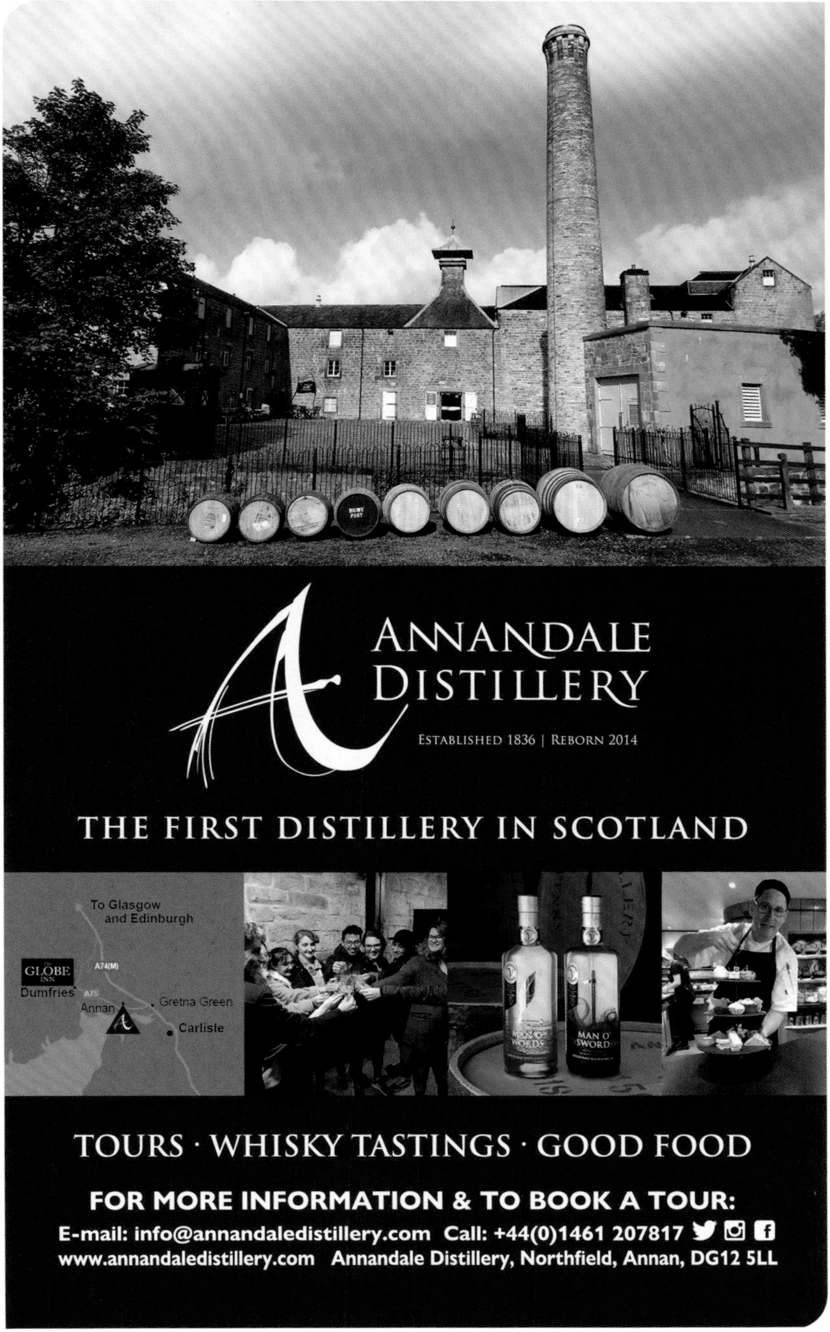

PETER HILL
ROUNDHOUSE

(See page 212.)

WHITHORN
TIMESCAPE
Come Close. See Far